1

Ph☺cked Up Philadelphia

Ghost Story

By: Arturo R. Martinez ☺

It is funny how some things work out in life; out of pure boredom I found myself writing again. It took a world changing event like the Covid pandemic for my writer's instinct to kick in again. Can't really say what the motivation was for me to re-start this past-time of mine; still to this point though, I can't seem to explain the method to my madness. Simply put it's a rare gift that seems to manifest itself when I relax and smoke some good weed; at 3am in the morning. Sick and tired of watching the news and all the politics that come with it; I turned off the TV and decided to do some basement cleaning.   I was going through some old boxes when I came across a book that belonged to my wife's grandmother. It was the Philadelphia Ghosts Stories book by Charles J. Adams III. This book was my starting point; my map and my compass that would become the foundation for my idea. I started going through some of the stories as I was smoking some really good "Supersonic Crystal Storm Weed" strain. It took only a thought and a couple of songs in random order; then, a spark went off in my head that would bring me to the "concept" for this project. I am glad that I wrote this book when I did; it helped me through a rough patch in my life that has only made me more resilient and eccentric. It really has been a weird 1 year stretch; where I've seen almost everybody I've come in contact with start to question the meaning of their existence, their purpose in life, and started pointing out all the injustices right in front of us. So as the world was turning upside down during the Covid Epidemic; I turned on my computer and went to work. I had decided to come up with a rather less complicated and more entertaining way to pass my time. I've decided to write my story in a type of script format; one that would facilitate the readers ability to see in more detail. I put all notes about the story and music information together visible to the reader; so it gives the imagination a better sense of the picture being painted. It sets up a more realistic feeling for the reader by having music accompany the reading material. Think of it as a cheaper version of an audio book, all you need is a copy of this book and a way to stream some music; preferably our Amazon music apps. (L☺L) Laughter can lift the spirit and help you look at life from outside the box and from a different angle; there for helping you cope with the unnecessary stresses of life.   It's a funny thing coincidences; a coincidence is a coincidence until it becomes a coincidence no longer. In my case, it was the moment when I finally accepted and understood that all the signs given to me in life; all pointed to the City of Philadelphia. It is in that spirit that I intend to leave my mark in this great city; the same way someone else from my same place of origin did.

I'm talking about a Philadelphia Eagles legend, Mr. Steve Van Buren who was born December 28, 1920 in La Ceiba, Honduras; my hometown.   The first hat I ever bought with my own money when I was 11 years old; was one with the Philadelphia Flyers logo on it.   The first baseball team I ever rooted for was the Philadelphia Phillies because I loved how the name was spelled in cursive writing. My first recollection of basketball was seeing a picture of the one and only Doctor J. along Moses Malone sporting their Sixers uniform. During the '93 World Series, I was the only one rooting for the Phillies in a room full of Anti Philadelphia assholes; nearly got my ass kicked. I love the eagles so much, that at an Eagles draft party when Donovan McNabb got selected in the draft, I was the only one in the room cheering for him. I nearly got my ass kicked for that one too by my fellow Eagles….lol.   I met a girl from Philadelphia and married her; now we have a beautiful daughter and we live a comfortable life in South Philadelphia. Needless to say; this is my home. Through my research I've discovered that many famous writers have lived here or have left their stamp in this city with their presence. Among them would be Edgar Allen Poe, Charles Dickens, Bram Stoker, and one Sylvester Stallone; that's right, I'm a fan. I got the Rocky theme song as my alarm on my phone; it helps to have a motivational song to tell you to get off your ass and get to work in the morning. I'm glad in my heart that I came here to Philadelphia, not because I chose Philadelphia; but because Philadelphia chose me. A place where I've lived the hard way; were "we the working class chase the American dream as we live an American Reality". My thanks go out to my friends at work Anthony, Matt Webb, Mrs. Hue, and Herbie; for motivating and encouraging me to fulfill this project. Also want to send a big thanks out to the Bostwick family who have made it possible for me to continue my goals as a writer. And now, without further delays; in the hopes of trying to lift everyone's spirits and spark the flames of brotherhood and sisterhood in our great city; I present to you a,

Ph☺cked Up Philadelphia

Ghost Story

Right at the heart of the Delaware Valley, amongst the clouds, the noise, and the pollution you'll find the city of Philadelphia. Surrounded by New York and Boston to the North, Wilmington and Baltimore to the South, Lancaster and Pittsburgh to the West, and South Jersey to the East. Philadelphia is one of the most unique cities time has seen; known in the past as "The Quaker City", Philadelphia is shrouded by mystery and intrigue. The Quakers, who by making religion a mystery, promoted faith in shadows. Whatever Quakerism may be now, it was, in its early days mysticism of the first order. Its very basis is the belief in the activity made manifest of spiritual agents. The city of Brotherly love, like all the great cities of the North East; contain many different types of Histories. The ones written down, the actual truths, and the ones nobody outside of Philadelphia has ever heard of. From its founding by William Penn and the Quakers, to the many different groups of people that have inhabited her throughout the centuries. To the Philadelphia Experiment at the Naval Yard and even over to Penn's Landing; where there is an actual boat turned restaurant that is haunted. The stories that were locked up in history, expected never to resurface ever again, have found their way into our time; in the most peculiar of ways. A manner so strange that it seems, "Destiny" is making an attempt to play a cruel joke on us; because these unique stories are about to be unlocked by the "most unlikely",

The psychotically dangerous,

And the mysteriously unexplained.

Chapter 1

The "Oh Face" ☺

Place: Center City, Jefferson Hospital

    Philadelphia, PA

    14th floor Thompson Building

(A busy day in the city of Philadelphia; people moving around everywhere accompanied by the never ending sounds of cars, buses, birds, and machines. A young man arrives at the Thompson building of the Jefferson Hospital; he passes the security desk and makes his way to the elevators. He then proceeds up to the Psychiatric Ward on the 14th floor; he is there to pick up a friend who was mentally unstable and is now only minutes away from being discharged. As he waits for his friend over by the front desk, he picks up a magazine and starts going through it with no particular purpose. He just starts browsing through to kill some time, as he comes up to an article about the history of Philadelphia; its Aristocracy, the old giant mansions, and the curse of William Penn. As he kept reading, he comes to a section about "Elizabeth Robbins" Philly's first ghost hunter and her book "Our own Ghosts"; then suddenly, a soft whisper slowly started making its way into his ears. He heard someone whisper, "Find us". He quickly turns around and sees no one is there; then someone taps him on the shoulder from behind. He turns around again a bit scared and then finally; he sees it's his friend Flaco (skinny). He lets out a huge exhale of relief and still with a bit a fear left.)

Matt: Bro!! You scared the shit out of me; I thought I heard a voice that came out of left field.

Flaco: Try spending 2 months in here, you'll hear all kinds of voices from every direction.

    Ones you don't want to hear one bit and then there's the scary ones. Well, it depends on

    what fucked up new medicine they want to put you on; know what I mean "homie". Oh

    yeah, it's good to see you too by the way.

Matt: Sorry Bro, it's good to see you too; let's hug it out bitch! (manly hug) Now let's just get

    the fuck out of here.

Flaco: (looks over to the secretary) Peace out, Mrs. Wallace!! (she just shakes her head and

    chuckles)

(They walk over to Matt's car and Matt opens up the trunk; he quickly takes out the magazine he was reading at the 14th floor out of his back pocket and throws it in the trunk.)

Matt: Let's fucking bounce bro! I got all the boys meeting us at the club. There's a

　　　lap dance with your name on it waiting for you.

Flaco: Fuck Yeah! Strippers here I come!! (LOL)

Place: Columbus Boulevard, South Philadelphia

Song: Handsome and Wealthy – Migos (0:00 – 0:35)

(They drive over to South Philly and pull up at the parking lot by the Wawa on Columbus Boulevard. There they meet up with their friends from work. 10 Pak and his cousin El Chino, a computer Hacker by the name of Paul "The Fire Wall", Lil Kev, Steve "The Pill", and the craziest of us all; fucking Herbie. As the pouring of shots commences followed by the pills, the weed, and the intrigue of it all; these non-voting, honest criminals, whose only crime is that of having the good luck of being born different, are now set on having a good time. These are your everyday people cursed with living from paycheck to paycheck; the struggle they embrace is not because they want to, it's because they have to. Simply because the world decided to conspire against them first, they are now forced to be the noise that interrupts the signal; their message is simple, "Fuck the status Quo". After a couple of bottles down; Matt begins to explain everything to Flaco about his idea to become ghost explorers. He explains the whole concept that all ghosts aren't assholes; that some are cool and all they want is some company to smoke, drink, chill, and laugh with them.)

Song: Strippers – Body Count- Slow Part (1:50 – 3:10)

(They finally make it into the club after an hour of celebrating Flaco's return to the living. As Flaco follows his buddy 10 Pak, all the beautiful women dressed in the proper work attire, seemed to be looking in our direction. Was it the glow of our energy that seemed to reverberate around the room? Or was it the fact that we didn't look like easy prey? Our waitress comes over and everybody puts money together, as we get Flaco his welcome back Champagne Room present. This consists of a 30 minute private lap dance in a private room. Flaco follows the waitress into the private room and then sits down on the soft leather couch; a beautiful dancer approaches him and sits on top of him, riding him slowly to the tune of the song, which has now switched gears to make time stop all around the club.)

(As she moves slowly and caresses his face, the room starts spinning slowly and seductively and fills itself with the excitement of the unknown. The unknown fate tomorrow will bring, the unknown woman in front of him, the unknown time he would be up tomorrow, and the unknown time of his life here on this plane of existence. Everything starts going dark slowly, till finally there is no light left. All you hear is the breathing of the stripper enjoying her job and the perks that come with it; when finally, nothing. The Infamous "Black out" some men go through. That's how you know you partied hard; when you can't remember shit the next day.)

Next Day ☺

Place: Matt's Apartment

    Hollywood St. and Reed St.

    Southwest Philadelphia

(House phone starts ringing, ringing, ringing and no one picks up. Matt, still in a partial inebriated state, opens up his eyes and starts growling and mumbling; the answering machine finally picks up.)

Flaco: Yo Matt! Wake up you fag! I got all that equipment that you need to start filming that

      ghost documentary of yours. I made those calls we were talking about

      last night and you were right, there is a shit load of money in filming ghosts and the

      occult and all that other crazy shit you mentioned. I got Vic the Realtor to show

      us a house in the old part of Queen's Village that's supposedly haunted. Apparently

      some construction workers have seen shadows walking back and forth in certain parts

      of the house. We got to meet him at noon, so get your ass up because if you're not here

      by then; I'm gonna steal your idea and keep all the money to myself. Just saying, hurry

      up. {End of message}

(Matt looks at the clock to check the time, it's 11:11am)

Matt: Fuuuuck Thaat!!! (Jumps out of bed like a champion with a purpose.)

Song: Assesment – Beta Band (0:00 – 1:00)

(Right on point; Matt is getting dressed in a bit of a hurry, grabbing the first items of clothing he can pick up off the floor. He starts rushing down the stairs, grabbing an old coffee and putting it in the microwave for 2 minutes as he continues to get ready; grabbing keys, cash, and weed. He grabs his warm coffee and runs out the door and starts driving the streets of South Philly. He makes it over to Queen's Village just in time; as he arrives, he sees both Flaco and Vic the Realtor standing there bullshitting with one another.)

(Matt parks his car and turns the music off and starts heading towards them.)

Flaco: Eyyyyy, there he is; just in time too. What's going on buddy?

Matt: You little fucking piece of weasel shit, you just had to make the appointment today;
       I'm hung-over like a mother fucker. Aren't you feeling the effects from yesterday?

Flaco: Of course, that's why I'm still drinking. (takes a sip of Fireball) How rude of me, Matt
       this is Vic Vinegerrete, the real estate agent I was talking to you about.

Matt: You mean the crooked real estate agent; we all know about this guy and the wonderful
       job he's done around here. Are you fucking serious? This guy is a piece of SHIT.

Vic: People should pay attention to the fine print because I choose my words, very deliberately
       my friend. Now, do you want to go through the property or not? Ok. Good, here are the
       keys, good luck, lock up when you're done. Give me a call; better yet send me a picture.

(Starts laughing as he walks away)

Matt: Wait!! Aren't you going to show us around? What kind of shitty real estate agent are
       you??

Vic: The kind that usually gets paid and since you guys are not paying me; you simply are just
       gonna owe me a favor. Well then, that means that my job here is finished; Koni chi wa,
       bitches. (starts walking away)

Matt: God damn Cock Sucker!!   I fucking knew it; what did I say!!

Flaco: What you bitching about, he's not the type to ask questions on why we are even here.
       Now let's go film some crazy shit, that's gonna get us paid mutha fucka!!

(They both walk into the darkness of the house; and not a moment too soon the front door slams shut right behind them. You start hearing sounds like they are being mugged, shouting, struggling, cursing and laughing. There were some voices with Enlgish accents saying something about "potatoes and beans" on the account of Matt being Irish and Flaco being Guatemalan. Laughter followed and then suddenly both Flaco and Matt were rushed out the front door really fast and harshly. It seemed like they were being pushed out by some strong wind acting like a big bouncer at a bar. The way they came out was not in the same fashion they went in. They had been stripped down all the way to their underwear; they had been tarred and feathered. In pure disbelief, Matt takes a deep breath thinking that things couldn't possibly get any worse; when suddenly, Vic pulls up in his car and takes a picture of them and starts laughing.)

Vic: Oh yeah, I might as well tell you now; since you forgot to ask. This house is infamous

    Amongst real estate agents, for being haunted by some very rowdy types back from ye

    olden times. (sarcastic) That's like, a long time ago. (glances at his camera) They're just

    gonna loooove this picture back at the office of you ghost hunters; nice work boys.

Matt: Mother fucker!! (Darts over to Vic to go kick his ass)

(As Matt starts running towards Vic's car; Vic starts laughing his ass off even more and quickly takes off in his car, as he takes one last picture of Matt.)

Vic: (yelling out the window) That's what you get when you don't pay me!!

Matt: I'm gonna fucking kill you!! (Looks at Flaco) Is this how you pictured it?? This great

    fucking venture of ours!! Is this how you saw us "getting paid". Fuck!!

Flaco: My fireball!! It's gone!! No way!!? Those ghosts took my shit!!!

(They both start walking down the street still tarred and feathered to where Matt parked his car. On their way to the car, some people from the neighborhood that were out and about, start staring at them and start laughing. Other people even started clapping and cheering while making pigeon noises; they were really letting them have it. Philly, enough said.)

(They get in Matt's car and a few seconds of silence go by)

Matt: We are going to need help; big time.

Flaco: (spitting feathers out of his mouth) Yup. I agree.

Matt: We need someone who knows about this shit, that's not going to make mistakes. We need

the toughest scariest person we know; someone who doesn't take shit from anybody, not

even ghosts!!

(A few seconds of silence go by and then they both look at each other with the answer.)

Matt + Flaco: 10 Pak!!!

Song: Caribbean Connection – Big Pun (1:18 – 1:40)

(10 Pak, this guy was Philadelphia through and through; old school, fearless, and hard core down to the bone. 10 Pak is cousin to the notorious, "El Chino" of North Philadelphia; one of the baddest mutha fucka's of all time, (as Dave Chapelle would say). Matt and Flaco just happen to be acquainted with a character such as 10 Pak, due to the fact that they currently work together at a Crab Cake factory in "Chester, PA".)

Next Day ....

Place: Chester, PA

Crab Cake Factory

(The sounds of machines working, people moving, food being made, and distant chatter clutters the hallways of the Crab Cake factory. Orders being made for places as far away as California on the West Coast and as near as Lancaster, Pittsburgh, Delaware, and New Jersey (all Exits☺).

(Flaco and Matt make their way to the kitchen section of the Factory, where 10 Pak is usually at washing tubs, pans, pots, and dishes.)

Flaco: Yo Ten Pak! What's up bro? Que pasa cabron? What's new with you?

10 Pak: Wuzz up boys, what you up to? (fist bumps all around)

Flaco: Bro, we need you to help us out on a little project that we are trying to do. We need

people, we need equipment, and most importantly; we need muscle.

10 Pak: What did you guys do this time?

Flaco: No no no, nothing like that.

Matt: Please, let's put that behind us, no need to bring up the past. (clears his throat)

10 Pak: Yeah; let's not. (starts laughing) okay, you got my attention; go on.

(They start explaining everything to him, including what happened to them the day before. They leave no small detail out; telling him even about how embarrassing it was for them, to have to walk through the streets of Center City Philadelphia, tarred and feathered. 10 Pak tells them that it sounds like a good idea and that they can count on him for support. He even tells them that he is going to go visit a Light Worker (Wiccan Practioner), to see if "the cards" can tell him anything about their project. After hearing this, both Matt and Flaco get a quick chill down their spines; because all of sudden this shit got real for them. They were both thinking about what they had just heard; and after processing it for about a half a second, they respond with.)

Flaco: What the hell is a light worker? Is that like a witch??

10 Pak: No genius, it's not like a witch.

Matt: A fucking Witch!!??

Flaco: Wait, what the fuck did we just sign up for??

Matt: A fucking Witch!!?? Bro; you for real?

Flaco: How the fuck you know a Witch bro??

10 Pak: She's not a witch you ding dongs!! Besides, I thought you guys were serious about this; unless you prefer having feathers shoved up ya'lls asses again. (starts laughing)

Matt: That's bullshit!! There was nothing shoved up there; although I did get punched in the nuts. Alright fine, talk to the Witch on behalf of all of us; I am going to hell for this.

Flaco: So wait, a light worker and a witch; is that like comparing a hooker and an escort? You know, during the course of the night she's your date, your Escort. But by the end of the night; when she's all coked up out of her mind, wrapped up in some dudes carpet while she is being put in a trunk of a car, then she's a Hooker. Is it kind of like that??

10 Pak: (shakes his head and laughs) Alright, all bullshit aside, I'll go find out what the cards have in store for us; see if it's favorable. In the mean time you two can go pick up a few things we'll need, at this address. (starts writing down an address and some instructions on a small piece of paper and hands it to them) Go here and ask for Karl. He is going to give you a duffel bag with most of the stuff we need to get started. When you get there say "Blueberry Muffin". He'll know you are with me, that's my personal pass code. Then take that over to my place, we'll meet there; Flaco I'll hit you up as soon as I know what's what and we'll go from there. Sound good??

Matt: What's in the duffel bag? Hold on, this just went from being a cool safe side project to a bad day in IRaQ!!

10 Pak: Insurance, that's what's in the duffel-bag Matt, insurance; plain and simple.

Flaco: Sounds like a plan; we're on our way out anyway, we'll head over there right now.

(A few moments later, they head out to a warehouse in South Philadelphia to meet the man named "Karl".)

Place: Water-Front Warehouse

    South Philadelphia, PA

(They arrive to the warehouse and as they walk up to the door they see an old school giant camera staring right down at them. They try opening the door but it's locked; a voice starts talking to them from the speaker next to the camera.)

Overhead Speaker: Can we help you with something?

Matt: (bumps Flaco on the shoulder) Dude, the password.

Flaco: Oh yeah; "hmm" (clears his voice) Blueberry Muffin.

(Buzzer goes off and they open the door and go in. They start walking towards the front desk; there are security guards on both sides staring at them, checking them out.)

Matt: Yeah, this is some serious shit here.

Flaco: Stay cool, I'll do the talking. (He walks up to the man behind the desk wearing a Jeff Cap

and hands him the note from 10 Pak) Yeah hi, we are friends with 10 Pak, he told us to

stop by and ask for Karl; we're supposed to be picking up a duffel bag from him.

(Karl just stares at them for a few seconds without saying anything)

Karl: I'm Karl; you're friends with 10 Pak? You look like a couple of low lives from Delaware.

Matt: Yeah we know 10 Pak, we're his muscle; you know, his backup.

Karl: (laughs) I'm having a hard time picturing 10 Pak needing a couple of stoned

" little cheeba monkeys" like yourselves, as back up.

Matt: Oh shit! Karl's got jokes!

(Flaco gets distracted by the multiple jars of different items on the counter in front of him.)

Flaco: What the hell are these? (pointing at the jars)

Karl: Call them, Vitamins.

Flaco: Vitamins huh; they get you high??

Karl: Ok see, NOW I believe you know 10 Pak.

Later that evening…..

Place: Pennsport Section

    South Philadelphia

(10 Pak arrives at his destination; he is received at the door by the "Light Worker" (Wiccan Witch) apprentices. They make their way to the back yard where there is a tent in the middle of a small, but beautiful garden. He enters the tent and sees the light-worker sitting down as she lays the cards out.)

 10 Pak: I appreciate you seeing me in such a short notice; I hope that job we did for you was to

your satisfaction. No more problems with the neighbors I hope.

Witch: Your help is appreciated; great grandson of the "Catalan Gypsies".

10 Pak: Excellent; now we can get down to another piece of business I'm interested in. I want to go film the unknown, the occult; those things that are hiding that don't know yet that they want to be found. Are there any rewards on a pursuit of this type of venture?

Witch: Let the cards speak; and let your path follow where it may.

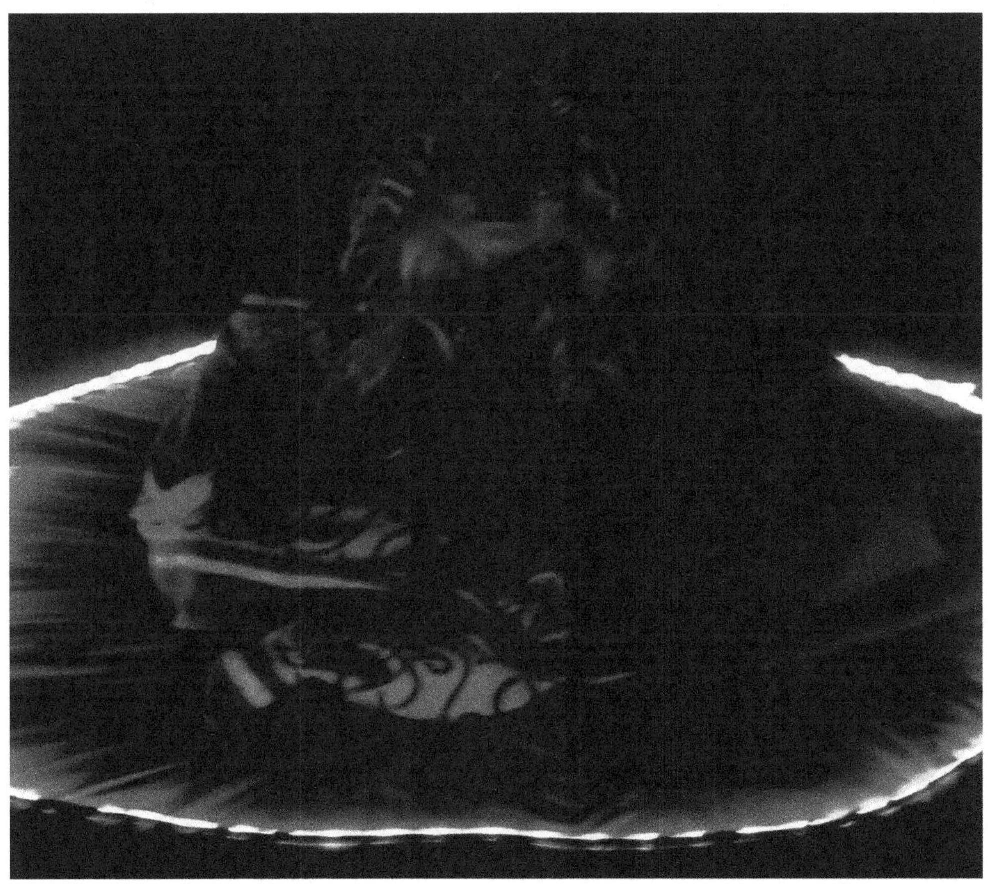

10 Pak: I woke up this morning with a peculiar feeling, then during the course of the day; this plan, this idea, falls right on my lap.

(She places the cards on the table and observes them, moves her hand over them to feel their energy; then she opens her eyes and interprets them in her own unique way.)

Witch: Fortune favors the bold, my old friend. If you are brave enough to withstand the "Obstacles" surrounding this venture of yours; then be assured that you'll find a pot of gold waiting for you, at the end of this particular rainbow.

10 Pak: Hmm.. I like the sound of that. So I take it that these "obstacles", are some kind of crazy scary shit I got to deal with before I get to my reward. Sounds promising, I guess that means green light then. (Gets up and drops a stack of Benjamin's on the table.) Thank you again. This is for your discretion of course, that is much appreciated.

Witch: My lips are sealed, may Death be the Judge; not a word to no one.

10 Pak: I'm glad we understand each other. Good day Madame.

(10 Pak walks away from the garden and leaves; as he's walking he calls Flaco and lets him know that it is on, like Donkey Kong. ☺ They are to rendezvous around noon at 10 Pak's place in South Philadelphia.)

Song: Marijuana Dreams – DubbleStandart (2:20 – 3:00)

Place: 3rd St and Tree St

10 Paks House - South Philadelphia

(Early Saturday morning ☺ Chilling and grooving; 10 Pak showing why he is so valuable to many different business people of different types of corporate cultures. You see him going through the process of making THC edibles. Lollipops with the Mary Jane leaf imprint, sticks of canna-butter, space cakes, tincture, and yummy gummies. La Da Mercy ☺ The clock strikes the appointed hour; Matt and Flaco knock on 10 Pak's door. He lets them in and they right away get a huge whiff of the good life. As they walk in they see that Vic Vinegerrete is sitting there hitting a little bubbler bong. Matt's eyes start turning red hot and not because of the smoke.)

Matt: 10 Pak what the FUCK, is this asshole doing here!!

10 Pak: Matt calm down, it's taken care of. Vic said he's sorry; ain't that right Vic?

Vic: (coughing from the bong hit, not really giving a shit) Yeah sure; whatever you say, that's right.

Matt: (sarcastically) How very sincere of you; 10 Pak come on bro…. ☹

10 Pak: Vic said he's sorry and he is giving us a good lead on a spot that has a ghost

sighting. Ain't that right Vic??

Vic: You said it buddy. (puts the bong down looks at Matt and Flaco) Money talks amigos; well

in this case a different kind of green speaks to me. The kind of green that gets me laid; if

you know what a mean?? You pay me, I hook you up with what you need; welcome to the

real world boys. This particular sighting is in the Old City section, an old Victorian

Mansion belonging to The Dutchess Lady Crane; an English woman of Patrician noble

blood, heiress to a great fortune. She died of depression after her husband and son died

mysteriously; sadness and loneliness over took her or some corny shit like that….

(Matt starts clearing his voice a bit loudly, interrupting Vic)

Matt: Yeah, I call bullshit. 10 Pak, don't trust this asshole piece of shit lowlife monkey fucker!!

10 Pak: Matt I appreciate you looking out for us; but Vic, doesn't have the balls to fuck me over.

That's why you brought me in remember; we take no bullshit from no one. Besides, I

already paid him, in weed. Matt he really does work well if you pay him; right Vic?

Vic: Absolutely buddy (as he hits the bong again) absolutely. (exhales) As I was saying, not

much is known, few scattered details here and there; you guys know what I mean. The

old mansion is up for restoration. I can talk to the security guys for you; they might want

some of that Cotton Candy Kush too for their troubles, just saying. They'll let you in, take

your cameras and take all the time you want in there and your good to go; and so am I if

I'm being honest. 10 Pak are my Lollipops and gummies ready to go???

10 Pak: Yes they are; don't forget to keep the gummies refrigerated. Here are your space

Cakes also (hands him a grocery bag with edibles). There you go.

Vic: Thank you kindly; any questions you got my number. Oh yeah, if you can; don't call past

8:00, I'll be with a special lady friend, that's what these groceries are for. (lifts up his bag

of edibles and waves them around) 10 Pak, take it easy bro (looks at Matt and Flaco)

Wingus, Dingus…hopefully I won't have to see you monkeys again.

Matt: Yeah well, the feeling is mutual asshole!!

Vic: Whatever!! (closes the door behind him)

Matt: Calls ME a fucking monkey; fuck that guy! I hope he gets mugged by some crack head on his way home.

10 Pak: (laughing) Damn bro, that's a bit heavy don't you think.

Matt: Fuuuck him; son of a son of a bitch!!

10 Pak: (passes Matt a special blunt to smoke) He got to you that bad huh?? Don't worry about him. He's a crook and a half, but he's on our side, trust me. He just played a joke on you guys, that's all.

Matt: Yeah well I'm tired of assholes like that picking on me because of my size.

10 Pak: Hey I got picked on too; a lot. I didn't have it horrible, but there were some assholes that did go out of their way to make my life miserable. But you know what I say to that. (as Matt passes him the blunt back, he hits one time and then exhales slowly) Fuck them, I've buried that anger and hatred in the past and I let it stay there. It does me no good in my life. Those memories are there only as fuel fire for when you're up against someone more skilled than you that could kill you. That's about the only time you let that rage out. That's why God invented weed, coffee, and bitches; you feel me bruh. (exhales slowly and gives Matt a fist bump)

Matt: Fuck yeah bro, I hear you. (smokes some more of the blunt and passes it to Flaco)

Flaco: What's this we're smoking??

10 Pak: This is Purple Punch, not bad right??

Flaco: Yo man, when are you gonna get that Juicy Fruit again?? That was my favorite; I think that's the best one you've ever had bro.

10 Pak: I agree, that shit was delicious. "Bill Gluckman is down with the bitches and Ho's,

Flaco: "Imma vote for him".

(They start laughing at the "Malibu's most Wanted" reference.)

Flaco: Ha ha; fuck yeah! We are gonna have some fun with this shit! When are we set to go?

10 Pak: We'll go see the security guards tonight and see what kind of edibles they want. Then

we will set everything up for tomorrow and we will go from there. I got Steve, Willis

and Lil Kev coming along with us as the sound guys and camera crew.

Next Day……………………………..

Song: You got me – The Roots (feat. Erykah Badu) (0:00 – 1:30)

Place: Crane Manor

Old City, Philadelphia

(Tomorrow comes today as they drive through the streets of Old City Philadelphia; they arrive at

the property. The day has come to an end as the sun is about to set; no matter where you are in

the world, those beautiful sunset colors never seize to amaze. As they walk up to the front gate,

they see the security guards coming up to them.)

Security Guard #1: Yo 10 Pak, those lollipops where off the hook; I passed the fuck out;

shit had me drooling.

Security Guard #2: Yeah bro, leave us your number so we can buy some more off of you.

Eating some gummies during work, I felt all nice and relaxed. You don't go

crazy from being bored all the time. The rest of the guys are gonna want

some too, so we are going to put in a big order; is that cool?

10 Pak: That won't be a problem gentlemen. Here's my card with my number; in case I

don't pick up please leave a message and I'll get back to you. I'm usually doing stuff

like this so I'm always a bit busy; but somehow I manage to get everything done believe

it or not. Is everything good to go?

Matt: Guys has there really been a ghost sighting here? Or is it all bullshit?

Security Guard #2: Nah, it's true; we've seen her ourselves walking by the windows. You see

her in her dress; she just seems sad and lonely. She doesn't feel like she is

evil or scary. You know like the ghosts on TV that are complete dicks, that

just want to scare you and attack you. All those movies are the same crap.

Security Guard#1: Sometimes the lights are turned on like around 3 in the morning on certain

nights; then when we go in, nothing, not a clue nor a sign of anything. No

footprints, no smells; not a fucking thing. So that leaves out the possibility

of kids breaking in as a prank or junkies breaking in to steal shit.

Security Guard#2: Seriously. She seems very nice; a real classy lady.

10 Pak: Is that so??

Flaco: You're getting an idea aren't you? I know that look.

10 Pak: I think I have an idea; but this one is WAY outside the box. (starts laughing)

Security Guard#1: Anything you need brother, you let us know. We'll let you do your thing

We're not gonna keep you anymore. (They start walking away to their guard

booth) We'll call you soon; real soon.

10 Pak: Thanks again brotha; much appreciated.

Flaco: Why you always so polite? As bad ass as you are at fighting, you'd think you be more

aggressive or tough speaking. Like "Nah motherfucker"!! Or "Scram BITCH"!!

10 Pak: That's because my momma taught me some manners son. You watch too many rap

videos Flaco, that shit is bad for your brain. Besides, you catch more flies with honey.

Matt: You can also catch plenty of flies with shit too you know.

10 Pak: True, but then again; who likes the smell of shit on their hands, compared to the smell

of honey.

Matt: Also true. So! What's the plan, how do you want to approach this? What crazy outside

the box idea do you have?

10 Pak: What's today Friday or Thursday?

Matt: It's Saturday night for fucks sake; you smoke way too much amigo.

10 Pak: You can never smoke enough bruh! Ha ha ha. Till the day I die. Ok, let me make a

quick phone call. (phone rings at the other end and his friend picks up) Yo Mario!! I

need a favor, I got a lady in distress and I need one of your boys to come help.

On the phone….

Mario: I got you, give me the address, he'll be there within the hour; give or take a few minutes.

10 Pak: You're the man Mario; oh and tell your sister to stop calling me, will ya.

Mario: (starts laughing) You wish you Mook!! Take care of my boy, talk to you later.

10 Pak: Alright Mario, peace out and thanks again.

Flaco: What, you ordering a pizza or something??

10 Pak: Not exactly (starts laughing) lets go boys, grab your gear; we are going in.

(10 Pak and crew make their way up to the House; they go in to the main living room and start setting up their sound and video equipment. 10 Pak is writing a letter addressed to Lady Crane and is not letting anyone else read it. He sets the letter on the table along with some flowers for the Lady and then asks everybody to leave. 10 Pak closes the door behind him and a few seconds go by and a ghostly figure makes her way to the flowers and the letter.)

Lady Crane,

I write to you in a most sincere manner to simply extend my friendship and services to you, dear Lady. I cannot fathom the loneliness you've had to endure throughout the centuries; I admire your courage for that. For I don't think that I myself have the intestinal fortitude to go through what you have been through. That is why I have taken it upon myself to send you a present. My intent is not to insult you in any way my Lady; but to give you some much deserved company on a lonely boring Saturday night. If it is your wish to accept my gift to you; then open the front door for us and we will send it in. If you decide that this is an invasion of your privacy and find us to be too "pedestrian" or too "bourgeois" for your liking; then I humbly apologize in advance and you shall never see us again my Lady.

Sincerely

Rafael Bertrand de la Plata

===

(As the crew waits outside the Mansion, the delivery that 10 Pak had ordered finally arrives. A handsome looking young man who seemed to be in great shape carrying a small boom box, walks up to the group.)

10 Pak: There he is, you're Mario's guy right? What's your name??

Marcus: My name is Marcus, what's up fellas?? So, what's the job??

10 Pak: Very high class customer, very well respected Lady, you understand?

(The rest of the guys looking at each other all confused and baffled; but nobody is saying anything. On top of that, they see that the front door started opening up all by itself.)

Marcus: Okay, I got it; no dumb shit, keep it professional.

(10 Pak sees the door opening as well and knows that this is his cue to send Marcus in.)

10 Pak: That's right. Oh, and you're gonna have to wear this right before you get ready to start. If you don't put on the blindfold you don't get paid, and I'll tell Mario that you were less than helpful. (hands him a blindfold) I'll walk with you and tell you where to set up. Once I leave you there, get dressed or undressed; whatever it is that you do and put the blindfold on, play your music and start the show. The lady will be there and you got to let her do whatever she wants. I'll throw something extra for you if you do a good job, okay??

Marcus: Clear as Crystal. I'm ready when you are.

10 Pak: Good shit, guys I'll be right back, I'm gonna help young Marcus here, get situated.

Matt: But…oh boy; never mind.

(They proceed up to the house and into the living room area. Marcus puts all his stuff down then 10 Pak tells him that he is to perform only in here and that the Lady would be watching him. He also tells him that he would know when it would be over because the Lady would tell him. He is saying all this out loud so that "Lady Crane" can hear him as well. 10 Pak wishes Marcus good luck and then leaves the house and goes back outside with the rest of the group.)

Matt: Bro, what are you doing?? A fucking Male Stripper!!

10 Pak: Giving the Lady something she hasn't seen before, on a Saturday night; I hope.

Flaco: This is gonna be interesting. Bruh, what if she eats Marcus alive and shit. How you gonna explain that to Mario?

10 Pak: The Escort and the Hooker; that's why in Chess, the pawns always go first.

Flaco: Damn, that's cold blooded bro…

Matt: I am not rolling up a dead stripper in a carpet!! I am…(hears music coming from inside)

(They all look over to the house; they can all hear the music.)

10 Pak: So far so good.

Lil Kev: Let me get this straight, you are giving a 300 year old ghost a fucking male stripper?
I don't think I've ever heard of anything even close to this. But hey, you are paying me
either way, so who gives a shit right.

10 Pak: Willis, how we looking??

(Willis, the camera man was monitoring the whole thing from his laptop.)

Willis: She's there; the infrared camera is definitely picking something up and it isn't Marcus.

 (Back inside, Marcus is doing his dance routine when he feels someone's hand on his chest; suddenly his pants are ripped off and he is pushed back on to the big couch. Lady Crane had pinned Marcus down and started giving him, probably, the best blow job he had ever had. The proof was in the craziest most intense "OH FACES" in the existence of mankind made by young Marcus. The ghost lady was sucking him so hard that Marcus's eyes rolled back into his skull and he shouted…all the while still being blind folded.)

Marcus: Fly Eagles Fly!!!!! Yeah!!!!!!!!!!!!! Holy fucking shit!!!!! Holy shiiit!! How'd you fit
my balls in there too??

Ending song: Bad Vibrations – Black Angels – Final part (3:20 – 4:20)
(Back outside, the crew couldn't believe what they were hearing as they were laughing their asses off. Little did they know it, but their theory had proved right. All ghosts are not assholes, well that was until young Marcus decided to get cute and take off his blind fold. He sees a pale ghostly looking women with her eyes turning red; Marcus starts going into an epilepsy convulsion now because of her.)

(He is scared and excited at the same time as her hair starts floating in the air all creepy like. The guys start hearing Marcus cry out for help and they start rushing for the doors to try to open them. All except 10 Pak and Flaco; they were just watching; letting things transpire to see what would happen. Matt and Willis are trying to kick the door down at this point when all of a sudden the screaming stops and the doors open up by themselves. They all go in to see what had transpired; they see young Marcus laying there half dead; although it wasn't young marcus anymore. The body laying there looked like that of a 90 year old man. The lady ghost had pretty much literally sucked the life-force out of Marcus. As Marcus laid there asking for help, the boys petrified from the shock slowly start helping him out.)

Flaco: So, should we go get the carpet now??

Chapter 2

For the Love

of

Money

Next Day back at Crane Manor……..

Place: Crane Manor

Old City, Philadelphia

Song: Say Ooh La La – Wiseguys (0:00 – 1:03)

(As we come back to the Mansion; we find that something new transpires behind its walls. Strangely enough; 10 Pak is presently demonstrating some dancing moves, trying to teach Lady Crane how to shake her hips to a modern beat. For the first time in a very long time; laughter fills the empty spaces throughout the hallways in the Mansion. Amazed at his lack of fear for the unknown, Lady Crane begins to realize that 10 Pak is not an ordinary person; but a bit of an "eccentric" with a dash of dangerous.)

Lady Crane: Are you sure your employers won't be angry at you for missing work today??

10 Pak: Nope; not at all. Everything is taken care of; now let's dance.

Lady Crane: I haven't danced in a very long time; I don't know what to do.

10 Pak: Look at it this way; at least you don't have to worry about stepping on my feet.

Lady Crane: (starts laughing) Oh my! That just looks so…(staring at his ass)..delicious.

10 Pak: Eyes up here Lady…Come on.

Lady Crane: Funny…(makes an attempt at shaking her hips)what do you call this??

10 Pak: It's called, having a good time. (They keep dancing)

Lady Crane: I do say; things have changed quite a bit since my time. I most certainly could of used a friend like you 250 years ago. (laughs) You would have loved it here in Philadelphia all that time ago. The City was so young, so vibrant and full of life, not knowing what the future had in store for us.

10 Pak: I love history; I think I would've liked to have seen it. The way you describe it; so full of life and hope.

Lady Crane: Copious amounts of good times. Out back on our property cooking, laughing, and smoking hemp with friends and family; watching the sunset. (sighs) Those were the happiest days of my life.

10 Pak: Wha wha what?? You say hemp?? You mean what we call Marijuana?? Ooh, What

you know about that Lady Crane?

Lady Crane: I've heard all the guards call it that, while I've seen them smoking the hemp. So

my guess is yes; M-A-R-IJUANA..Is that how you say it??

10 Pak: Close enough. Tell me more; did you smoke a little, a considerable amount, or every

chance you could get??

Lady Crane: What do you mean, did??

10 Pak: As in past tense, did. (pause) What? No way; you can still smoke? How's that

possible??

Lady Crane: Why do you think they just call me "Lady Crane" and not "Old Crazy Lady". I

would have gone MAD without my regularly appointed hour of Hemp

consumption. As for the how? Don't know how to really explain it; I just know

that it is possible. You're going to have to ask my hemp guy.

10 Pak: How very interesting; I can't believe this. This is like, major discovery here. If this shit

weren't this crazy; I'd probably be nominated for something…like a Nobel prize or

some shit like that. Who am I kidding, I'm a Latino from Philadelphia; we don't get

nominated for shiiiit. Does your dealer deliver??

Lady Crane: Oh no need; I have plenty here.

10 Pak: Interesting….☺

Place: Crab Cake Factory

    Chester, PA

(Back at work at the Crab Cake Factory, Matt and Flaco are going through their daily routines;
somehow managing to work hard and hardly work at all.)

Matt: This sucks, 10 Pak is off having a good time while we're hanging out here with

these fugazzi crab cakes; not doing dick.

Flaco: How cool was that, we got a ghost a stripper; you can't make this shit up bro.

(One of their other fellow employees by the name of Scott, grabs a piece of rolled up plastic and tries throwing it in the trash can, but misses.)

Matt: Damnnn you suuck!!

Scott: You don't think I can play basketball??

Matt: I don't think you can't play; I KNOW you can't play.

Scott: Fuck you dude!!

Flaco: Maybe he played baseball. (laughs) ☺

Matt: Yeah for the girls team; and I believe it was softball. (starts laughing)

Scott: Shut the fuck up Matt!! You were the teams WATER boy!! (starts laughing)

Matt: Yeah; but not for the GIRLS team. (other employees start laughing)

Back at the Mansion……

Place: Crane Manor

Old City, Philadelphia

Lady Crane: Rafael, listen to me; life is nothing but a series of moments; and somehow, you have to find something to do with your time in between those moments. Usually, that time is spent with the ones you love; and if it's not, then it should be.

10 Pak: I agree. (brief pause) Lady Crane are you a religious person?? I only ask because you don't seem to be blessed with the weight of its burden.

Lady Crane: Please; can we not talk about God nor religion. The worst things imaginable in History and all over the world have transpired in the name of Religion.

10 Pak: Lady Crane, a thousand apologies; it will not happen again. Just, allow me to say this; I will not question your reason as to why…but know that I understand. I also believe that there is too much injustice in this world, for me to believe that there is such a thing as a benevolent and merciful God. I refuse to believe in that; whole heartedly.

Lady Crane: You really are a clever one; I like that about you. You've figured out at such a young age, what most people can't in a whole lifetime.

10 Pak: (turns off the stereo and grabs his guitar) How about your family? Do you miss them??

We don't have to talk about this if you don't want; I don't want to impose …

Lady Crane: Never had anyone to speak too about them. Truth is that I do miss my husband

and my son; so much. I miss their presence, their laughter, the debates, and the

sunsets with them. (Starts crying)What did I do to deserve this penance? Did I

not pray enough; did I not give enough money to the poor? What did I do wrong?

(10 Pak seeing how distressed and sad Lady Crane was, starts playing a song that he knows; a song to sooth the soul from the sadness within. The song is called; La Guitarra Triste, which translates to, "The Sad Guitar".)

Song: La Guitarra Triste – Window Psychosis (0:00 – 1:00)

Lady Crane: That is a pretty song; did you compose it?

10 Pak: Yes; I composed this particular arrangement; it's a hint and a whisper of two songs I

Like with my own sad little twist.

(She keeps listening to the song for a moment longer)

Lady Crane: Beautiful song, I like it. That just put me in the mood for some of my sticky icky

hemp. Now…. Would you like to try some of my own MA..Ri….JUANA?

10 Pak: (his eyes almost pop out of his head) Sure, why not...☺ Don't have to be at work till

tomorrow. (starts laughing and puts down the guitar)

(Lady Crane takes out a little glittery shinny bag with her weed in it. As she opens it up, a light blue glow starts resonating (fucking beautiful). She grabs a bud and puts it in the palm of her hand and says the words.)

Lady Crane: From start to finish. Turn wind to mist. Reverberate and diminish.

(The bud turns into this cool smoky mist in the shape of a flower and makes its way up her nose and also 10 Pak's nose)

(few seconds later)

Song: Sing – Blur (0:00 – 1:10)

10 Pak: (eyes start turning red) Hoollllly shiiiitittttt!!!!! (starts coughing a bit and rolls over
on the floor and exhales slowly) Lady Crane, this is the best Hemp I've ever smoked. I
feel so….light, weightless.. I feel …free.

(10 Pak lays down slowly on the white fluffy carpet; Lady Crane lays down next to him. She
makes the room spin in slow motion, as she also makes the trees from the Van Gogh paintings on
the walls start moving; as if there were real wind blowing inside the paintings. The sunlight
from outside, was temporarily blocked by a couple of passenger storm clouds roaming the skies
above Center City. A few minutes go by and then a silence takes over.)

Lady Crane: If I may be so bold now, let me ask you something; are you an honest
man?

10 Pak: I try, but with the cards I've been dealt; it's a bit hard. But to answer your question
truthfully; I would never lie to "you" Lady Crane.

Lady Crane: Good answer; I believe you. (brief pause) What is it that you want from me;
Rafael??

10 Pak: Knowledge my Lady; money and objects are just trivial things to me. I want to know
what's beyond the realm of possibilities. I wish to know if this thing called life is really
worth it; I must know. I do not believe in Religion or in God nor any Gods; therefore I
am left alone without any answers to the questions I have.

Lady Crane: What about your friends; I don't think they share your same beliefs about earthly
possessions.

10 Pak: You are right, they don't. I made them a promise I don't think I can deliver. I promised
them, adventure, riches and fast easy women (strippers and ho's); all the while that was
never my goal. I guess in the end, after it's all said and done; to them I'm nothing but a
charlatan.

Lady Crane: That my young man; is something you are not. You have a positive good natured aura. It glows bright and proud. (few moments of silence go by) Perhaps I can help you with the finance of such endeavors; if you help me find my way back to my family. Help me get rid of this "curse", this purgatory I'm in and I shall provide the coin to make amends with your friends with plenty to spare.

10 Pak: My Lady, I will help you find your way to your family; I give you my word. Money, it doesn't move me or motivate me; I've seen it bring out the worst in people.

Lady Crane: You are right; money is a form of control. An illusion set forth by those who seek to tell people that they have all the answers; when they really don't. See that painting; slide it to the left and pull the lever behind it.

(10 Pak does as she says and a secret door slides open right in front of him. Behind this secret door was an un-measureable amount of treasure just sitting there. There was treasure ranging from old paintings, to gold and silver coins, to priceless statues, and beautiful artworks. Also visible, were documents of tremendous value; depicting implications of ownership of properties within the Commonwealth of Pennsylvania. All put together, it was just about the same amount of money as the Lottery winning ticket. Cha Ch'ing!!)

Lady Crane: The renovators are coming; don't want them to keep all this money now do we?

10 Pak: Lady Crane; exactly how rich were you?

Lady Crane: Filthy Rich, my good friend.

10 Pak: My Lady Crane; this is a fortune. This is too much money how in the….Lady Crane I will help you get back to your family but; I don't need this much money.

Lady Crane: Then give it away to the poor, people that need it. Feed the hungry and the Unfortunate here in Philadelphia; if nowhere else. Do not let this money fall into the hands of the corrupt and the unworthy; people with no scruples nor decent morals. Please Rafael Bertrand de La Plata.

10 Pak: You truly are a Lady; you have a kind heart and an understanding manner. On my life; you will see your family again. Even if I have to go to the gates of hell and face its Demons for you my lady; you will see your family again.

Lady Crane: You really are fearless my friend. If I only knew what was keeping me here; I

wish I knew what wretched reason has me bound to this realm away from

those which I love the most.

10 Pak: That is what we are going to find out, let me call the realtor I know. I'm pretty sure

he'll set me on the right path; once I fill his pockets with gold and silver.

(10 Pak calls Vic and sets up a meeting for later on in the evening; he then sends Flaco a text message letting him know what's up. Back at the Crab Cake factory Flaco takes a quick look at his phone and sees the text message.)

Flaco: Yo! Speak of the devil..It's 10 Pak. He says to meet him tonight over at Strawberry

Mansions. He says he has another spot for us to go check out; he has a surprise that's

gonna make us "really" fucking happy he says.

Matt: Now we're talking!! FUCK your crab cakes Scott; (starts singing Scotty doesn't know)

Scotty doesn't know, Scotty doesn't know!! Don't tell Scotty!!

Later that night……………

Place: Strawberry Mansions

  North Philadelphia

(10 Pak and a few of his very close friends (gunmen) wait up at an old warehouse for Matt and Flaco. Herbie's phone starts ringing, he takes a quick look and sees that it's a "Collection Agency" calling for an overdue bill payment.)

Herbie: These assholes; watch this. (answers the phone in a loud voice) Hello!!! Is this Porn

Hub calling about my 10 inch Cock!! Hello!! Did I get the job!! Cause I'll bang

Anything!!! (Collectors hang up quickly; Herbie and friends start laughing) ☺

10 Pak: What's that, 6 out 6?

Willis: I can't believe that actually works; I'm gonna definitely try that.

Herbie: It'll be a couple of months before they dare try again. LOL…

(Matt and Flaco finally arrive, followed immediately by Vic "the Realtor". Herbie starts pointing at his watch letting them know they are late.)

Matt: Eat a dick Herbie; don't start with me. (everybody starts laughing)

10 Pak: Okay, we're all here now; we can finally start. First order of business (starts handing everybody schoolbags full of cash) here is the payment for everybody; Lady Crane sends her regards.

Flaco: How the fuck?? Jackpot!! The stripper idea worked!!

10 Pak: Yes it did.

Matt: (going through his bag) There's like 50 grand in here.

10 Pak: It's actually 65grand a schoolbag. Oh and Vic, here is yours as you requested.

(hands him a bag full of old silver and gold coins from the 1700's)

Matt: Why the fuck does he get paid in that???

Vic: Here we go....

10 Pak: That's what he wanted; so that's what I got him.

Vic: Just for once, I want to feel like a pirate and hold real treasure from way back in the day. I'm excited, why can't you be excited for me Matt?? Dear old buddy of mine.

Matt: I got your buddy right here asshole!! (grabs his junk)

10 Pak: Guys, please! (separating them)

Herbie: Queers. Good thing you're paying me to be here 10 Pak; because I would not be listening to these two fems, for free. Just F.Y.I

Flaco: Nice team work speech Herbie.

(Vic walks over to 10 Pak and hands him a couple of folders with information about all the addresses with ghosts' sightings and its histories here in Philadelphia.)

Vic: Everything you need is all there, just like you asked. I still can't believe you struck gold on this one my friend. You got quite the talent; I wouldn't bet against you. (They both start laughing)

10 Pak: Okay, new order of business; our next spot to visit. That's if you guys are still

willing to be a part of this, thing we're doing. (they all give him the nod of approval)

Okay then let's proceed; Vic give us the 411.

 (Vic tells them about a ghost sighting of an old janitor at the Founders Parish in Kensington. This place was rumored to have had the history books of the old families in Philadelphia hidden in the basement. If there was anybody that could point them in the right direction, it would be that Janitor's Ghost.)

Vic: If your theory holds true about ghosts being cool and not "dickheads"; then you might be

able to get his attention with normal bullshit one would want. In this case maybe a radio, a

Phillies Team Poster, a Hustlers Porno Magazine; I'm sure you'll come up with something.

Song: The Good Old Days – The Libertines (0:00 – 1:10)

On the way to Kensington….

(They take the trip across town, with all their equipment and head straight for the old parish. On the way there, they take the scenic view through town. As far as scenic views go; Philadelphia has plenty and then some.)

Place: The Founders Parish

Kensington, Philadelphia

(Vic managed to talk to the grounds keeper and sweeten the deal with a 50 year old bottle of Chivas Regal whiskey; so now they have access to the basement. The crew sets up the cameras, sound equipment, a ping pong table, chairs, beer, alcohol, weed, playing cards, a TV for sports news; and a radio with 94.1fm sports on the tune. 10 Pak tells everybody to step back a bit as he takes out some of the "Ghost Bud".)

10 Pak: From start to finish. Turn wind to mist. Reverberate and diminish.

(As the misty smoke engulfs the whole room, everybody starts cheering and going "whoah" in amazement!! Let the good times roll; right☺. A few minutes go by and some of the crew members were playing cards and the others were sitting on the shitty furniture drinking, watching the Phillies game on the TV; when suddenly someone appears out of thin air.)

Old Janitor: Hey fellas….(everybody stops what they're doing) You guys mind if I watch the

game with ya'll. Its sure been a long time since I saw the Phillies play.

Matt: (pulls up a chair) You can sit right here sir; there you go (sets a beer there for him.)

Old Janitor: You boys know I can't touch that.

Flaco: Because you're working??

Old Janitor: Because I'm a ghost; foool…

Everybody: Ohhhhhhh… Heyyyyyyyy….OOHHHHHHHH LOLs

Old Janitor: Okay; enough with the OHH"s.. I will take some of that ghost bud from the

young brother right here. (pointing at 10 Pak)

10 Pak: Thought you never ask; Sir.

Old Janitor: Enough with the Sir shiit; I aint your papppy!! (sees the Hustler's Porno Mag)

Is that for me?? Well shiiit; the fuck ya'll waiting for?? Pour the drinks young

Blood and light that shit up; let's get this party bumping, for real!!!

Song: Budha Lovaaz – Bone Thugs N Harmony (0:00 – 1:20)

(Four hours go by of smoking ghost bud, drinking, and playing cards with a man that could never be out smoked, out drunken, out played, or out hustled; a sharp mind in deed. Time slowly creeps in and out of existence; a moment disappears within the thin layers of smoke floating peacefully within the room. It is now 4:20 in the morning and everyone is passed out, except for 10 Pak and Flaco.)

Old Janitor: Okay young blood, I can see that you boys went out of your way to do this for me;

you could've brought over some bitches though. What can I help you with??

10 Pak: I need to help a friend find her way home; and I need your help to do this.

Old Janitor: Is that it?? (thinking the young man would want more)

10 Pak: That is it..

Old Janitor: Honesty; rare character trait around these parts.

10 Pak: I bet you have about a million and one stories to tell; don't you? I'm interested in the

history of the old families; one in particular, Lady Crane's.

Old Janitor: Lady Crane; somehow I knew I would hear that name again.

10 Pak: So you DO know something

Old Janitor: Leave me the radio, the TV, and the porno magazines and you got yourselves a

deal. Oh Yeah, definitely more of that Ghost Bud and I'll tell you everything you

need to know.

(The Old Janitor starts telling 10 Pak everything involving the case of Lady Crane; as he starts rolling himself a Phillie blunt with some ghost bud. He informs them that the old family records found in the basement wouldn't help. They need to go into the Church's records; into the files about spells and incantations of the old world. There's a particular spell there, that has been used and handed down from evil priest to evil priest throughout the centuries; with the sole purpose of obtaining that which cannot be obtained by force; TrUe LoVe.)

Old Janitor: I believe it was a certain priest that put that spell on Lady Crane; then he had her

husband and son murdered by evil magic. But the evil that he summoned through

the spell wasn't satisfied with taking just the lives of the husband and son; so it

killed the next closest thing it could find, that happened to be the priest himself. The

crazy jealous priest killed by his own spell; a spell he wasn't able to finish and

enclose. Which means that whatever he let out.. is still out there roaming around free;

and as long as it's out there, Lady Crane will always remain a prisoner. Until the day

the beast is returned or killed; that's what you'll find in those files locked up nice

and tight.

10 Pak: So there is an evil force keeping Lady Crane hostage there. I need those files, I need to

find this fucking thing.

Old Janitor: Boy you crazy!! This is some evil shit that don't play around!! No remorse, no

emotion, and no empathy. It's too much darkness and negative energy; what in

the world would posses you to even think about fucking around with something

this dangerous?? Weren't you paying attention to what the fuck I said?

Flaco: Bro…this is some serious heavy shit you're talking about. I didn't sign up for some

crazy dangerous shit like this. We got paid bro; what makes you want to do this; really??

10 Pak: Honestly….I don't know. What I do know; is that this is not fair to Lady Crane. I

barely know her, she's a ghost; and yet I have this sense of loyalty that my conscience

seems to be tied too. I have to do this. I am going to do this; I get to slay a "demon".

Old Janitor: If you sure you want to do this, you're gonna have to have your balls screwed on

tight then. Some of the shit you're gonna hear and see about this place makes Jerry

Sandusky look like a choir boy; no pun intended. This will fuck with your head in so

many levels you're gonna lose your mind if you are not careful..

Flaco: Ha, the Jerry Sandusky thing; that's a good one. You called him a choir boy; you know

because of the thing. (starts looking puzzled) Why aint, nobody laughing; that was funny

god dam it.

(They keep talking about a great many things; information that 10 Pak finds useful to the cause. Moments later, the sun finally began to make its presence felt; slowly but surely the night sky started to turn into a beautiful fiery orange and red beginning. As the dim light made its way through the old parish, the janitor slowly started fading away with the light. The crew started waking up and they were hung over like crazy; now having to be at work by 8:00am.)

Place: Chester, PA Crab Cake Factory

(The struggle commences as the still inebriated group prepares for clean up duty at the factory on a Saturday morning. Water starts being sprayed, hoses everywhere while listening to one of the only two radio stations they could tune in at that part of the factory.)

Herbie: Well, it looks like this or talk radio. I'm kind of leaning more towards this. (turns the

radio up. (Herbie starts following the beat of the music and starts moving some empty

boxes so he can break them down and put them in the trash cart.)

Song: Safety Dance (remix) – Men Without Hats (0:30 – 2:30)

(Present for duty is Matt, 10 Pak, Flaco, and Herbie.   Flaco present only in body and not in spirit; is currently staring at the wall with a blank stare because he's half asleep. Matt grabs him and turns him around so he can keep spraying the floor instead of the wall.   10 Pak starts bumping along to the song up and down the room; with sunglasses on for some reason. ☺ Matt falls on his ass sliding along the floor as if where on a slip n slide. Flaco finally comes too and with his drunken reflexes starts dancing one hand over the other and one step at a time. Matt hops along to the song, while jumping over the hoses side to side and it keeps on like that for 4 straight hours; therefore finishing their Saturday morning 80's stoner montage.)

Saturday Night.......

Place: Camden, New Jersey

Underground/Ilegal Pawn Shop

(Vic takes his newly acquired wealth over the bridge to a man in Camden, South Jersey. This particular man trades in stolen goods and rare artifacts; like the gold and silver coins that Vic presently has. He wanted to have them appraised himself to double check their authenticity. From there, he would find an idiot buyer with deep pockets who would pay more for them; therefore Vic could double or triple what he originally got from 10 Pak. Unfortunately for Vic, today was not his lucky day; the pawn shop he had just walked in to was presently being robbed, by some very nasty individuals. Vic's bad timing had just put him in the hands of a group of "south jersey devils" led by an extremely dangerous asshole nicknamed; "The Black Frog". Unaware of the predicament he was in; Vic unknowingly just starts blurting out a lot of the details about the coins and where they originated from.)

Vic: (as he walks in the Pawn Shop) Hey Earl!! You are not gonna believe what I got my hands

on; these gold and silver coins from the 1700's. My boy just pulled off the most amazing

job; you are not gonna believe how much money there is to be made. Oh man!! And this

new weed he found; they call it Ghost Bud. Shit is not from this world; literally. Hey Earl!!

You're not taking a shit are you??!! Earl??

(He sees 3 men in masks with guns get up from behind the front counter and four more come out from behind him. One of them approaches Vic and slowly points a gun to his head.)

The Black Frog: You were saying???

Vic: (looks down to his pants; he just pissed himself) Awh Shiiit….(Black Frog starts laughing)

Song: No More Pain – TUPAC SHAKUR (0:00 – 2:00)

(The Black Frog sees what Vic has on him and decides that he wants to know more about those coins and where they came from; because it's not like you can just get them off of any ATM machine. Vic "the real estate agent" is now praying; and if he isn't, he fucking should be.) (Everything goes dark as it fades.)

R.I.P 2PAC

Chapter 3

The
Coming
Storm

Song: Rise – Eddie Vedder (0:00 – 1:00)

 (Chapter dedicated to the memory of Chris McCandless – Into the Wild)

(The day starts out with many people smiling; rising up with a renewed sense of hope for humanity in the city of Brotherly Love. Help had finally arrived in the most unexpected of ways.)

Philadelphia "MOX" News Room, Morning Edition

Market St., Philadelphia

Reporter in 3…2…1…

Jerome Khoppel: Good Morning!! And Hello to you ALL! My name is Jerome Khoppel big K Khoppel reporting today about a very, unusual event. A rare gesture, a promise kept, a life saved, a smile made, tomorrow WILL BE a brighter day. (looks over to her assistant) Write that down baby; I said write it down, dam it!! (looks back at the camera) Someone has donated BUcket loads of money throughout the whole city. An act of extreme generosity, simply distributing money amongst the groups that needed it the most. Schools now being more self sufficient with solar panels powering up their buildings; which means no more electric bills for the schools. Hey brotha! You forgot to stop by my neighborhood; where is MY fancy antenna?? You know what I'm saying (slowly stops laughing and clears his voice) All schools and day care centers' meals for the next five years have been paid in full already. The soup kitchens and homeless shelters have received food, clothes, and foot wear donations. Who is this mystery philanthropist taking care of "the People" in the WHOLE city of Brotherly LoVe?? Jerome Khoppel Reporting here; and remember, I don't care what you think! Peace!!! (Cameras Stop rolling) Can someone get Howard Eskin on the phone for me; having lunch with the man, just gotta make sure he's paying this time. Last time he stuck me with the bill; that shit ain't happening again, you hear!

Place: Crane Manor

   Old City, Philadelphia

10 Pak: (Showing Lady Crane the Newspaper's front page) "Anonymous Donation made to every school and health care center in the city by "Mystery Philanthropist" See, as promised; with more yet to be done.

Lady Crane: Excellent work my dear friend; you've done a very good deed young man.

10 Pak: Lady Crane you did this; none of this would've ever been possible without your donation. I was simply the delivery boy on this; a trained monkey could have done what I did. But I did it for the people that needed it the most; like you asked me to do.

Lady Crane: Nevertheless, you did the honorable thing; instead of just running away with all that money and not help out at all. Is this the most honorable thing you have ever done for someone?

10 Pak: Actually, it is.

Lady Crane: Feels good doesn't it?? If this is the most honorable thing you have ever done? What is the "craziest" thing you have ever done?

10 Pak: You mean besides giving away millions of dollars to people I've never even met. Some would consider this, at the top of their lists. Okay, craziest thing I've ever done….Back in the day I was delivering pizzas for a real shitty pizza place, when I got ambushed by like 14 teenagers on my last delivery of the night. To some skilled fighters this is no impossible task; but then again 14 three legged dogs can still kill you; if given the chance. Luckily for me I had been a bouncer for over 15 years and I knew what to do in a situation like that. I fought more than 10 people in one go, that's as crazy as it gets in my book.

Lady Crane: Oh my…were you scared?? I feel like I'm there…

   (as she hits her little bubbler bong and then exhales slowly)

10 Pak: Honestly, the adrenaline rush doesn't allow you time to be scared. You think fast, you

re-act fast, and then you act fast. You kind of have to make an example out of the first

two, so the rest can understand that you're no prey at all; a cornered beast is ready to

kill, if pushed to it. You let THAT sink into their heads; and you have already won half

the battle. The technique to control pure violence can only be achieved by an astute

natural born killer; or someone with no fear of death. Out of these two, I am not the

former; but I do believe in the latter.

Lady Crane: Dangerous indeed; and all this just to deliver some food. A life is worth so much

More; how sad has this world turned into?

10 Pak: Very Sad; Silly world isn't it?? Companies don't make money off of healthy people.

Lady Crane: Indeed; let us change the topic. How about, okay I got another

one; what is the funniest thing you have ever done?

10 Pak: Back in college I was at a party and I took some acid sugar cubes.

Lady Crane: Acid??

10 Pak: Oh shit, I keep forgetting. Think of acid, like you would hemp x 1000.

Lady Crane: That is just too much; anyway continue.

10 Pak: I knew the effects were going to hit me soon; so I barricaded myself in the down stairs

bathroom, where I spend the next 4 hours talking to a poster; I mean a printed image of

Pamela Anderson on the wall. It was a full conversation and all; she really understood

me, like we were best friends.

Lady Crane: 4 hours you talked to the wall; that is…..insane. (starts laughing)

Since now we are in the topic of women; I'm curious, what does your dream girl

look like, or better yet who is she?

10 Pak: That's' a deep question; you're gonna have to let me have some of that ghost bud if you

want me to tell you about my dream girl.

(He goes ahead and starts smoking as he puts music on for them to listen to. As the song plays

along, he starts exhaling slowly watching how the smoke makes its way towards the ceiling.)

Song: Hayling - FC/Kahuna (0:00 – 1:00)

Lady Crane: This has to be good, you got to sit down, relax, and really think about it don't you?

10 Pak: Its complicated and at the same time it's not complicated. I'm a drummer by nature; so
I'm already a complicated mind according to my stars and planet alignments.
(lady Crane interrupts)

Lady Crane: Lord almighty man; All I wanted to know was about your dream girl not your
thoughts on life. (they start laughing at each other because they are both stoned.)

10 Pak: I'm getting there; ok, as I was saying and don't laugh. Men are from Mars, Women are
from Venus; and drummers are from Pluto; it's a saying drummers have.

Lady Crane: That goes without saying; okay relax and tell me about your dream girl.

10 Pak: Out here in the perimeter there are no stars; out here we is Stoned, Immaculate.
That's Jim Morrison by the way. Let's see, my dream girl is a talented actress named
Kaley; a rare beauty who was in this show with four geeky dorky guys that lived in the
same apartment building. She played a struggling waitress who wanted to be an actress.
In my opinion she is the most talented one out of that whole bunch.

Lady Crane: Let me guess, A blonde??

10 Pak: Hair as golden as the sun. Like rain and fire in one; a smile that could stop time itself
and start it back up again; complimented with a very nice sized ass, for a white girl.

Lady Crane: Spanish men. Why her? What makes her so special to catch the eye of the
fearless Rafael de la Plata?

10 Pak: The one thing we both have in common; an "empty sadness" behind our smiles. It's
like the expression, an empty victory. You've accomplished so much and are blessed
with success; but still, there's an empty space where our hearts used to be at. An empty
space that no amount of money or fame could ever fill; I recognized that in her eyes
right away.

Lady Crane: How Shakespearean of you; I'm curious then, a brave man like you would've
found a way to meet her already. What's keeping you from meeting her?

10 Pak: It isn't really that easy to do these days; she's L.A. royalty and I'm Philadelphia

Underground. I have a better chance of winning the Powerball lottery than ever

meeting her. Besides, I don't think that to be the hard part; the hard part is, how do

you tell a beautiful girl that she's beautiful; without actually telling her so.

I'm sure she hears that every day from everybody around her; including all the assholes

that hit on her all the time. I wouldn't go about it that way; but, if ever given the chance

I would definitely not waste any time and I would tell her what I think.

Lady Crane: What would you say to her??

10 Pak: The only way I know how to describe an exotic flower like her. By comparing her to a

breathe taking painting. A painting that shows a city landscape with dark storm clouds

everywhere; as you see a ray of light piercing through the dark clouds with such great

clarity. Through the light projected you can see a dream, imagination; you see, her.

Lady Crane: Very nicely put..I take it she is the light??

10 Pak: No, she is not just the light; she is the whole painting.

Lady Crane: You are quite the poet my friend, very thoughtful and observant; delicate yet firm

and straight to the point. I'm sure fortune will lead you to her someday because

fortune favors the bold; don't ever forget that

10 Pak: Oh yeah, almost forgot the good news for the Lady; I found a trail and now I know how

to go about finally getting you back home. Might not be easy, but I think it can be done.

Lady Crane: (she starts smiling) Really, that is wonderful news.

(10 Pak's cell phone starts going off, he sees that its business that needs his immediate attention.

Its Herbie calling; he picks up the phone.)

On the phone......

Herbie: Yo!! Don't forget about tonight; the boss wants us all there. You know how he gets

when all the families meet under his roof. We are on point this time, so make sure you

are wearing your bullet proof vest you hear me.

10 Pak: Don't worry; I'm on my way to pick you up. Ok. See you in a few. (hangs up)

> That was someone from my real job. Lady Crane I have to go for now; I promise
>
> I'll give you all the details when I come back tomorrow.

Lady Crane: Very well, please be safe. I want to hear more of your stories when you get back.

10 Pak: You have my word; good day to you Lady Crane

(He Exits the house and Lady Crane turns into mist and disappears into the thin air. He is now headed to South Philadelphia to meet up with Herbie and his cousin, "El Chino".)

Place: Broad St. - South Philadelphia

Song: The Mental Traveler – David Axelrod (0:40 – 2:20)

(The boys start driving down Broad Street as the lights reflect off the shiny black SUV they were driving in. They make it to their destination at 8th and Chestnut, where they are met with other associates from very different types of corporate cultures. These are Men from a different generation who never knew how to compromise with anything; nor anyone. Due to this simple fact they now sit as Kings of the North-East.   This happens to be an "Organized Crime" meeting to address the changing times and how to proceed forward accordingly; so that they don't become a thing of the past. Hit-men, Bodyguards, Crooked Cops, Union Leaders, Bookies, Loan Sharks, Casino Bosses, Bosses, UndersBosses, Capo's, and the Lieutenants along with plenty of their men; they were all there. The type of people you wouldn't want to fuck with; simple as that. All this, under "our" Bosses' roof; we had to set an example and impress the other families. Boss Carraffa calls for silence so he can address everyone.)

Boss Carraffa: I see some beautiful people around tonight and I see some ugly ones; you

> mooks. (Everyone starts laughing) I want to welcome you all to my
>
> Establishment, "Nostra Patria" (Our Country). Please feel at home, enjoy
>
> Yourselves; and remember, we count "the silverware" here. (a roomful of
>
> criminals laughing at a joke about stealing; fucking priceless.)

(As the event progresses into the night and with the main business meeting being over; everyone becomes more relaxed. Smiles, songs, and laughter fill the air around the room; except for a couple of the waiters who were there on behalf of the Black Frog.)

(The Black Frog now knew about Lady Crane, the money, and the Ghost Bud because he had beaten it out of Vic. It didn't take long for Vic to tell them everything, due to his low tolerance for "torture". Waiting for the right opportunity to approach 10 Pak, they wait patiently. 10 Pak goes over to the Bar for a drink when one of the waiters approaches him. The Waiter places one of the gold coins that they took from Vic right in front of 10 Pak. He notices the coin; he takes another sip of his drink and clears his throat.)

10 Pak: (keeps his cool) Where did you get that?

Waiter: I think you just dropped it.

10 Pak: Did I!!

(Both of them are unaware that a third person at the bar has also set their eyes on that gold coin.)

Waiter: We need to talk, let's go out to the parking garage; and don't call for help. Otherwise

your friend Vic is gonna end up with a bullet or two in the head.

10 Pak: Fucking Vic. I see; well let's go then.

(They make it to the parking garage and as they are walking along some cars, the other waiter comes up from behind and hits 10 Pak on the back of the head with his gun. 10 Pak falls on the ground and right as both waiters start aiming their guns at him, they get shot from behind by someone using a "silencer". One of them dies instantly and the other one falls against a car wounded. Out of nowhere the mystery shooter comes out and grabs the wounded waiter by the face; sinks his fingers into his eyes and then crushes his hole head to mush(pretty gruesome) ☹. He walks over to 10 Pak, who is now getting up off from the ground and grabs him by the throat and pins him against a Van with a good amount of force.)

Mystery Shooter: What kind of stupid fucking asshole's, go around waving a gold coin from the

late 1700's with king George's face on it. It's a rhetorical question; so

please don't stress yourself trying to come up with an answer. I do think

these men wanted to kill you; your welcome, by the way. So you are the

genius trying to free Lady Crane.

10 Pak: Where the hell did you come from?? Who the fuck are you??

Mystery Shooter: I'm the evil that took her husband and her son; I'm the evil that ripped out

the guts of that priest who ordered her families' death; and I will be the end of

you, unless you start talking and tell me everything. *"Capiche"*.

10 Pak: (gasping for air) Got to admit, you're pretty clever; hiding within the "Mob" as

their best hit-man. But, I can't really talk with your hand on my throat.

Mystery Shooter: Figure out a way…

10 Pak: (looks at him dead in the eye) Fuuck You, kill me if you want; but that intimidation

shit doesn't work on me. If you want to talk, let's talk, if not; go fuck yourself!!

(Mystery shooter just starts laughing slowly, then louder and then finally lets go of 10 Pak.)

Mystery Shooter: I guess Carraffa's boys do have some balls, I'll give you that.

Now, start talking. (as his eyes start turning red)

10 Pak: Do those come in different colors?? (referring to his red eyes) You're Boss Franco's

hitman, Zepi Petri. Fan of your work, now I know how you were able to pull off all

those jobs as easy as you did; coming in and out of the shadows. The North City Casino

job; fucking masterpiece. Honestly, it was by pure coincidence that we ended up at

Lady Crane's. It was this idea my friend had to go record paranormal phenomena and

someone very clueless pointed us in that direction. You said you killed her husband,

her son; and also the priest that summoned you??

Zepi Petri: He was a bad man. Truth is, Lady Crane is stuck there because I'm also stuck in

this plane of existence. I don't know how to get back; if I could, I'd go back in a

heartbeat. You find a way to send me home then you have your way to send

Lady Crane home; its two birds with one stone. To live for an eternity can get

pretty fucking boring.

10 Pak: The priest, the book he used. Where is it??

Zepi Petri: Exactly!! Find that book and we all get to go home.

10 Pak: Shit, they have Vic; he told them everything, that's why these assholes are here.

Zepi Petri: You sure he told them everything??

10 Pak: The guy is a snake in the grass; believe me, he told them everything.

(Zepi starts searching the dead bodies for a cell phone or anything that could help find Vic.)

Zepi Petri: Here we go; let's see. (Phone starts ringing) Love it when I'm right. (answers in a

deep voice like the waiter's) We got him.

Voice on Phone: Good, bring him over to Pier 17 by Penns Landing; and no fucking around

okay, come straight here.

Zepi Petri: (disguised voice) On our way. (hangs up phone) Okay, there you go; I'll take care of

these guys for you at that Pier. You find a way to get me home and it'll all be over;

for me at least. You look like you got a long road ahead of you kid.

10 Pak: What about Vic?

Zepi Petri: You said he told them everything. Then he was of no use to them anymore; Vic is

already dead. But I'll go in and check, if I find his body I'll bring it back. But first

we need to get rid of these bodies. (He snaps his fingers and the bodies turn

into dust and a sudden wind blows them away.)

10 Pak: If he is dead; at the very least I owe it to him to give him a proper funeral. Give him

the proper send off, just like he would of liked.

Zepi Petri: (walks away into the darkness and disappears) The Clock is ticking my friend; you

take care of your end of the bargain and I'll bring your friend back, dead or alive.

Place: Pier 17 Penns Landing

Columbus Blvd, Philadelphia

(At the Warehouse there are a dozen of the Black Frog's men waiting for 10 Pak. Already there among them, is Zepi Petri moving along the shadows planning his course of attack. He picks his point of entry; he puts his headphones on and picks a song off his phone play list. A few moments later a light fog starts entering the room, making its way all over the place. It starts covering the whole entire floor in the Warehouse. All of the Black Frog's men are freaking the fuck out because they've never seen creepy shit like this before. Suddenly, they start noticing that they are slowly sinking into the ground as if they were standing in quicksand.)

Song: Opera - Emmanuel Santa-Romana (0:10 – 2:00)

(As they sink and become completely helpless; they quickly start panicking because they see things move within the fog. Some start yelling for help, as others are now being dragged down into the fog by some creepy looking creatures. All of a sudden, out from the fog comes this tall figure in a dark cloak that starts catching fire on its own. The men that where left, could only watch helplessly as their inevitable deaths approached; the Day of Judgment had come for them.)

(After he kills every single one of the Black Frogs' Men, Zepi Petri walks over to a holding cell where they had Vic in; a very much alive Vic. Zepi Petri sees Vic and the horrified look in his face.)

Zepi Petri: You look like you just shit your pants; You Vic??

Vic: (sounding like a little bitch) Yes. That's, me. You here to take me back? Did 10 Pak sent you?

Zepi Petri: Yeah, he did. (point his gun at Vic)

Vic: Wait,w ait wait…

Zepi Petri: I told him I'd bring you back dead or Alive; I prefer dead. Snitches don't get to live; you fucking rat!!. (shoots him in the head twice. He then grabs Vic's body and then disappears into the fog on the ground with it.)

(Couple of hours later the police arrive, and then followed by the news crews, paramedics and firefighters. The officers that were there first on the scene described as so gruesome that it should be considered top priority to apprehend the culprit responsible for these ungodly actions. Outside the Warehouse among the reporters present there was the one and only Jerome Khoppel. He had an interest in these particular cases because he had a hunch; a hunch that all these strange occurrences were all connected somehow, due to the bizarre nature in which they happened. Khoppel turns to his camera man to report.)

Jerome Khoppel: Needles to say Philadelphia, there's some funky shit happening here tonite!!

        As always, your man Jerome Khoppel will get to the bottom of this. Peace

        Out Philly; and remember, I don't give a damn!!.

Couple of Days Later………….

Place: Funeral Home 3rd and Snyder St.

>   **South Philadelphia**

Song: Goodnight Moon – Shivaree (0:00 – 2:00)

(All the guys walk into the funeral home and right away you hear the song playing while some models (strippers) in Lingerie are dancing, drinking, and smoking good ganja. Herbie starts dancing with one of the Strippers right away.)

Flaco: Now this is what I call a funeral!! (takes a sip from his drink and shoves his face into a pair of tits as they all start laughing)

Matt: Son of a bitch gets a cool ass funeral like this; I kind of feel a bit bad about all that shit I said about him.

10 Pak: You know he was a Cowboys fan, right?

Matt: I hope he burns in HeLL!!

(They all start walking towards Vic's body in the coffin when they see a few women in line in front of them.)

Woman#1: You piece of shit! (walks off and the next woman walks up)

Woman#2: You finally got what you deserved didn't ya?? I hope you get BUTT fucked by the worst kind of shit possible down there in HELL!! (She walks away as well)

Willis: Damn; he really was an asshole.

Flaco: That's a bit heavy on her part don't you think?

Herbie: Fuck him…he was a real asshole.(they all start laughing again)

10 Pak: (raises his rum and coke) Here's to Vic then…

All Together: Rest in Peace Asshole.

(A few moments go by when they resume their talks about the next job they were going to do. This time around, they decide to each go on their own and keep whatever treasure was found for themselves, without having to share. 10 Pak writes down the addresses that Vic left him; a whole bunch of different addresses on small pieces of paper and throws them all in a hat.)

10 Pak: There you go boys; take a turn and pick one piece of paper; and you know, good luck. (They all take their turns and grab a piece of paper.)

Flaco: I got Washington Square

Matt: I get the garden at 27th and Walnut.

10 Pak: Herbie, Willis; looks like we get to go eat at the "Moshulu" on Penns Landing. Dinner and drinks are on me Amigos.

Willis: The "what" on Penns Landing??

10 Pak: The "Moshulu", a boat turned restaurant on the water; it's supposedly haunted by two different ghosts, apparently. You couldn't even begin to imagine the history of this boat and how many trips around the world it has made. How in the hell is a boat like this just parked in Philadelphia's front yard?? Your guess is as good as mine, but I intend to find out; I can't wait to see what we find there. Having said that, when we are all done with our individual adventures; we all get to go to Fort Mifflin or Eastern State Penitentiary, see what we decide. We'll cross that bridge when we get there.

Herbie: Well if you're buying, then I'm bringing a date.

Matt: Oh yeah, what's "HIS" name? (they all start laughing at Herbie)

Herbie: Shut the fuck up Matt!! You wish you could get as much pussy as I do motherfucker!

Matt: Whatever, Herbie.

(10 Pak hands Matt and Flaco some folders with information and notes about the addresses and their ghosts. Outside the box ideas that could help them solve certain riddles; not achievable by a normal mind. They spend a few more minutes going over some more details and then they call it an evening as they go their own ways for the time being.)

Matt: I gotta take a piss real quick, I'll be right there with you guys.

Herbie: Don't forget, you got to wipe front to back. (they all start laughing at Matt)

Willis: In his case it wouldn't matter what hole goes first!! LOL You dirty ho!

Matt: Ya'll got jokes; not funny you cocksuckers.

Flaco: Speaking of Cock suckers; remember when we caught Bruce sucking dick for money under a bridge by the 95 overpass.

Willis: Yeah, I remember that one; that shit was funny, the look on his face was priceless.

10 Pak: Fuck that bitch, Bruce; never liked him.

Matt: He was never broke; that's one way of putting it.

Flaco: If 10 Pak hadn't of come through with all this money; I don't know, I'd be thinking about sucking dick for lots of money.

Herbie: What the fuck??

Matt: Here we go…

Flaco: It's only till I die; after that nobody will ever know.

Herbie: Bullshit, nobody will ever know. One way or another it's going to come out and bite you in the ass. In life or in death, you'll see; because whether I see you in Heaven or in Hell or around the corner from here; I'll be telling my buddies, "Yo, there goes that cock-sucker", when I see walk by.

(They all start laughing at Herbie's response to Flaco's new found curiosity to oral fixation. As the laughing starts dying down; they all eventually start making their separate ways.)

Chapter 4

Into the Mouth

of

Madness

(William Penn incorporated five public squares into his plan for Philadelphia. As Quakers frowned on naming things after people, the Squares were simply named for their geographic positions in Penn's rigid grid: Center, Southwest, Southeast, Northeast, and Northwest. City Hall now stands where Center Square used to be. Upon Northeast Square rises the ramps of the Ben Franklin Bridge. Southwest is now Rittenhouse Square and Southeast is Washington Square; and last but not least, is Northwest Square which is now known as "Logan Circle". A fact that is <u>NOT</u> well-known is that both Logan Circle and Washington square also hold within their soils the bones of thousands of bodies. They range from both British and American Revolutionary War soldiers to Native Americans, paupers, vagrants, thieves, and yellow fever victims. Logan Circle was mainly a Potter's field, where unidentified or unclaimed corpses were unceremoniously buried. Washington Square also served as a burying ground for the indigent; but it has a more honorable role as the final resting place for an estimated 2,000 soldiers from both sides of the Revolution. A memorial to the "Unknown Soldier" of the Revolutionary War is situated on the western end of the square.)

(Due to this fact, it is known around Philadelphia that Washington Square is renowned for its ghost sightings; especially one in particular, that goes by the name of "Leah". There was a time when grave diggers and even Superintendents of these "Potter Fields" were known to supplement their income by turning over bodies to medical students and physicians for research. Late in the 19th century, a strange woman known only as "Leah" could be spotted in the dead of the night; prowling Washington Square as a self appointed protector of the dead and keeper of the graves there. It was her presence that kept many a prospective grave robbers from the square; this is of course, according to the stories handed down over the generations. As mysteriously as she lived, she died; her true identity went unnoticed by the world around her except to those that had witnessed her graveyard strolls. Yet, for many years now, people passing through Washington Square at night and at dawn have reported seeing the hunched, cloaked figure of a woman gliding ghostly through the park. Why the history lesson you ask?? You are going to have to keep reading to find out how it ties into the story. ☺)

Place: Center City, Philadelphia

Song: Who Am I – Peace Orchestra (0:25 – 2:00)

(It's close to noon and Flaco is traveling on the "Septa" bus, currently on Broad St. heading towards Center City. Through the light projected on the glass, he can see himself up close. At the same time he also sees the beautiful murals on the high buildings all over the city; paintings that embody Culture, Heritage, and Character. He finally arrives at his stop and as he exits the bus he jumps on his skateboard and starts heading towards Washington Square. Completely oblivious about what he is getting ready to uncover; he goes about his business in a very cool, calm, and collected manner. His ability to just blend in with his surroundings, as he glides ever so effortlessly through some of the busy streets of Center City, was uncanny. He finally closes in on his destination and crosses one more street and enters Washington Square. Flaco glides on his skate board all the way to a bench in the middle of the park. He takes his backpack off and sets it on the bench; he starts stretching out and getting comfortable as he lights up a joint. He sits down and pulls out a folder and starts going through 10 Pak's notes, which he left for him. About a half hour goes by when a Jehovah's Witness comes up to Flaco; trying to preach the word of the Lord.)

Jehovah's Witness: Good morning to you good Citizen; may I interest you in the…

(smells the weed as Flaco looks up to see who it is)

Flaco: Is the Mary Jane bothering you; Good Citizen? You're not from around here are you?

Jehovah's Witness: Is that what you call it; and no I'm not from around here, I'm from Utah.

Flaco: Well then my fellow American, welcome to Philadelphia. To be quite honest with you
I'm surprised that you guys are still walking around going door to door, when everything
you have to say I can read on the internet. How much do you guys get paid? Do you
get a commission on every book you sell? Do you get taxed? How much? Did they offer
you a 401K plan? What kind of life insurance comes with your benefits? Surely the lord
provides for all these essential things; doesn't he?? Is Utah a Commonwealth like
Pennsylvania?

(The Jehova's Witness sits down from amazement.)

Jehovah's Witness: You seem to be pretty well informed; and to be quite honest with you, we don't make much. I want to say that spreading the good news of the lord does bring joy to my heart; but deep down I don't believe it to be my true calling. You know how much money I would have to pay to get married at our main church in Salt Lake City?? It's more than a lot. I already did the college thing at B.Y.U. I feel that there should be more to life, it feels like there is an empty void there that hasn't been fulfilled. My faith has not been rewarded and I'm not getting any younger.

Flaco: You need to hit this Amigo. (offers him the joint)

Jehovah's Witness: Amigo? That means friend right?

Flaco: Fucking right bro, you need to relax. I bet you haven't even looked around and enjoyed the fresh air on this beautiful day in this beautiful park; you're too busy trying to make up sales numbers to please some asshole back in Utah, am I right??

Jehovah's Witness: I'm finding it hard to disagree with what you're saying; you make perfect sense. I still don't know what to do with myself. (takes a deep hit and then exhales slowly and starts coughing; rookie ☺) You only live once, right?

Flaco: No my friend, you only die once; we live every day.

(The wind picks up again and makes its presence felt with its cool embrace. The statement Flaco just made; seems to have made quite the impact on the young religious man.)

Jehovah's Witness: What exactly do you do for a living??

Flaco: I'm an outside the box type of entrepreneur baby. (Reaches into his back pack and grabs $1000 and just hands it to him) This, is me helping you find your way; maybe God is making me do this or maybe not. Either way, here is me doing my good deed because I choose too; and that in itself is the gratification I look for in life.

(He tells him a couple more of his views on life as he smokes his joint. He actually convinces the young man to leave his church and grab some of that money and go blow it all on strippers and hookers. He tells him that, this money is to buy himself an experience that will last forever; the young man says his thanks and leaves, never to be seen again. Flaco starts going about his business again, but little does he know that he was being watched the whole time by one of the Black Frog's Men. These guys were ordered to start questioning harder, to include the use of lead poisoning {that means shoot to kill} if necessary. The Black Frog was now in red alert mode, having lost the amount of men he had, he felt that retribution was in order. As a result of that, he sent more of his men to locate anyone of 10 Pak's crew members and eliminate them. Flaco starts walking around the park reading his notes; he puts his notebook down and walks up to a tree and gives it a huge hug. He then starts picking up trash and fallen branches and leaves. As he sits on a bench from a far; the hit man looks in amazement as he can't believe what he is witnessing.)

Black Frog HitMan: (talking to himself as he watches Flaco) Fucking great… these guys get all

the cool action and I'm stuck here in Philly with the tree hugging hippie.

This is some buuuullshiiit.

(Little did the Hitman know; that watching both of them from everywhere and anywhere; was The ghost of Washington square.)

Meanwhile…. nearby Center City………..

Place: 27th and Walnut

Center City Philadelphia

(Matt makes his way to the house on 27th and Walnut in an old abandoned section of the city set for demolition. Little did he know that on this one; he ends up with the shitty end of the stick, literally. As he goes through his notes, he realizes that he failed to pay attention to one very important detail that was underlined by 10 Pak. <u>Never go in this old house between the hours of 10am and 2pm on a "cloudy day".</u> As Matt is reading this important note, he turns around and sees right in front of him; a grouchy old fucking crazy looking, toothless, maniacal, whatever the hell you call it kind of ghoul ghost.)

Song: I'm your BoogeyMan – White Zombie (0:18 – 0:50)

(Matt literally in less than a second shits his pants and pisses himself as he starts running for his life. He looks back as he runs and this fucking thing is at his heels trying to grab him by the shirt.)

Ghoul Ghost: (screaming at Matt) come here you little fucker!!! I'm going to shove your ass!!

Up your ass!!!!!!!! (laughs hysterically)

(Matt gets to the end of the hallway and barely manages to get out of there as he closes the front door to the house. As he slams the door shut, immediately after; all you here is the door being punched and clawed at. The cursing and swearing went on as people on the street were looking at Matt all weird as he catches his breath; he then starts walking away in disbelief with his pants full of shit, piss, and shame.)

Back to the tree hugging hippie at Washington Square.................

Place: Washington Square, Center City

(The Black Frog's hitman starts approaching Flaco and hears him talking to himself.)

Flaco: (checking things off his list) Ok let's see; hug a tree, pick up trash, help the homeless,

feed the pigeons; do outside the box shit that is not gonna get you killed by being on

Leah's good side.

BlackFrog Hitman: Hey asshole…(straight out just punches Flaco in the jaw)

Song: Feels like we only go backwards – Tame Impala (0:00 – 0:25)

(Flaco starts falling in slow motion; as he falls back unconscious he puts out a smile in his face. The hitman walks over to him and retrieves the notebook off of Flaco.)

BlackFrog Hitman: So much for the fucking Hippie…(as he turns around he see Leah's ghost

right in front of his face)

(The hit-man out of nowhere started sinking into ground, like quick sand; till you could see him no more. A few seconds go by when the wind starts to pick up; the fallen leaves on the ground start covering up Flaco as to protect him by concealing him from prying eyes. As the leaves finally cover up all of Flaco's body; two more of the Black Frog's men pop up looking for their associate. They walk around the park from one end to another; baffled that they couldn't find or see anything nor anyone, they end up leaving.)

Place: Philadelphia Zoo

North Philadelphia

(10 Pak's cousin, the notorious "El Chino", gets on the phone and calls 10 Pak to warn him that a group of South Jersey assholes were looking for him.)

Phone ringing………

(At the moment 10 Pak is with a couple of lady friends chillin in a Jacuzzi bathtub, smoking the ganja in a Penthouse at the new Casino in South Philadelphia.)

10 Pak: Yo Chino!! What's up cous??

El Chino: You in some kind of trouble you haven't told me about??

10 Pak: What you talking about??

El Chino: I just got word that a couple of the Black Frog's little bitches were in town trying to gather up information on you. Not only that; these fuckers looked like they were serious about their business because it seems like they are packing heavy. What the fuck is going on??

10 Pak: Is it just me their looking for??

El Chino: Nah, their looking for Flaco and that little shit Matt too.

10 Pak: Chino I swear I'll tell you everything, but I got to go now. I'll call you back….

El Chino: Do you need ….(10 Pak hangs up) back up??

(El Chino looks at one of his associates and tells him to go to center city with a group of no less than 10 to go find his cousin. As for 10 Pak, he immediately calls Flaco's phone and waits for him to pick, but there's no answer.)

10 Pak: Ladies, it looks like there's a friend of mine who might need my help; so, let's skip the foreplay and get straight to the fun. (Both girls start caressing and kissing him and each other.)

Place: Washington Square, Center City

(It is now nighttime, the sun has set and the traffic rush hour is now long gone. The sounds of people, cars, and the Septa buses start to die down; replaced by the sounds of the night that gradually start making their presence felt. Back at Washington Square, Flaco finally wakes up; he sits up and sees himself covered up in leaves as he starts spitting some of them out. He realizes that someone was right next to him; it is Leah, the ghost of Washington Square. At first glance her face was blurry but then it became noticeable; a pale fair looking young woman.)

Leah: We have to hurry, trouble is coming; you have to follow me..

Flaco: Wait, what the fuck!! Who are you; girl I don't think a quickie

out here in the open is….. (she interrupts him)

Leah: Think not with your cock, if you do not want to get shot!! You jackass!!

Flaco: Holy shit!!! Your Leah!!! The whole, quickie thing; I was joking. Please don't rip my tongue out of my throat.

Leah: Will you cometh with!!

Flaco: Ok, ok. But for the record, I don't just walk off with strange women like this; I have standards.

Leah: I very much doubt that, short stuff.

Flaco: Wait, did I just get punked by a ghost?? That's gotta be a first for me; seriously!!

(They start heading over to the statue of the Unknown Soldier, as they see headlights come into Washington square; another set of lights start appearing from the other end of the square. Shit was about to get real; on one end you have about 20 of the Black Frog's men show up with one of his Capo's, Hannibal. Hannibal was a harmless funny looking asshole with a big mouth, who was as ruthless as the devil himself. Down at the other end; 10 Pak shows up with 15 of his cousin's men from North Philadelphia. Both groups come up to at least 30 ft from each other when they all stop. As they stand there facing each other at such a close distance, they all realize that they all know who is who in each group. Facing each other were the most dangerous groups from their respective areas; "Death", had front row seats to this show. It was like that moment of silence; right before the lightning strike hits and then is followed by the roar of thunder. Within the eternity of a few seconds, these men are all staring at each other dead in the eyes; the truth sets in and everybody realizes that there is only one thing left to do. The Way of the North East.)

10 Pak: Awwwhhhh shiit….

Hannibal: What the fuck you waiting for!!! Smoke these fools!!!

(The firing commences and within a matter of seconds the whole place is starting to look and sound like a full out battle zone. Watching it all unfold from a close distance was Flaco.)

Flaco: What the fuck!! We have to do something!! Those are my friends!! We have to help
     them!!

Leah: This is the place where the statue of the memory of the Unknown Soldier is at; a great
     secret lies beneath. You need only flip the page on the book on the statue and the door to
     a great power shall open unto you.

Flaco: (checking out her ass) Damn girl you fine! But this is too much shit you're laying on me,
     I'm still a bit toasted from before and…(she interrupts him)

Leah: Will you cometh!!!

(As he proceeds to turn the page on the statue; one of the slabs of stone on the ground slides over and reveals an opening into the ground. As Flaco steps down into the hole, he comes into a small room; the ceiling was covered in Native American dream catchers. At the end of it, was a dark evil looking book propped up on a podium; the cover was made from the peeled face of a demon. It was a very dark kind of magic; set forth by Warlocks with plenty of hatred and rage.)

Flaco: What the fuck did I get myself into?? (Flaco sees right before him one of the 7 books of

the Warlocks of Philadelphia.)

(He walks up to it and touches it gently, as his hand shakes from fear .)

Flaco: This is some heavy shit…..are those dragon scales??

Leah : (shouting from up above the ground) Hurry!! It's insanity out here!!!

(Flaco grabs the book and runs back up to the surface and walks over to a bench and places the book on his lap.)

Flaco: Ok Leah, what do I do??

Leah: Open the book and read one of the spells to help your friends.

Flaco: Ok, which one?? There's like a whole bunch over here!!

(The wind picks up and moves the pages all the way to the middle of the book; to The Resurrection Spells. Leah leans in closely and whispers to Flaco to start reading. Having noticed Flaco at the bench with the book and with Leah's ghost over his shoulder; 10 Pak tries to get Flaco's attention.)

10 Pak: No!!! Flaco!!! Don't read from that book!!!

(As he screams, 10 Pak sees Leah cover Flaco's ears with her hands as she looks up to 10 Pak with eyes as red as the sun. She grins at him and then shooooshes him, as Flaco continues reading the spell; until he is finally done. Then suddenly, a blue ring of light goes off like an EMP stretching out for about a 3 mile radius in circunmference. Leah starts laughing hysterically and disappears; 10 Pak runs over to Flaco while the shooting escalates to a crazier level.)

10 Pak: Flaco you okay!! What happened?

Flaco: Did we win?? I got the victory spell to help you guys; what's up??

(As Flaco is saying that, they start hearing sounds from below the ground. Angry moans full of hate and revenge, stirring underneath the hard cold ground of Washington Square.)

Flaco: Dude, please tell me you haven't eaten and that what I just heard, was your stomach

      singing the national anthem.

10 Pak: I ate some pussy earlier, so no; that was not my stomach. Flaco we need to get the fuck

      out of here, now!! We are in the middle of a shit storm!! Let's go!!

(They start heading towards their crew and their cars close to the exit. They fail to notice that there were shadowy figures with bright red eyes, starting to pop up everywhere from underneath the ground. They make it over to their peoples side as the shooting still lights up the dark night at the park; the shooting all of a sudden just stops. Both groups start hearing the sounds around them as dark figures move slowly towards their positions. Glowing red eyes now stand everywhere; silently watching the living stare back at them.)

10 Pak: Flaco, some of them seem to be looking at you and that book; put the book away…..

Flaco: Uh oh….(in a split second Flaco finally makes sense of it all)

Flaco's Inner thoughts:

{It seemed Leah had an ulterior motive all along; I mean, why else would she show me where a book of such magnitude was hidden at. This motive, I'm sure with no doubt in my mind, she knew that the end result would be the awakening of thousands of dead people; from the Center City area. From the mass graves in Logan Circle and Washington Square to the old historic cemeteries all around the city, including the old historic houses and old museums; they would all be awakened. A real fucking shit storm; what the FUCK, did I just do?}

(A loud scream is let out by one of the zombie looking fuckers. Hannibal stands speechless with what's before his eyes because he's never seen crazy shiiit like this before; I mean, who has?.)

Black Frog Gunman: Hannibal!!! What do we do!!

(Over at Flaco's end)

Flaco: (all scared and shook) What the fuuuck??…..

(Have you ever been in a situation where it goes from really bad, to nuclear fucking disaster bad in a matter of seconds? It happens right before your very own eyes and there is absolutely nothing you can do about it; all there is left to do is "FUCKING RUN". The zombies begin to charge and all hell breaks loose (literally); everybody starts shooting in every direction, while others start running for their lives trying to get into their cars.)

Song: Amoeba!!!! – Adolescents (1:58 – 3:07)

(Some people start getting hit by friendly fire as they are flanked by waves of Zombies never to be seen again. Like a stampede, everybody heads for the exits and out of nowhere; Hannibal bumps into 10 Pak by sheer coincidence.)

Hannibal: YOU!!!

10 Pak: HANNIBAL?? What the fuck are you doing here you traitor piece of shiiit!!!

(They quickly draw their guns at each other and fire (click click click) out of ammo, both of them. They throw their guns at each other and start throwing punches but none connects; too much craziness and people getting in their way. Hannibal manages to mess up 10 Pak's hair; he then slips away into a crowd of more people running through them, as he laughs his ass off.)

10 Pak: My Hair!!!! Get BACK HERE you FAT BEARDED BITCH!!!!! ☺

(Both groups are over run by the zombies and bodies start dropping like flies, fast. The few survivors now make it to the streets of Center City and scatter off through its blocks trying to save themselves. Like mice in a maze being pursued by a rabid fucking Cobra snake that hasn't eaten in days; they run like they've never ran before. Flaco, who is the fastest of them all, had taken off like the wind and was already out the park down two blocks when he turns into a main intersection.)

(He jumps on his skate board and starts kicking with a purpose, because the six zombies that are after him mean to kill him; and he knows this. 10 Pak, his boy Danny, and Matt are running like crazy on Arch street being pursued by a horde of zombies at this point; as there where many more heading in their direction coming from Logan Circle almost two miles out. They see one of those "Horse and Carriage" services they have all over Center City; they'd also noticed that the driver was actually taking a piss by the dumpster. So, without asking (like the bad non boy scouts that they are) they take the horse and carriage and make a run for it as they head up Race Street. Now passing the Cathedral Basilica of Saints Peter and Paul, 10 Pak pulls out his cell phone and dials out to Flaco; as Matt steers the horse and carriage.)

10 Pak: I hope this works; pretty fucking please I hope this fucking works!!

    (phone ringing….Flaco picks up) Thank fucking Mary Jane!! You

    mother fucker!!Where are you??

Flaco: I'm on 21st and Spring Garden heading towards the Art Museum!!

10 Pak: Why the Art Museum???

Flaco: I don't fucking know; in my head it sounds like a place that would repel evil. Shit!!

    Those are the Rocky steps; all of Philadelphia believes in those steps. I don't know

    god dam it!! I'm thinking outside the box here!!!

10 Pak: Don't know what you're on about!! But you know what; Fuck it!! We'll meet you at

    the Art Museum, you better have a plan.

Flaco: I do!! Just meet me there, hurry!!

(The three of them finally arrive at the base of the steps by the Rocky Statue; they see Flaco already gone up the first set of steps. Danny is carrying a shotgun on him while 10 Pak has an A.K. and Matt is only armed with a two 9's.)

10 Pak: There he is!! Flaco!!

Flaco: Come on!! (Looks up) Holy Fuck!! Here They Come!! Hurry!!!!

(Keeps running up the steps)

Danny: Let's go!! Fucking go!!!

(Making their way up, they start shooting at the creatures right behind them coming up the steps. They finally make it to the top of the steps, at the plateau with the circle in the middle. They reach the middle of the circle, immediately checking the few ammunition they have left and get ready with their backs to one another for the next wave of zombies to approach. Flaco, already going through the book of spells, has no idea what the fuck he's looking for.)

Flaco: God damn it!! Just give me a fucking break, you bitch!!!

(Just as he says that, a swift wind comes along and abruptly flips the pages all the way to the Vanishing Spells section of the book. He starts skimming through it and he sees a word being repeated over and over that seemed like our word "Amoeba". Flaco says "Fuck it" and makes up his mind and fills up his lungs with air and starts screaming over and over really fast.)

Flaco: Amoeba!!!Amoeba!!!Amoeba!!!Amoebaaaaaaa!!!!!!!!

(The zombie looking creatures are almost right on top of them; specially the six little people zombies running all creepy like towards Flaco. Suddenly; strong winds start blowing from everywhere. The winds immediately turn the zombie creatures into dirt and dust; as it covers all four of them. In pure disbelief with how lucky they were to have survived this insane ordeal; they stand up and start walking around. From where they were standing, they could see certain parts of the city engulfed in flames and smoke; lit up with the lights of ambulances, police cars, and fire trucks. Oh yeah, did I mention the Art Museum cameras had been rolling the whole time; yeah, everything that had just happened there got recorded. I mean everything.)

Chapter 5

The Legend of the South Philly Sticky Icky Ghost Bud

"If spirits may revisit Earth only to talk nonsense, if they can do nothing but prattle and look pretty, and can impart no information on man's state, either present or future; then it seems to me that "Spiritualism" is a fraud of the biggest kind. And that the "Spirits" would do much better to stay at home and let us form for ourselves other views of the hereafter; then we must regard it as simply as an asylum for feeble-minded ghosts."

"The Anonymous Times Reporter"

Next Day…..

Place: City Hall, Broad Street

> **Center City, Philadelphia**

Song: Fight the Power – Public Enemy (0:35 – 1:35)

(At city hall the next day, a plethora of reporters and news crews in the middle walkway at the Garden Area wanting answers to all their questions. Certain City Officials also there trying to calm the situation down as they make their statements to the cameras. As it became apparent that these officials had no clue of what the hell was going on; they started being ridiculed by the Philadelphia Press Reporters. Among them was the one and only; the infamous Jerome Khoppel.)

(talking straight into his Camera man's direction)

Jerome Khoppel: That's right Philadelphia!! Jerome Khoppel!! big K Khoppel here reporting from City Hall, trying to find out WHAT in the HELL happened last night. Because that was some crazy shit, wasn't it?? Now, was it a planned attack?? Are we being invaded?? Is it judgment day?? And I don't mean SkyNet you "heathens"! Just know this, whoever is responsible for this insane occurrence; has a lot to answer for, I mean deep shiiit brotha! Philadelphia!!! Do not worry one bit, I, Jerome Khoppel big K Khoppel will get to the bottom of this. And remember Philly, I DON'T give a DAMN!!! Khoppel OUT!!

Place: Germantown

       Northwest Philadelphia

(Watching all this on the "News" on the T.V is Ten Pak, Flaco and "El Chino". Chino grabs the TV remote and puts the TV on mute and looks at them with a very pissed off look. I mean shit, he just lost more than 10 men in one night.)

El Chino: Alright you two shiitts; start talking and don't even think about bullshitting me!!

(They both explain to him their sides of the stories as it went down all the way to the part at the "Art Museum". Hesitant at first to tell him anymore, 10 Pak finally decides to tell him about what happened after the Art museum; where things got even worst for them, a lot worse.)

BackFlash……

The night before at the Art Museum….

Matt: Guys, we need to get the fuck out of here; and I mean now!! I do not want to answer any
       questions about this; this is some serious shit.

10 Pak: I agree; Flaco you okay?

Flaco: Fuck No!! This is my entire fault; and what the fuck are we supposed to do with
       this book??

Danny: Can we talk about this on the way out of here; shit we don't even have a car. So let's
       get moving, we got a long way to walk.

Matt: Back to Washington Square??

Danny: What if the cops are there??

10 Pak: Guys?? The "horse and carriage" are still down there; let's use that to get to
       Washington square, if the cops are there we'll start walking back down to
       Oregon Ave. I'll get my cousin to send someone to go pick us up at the safe house.

Flaco: We're going to have to lay low for a bit. I'm sorry guys!!

Danny: A bit late for that you little fucking weasel!!

10 Pak: Danny, that's not helping; let it go.

Danny: How the hell do we tell Ramon we just lost 11 of his guys; and to what, exactly again??

I'm gonna sound like a whack job. 10 Pak, this is your fucking mess, so you're the one

that's gonna explain this to your cousin!! I fucking mean it!!

10 Pak: Fine; you pussy….fuck!! Shit just keeps piling up on my plate!!

(They finally get on the carriage and Matt gets them out of there as they start making their way back to Washington Square. On their way back, they see the aftermath of the zombie attack. Dead people half eaten torn from limb to limb everywhere. Cars turned over and a lot of others crashed into buildings and into other cars. There are hundreds of people out on the streets of Center City wandering about, trying to make sense of what had just happened. Our anti heroes finally arrive at Washington Square and they see that there are no cops around; so they make their way to Danny's truck. As they get there, they see a woman talking to someone all dressed in some real old style clothes; looked like 1800's fashion. This was no regular zombie she was talking to; this dude looked like the real fucking deal. This guy was the reason Leah tricked Flaco into reading that book, so that this guy could be freed. A man who was wrongly accused of being a devil worshipper after the end of the Civil War; and put to death in the most brutal of ways at Washington Square. Leah, having witnessed it all, knew of his innocence and his wish for revenge if ever awakened….She was very much inclined into helping him.)

Danny: Who the fuck is that??

Flaco: That's Leah…the ghost of Washington Sq. Don't know who the zombie is..

10 Pak: Keep it down assholes and let's get the fuck out of here…

(Out of nowhere someone just flat out farts; not a small weak fart, but a big loud one that lasted at least 5 seconds. They all look at Matt and move away from him; the fart was so loud that the sound traveled across the park; Leah hears it and looks at them and starts laughing her ass off.)

Leah: (turns to the Zombie) Tommy; they have the book. (pointing at the guys)

(The crazy looking but fashionable zombie, turns and looks at them and starts walking towards Flaco and company. They all start yelling pretty much at the same time.)

All together: Go!!! Fucking Go!!! (They all start jumping in the back of the truck in a hurry)

(10 Pak gets in the driver's seat and puts that bitch in gear and lets her rip. He starts going up 6th street pass Independence Hall and the Liberty Bell all the way up to the Christ Church Burial Ground. Out of nowhere a Septa Bus runs a red light and crashes into Danny's Truck; everything goes dark for a few seconds. Moments later as they slowly come too; they all get out of the crashed vehicle. They start looking around and they see that the zombie that was following them, was gone; no trace of him whatsoever.)

Back to the present…..

Place: Germantown, Northwest Philadelphia

(finally finishing their story)

Flaco: Yeah Chino, that was pretty much it; no bullshit bro..

El Chino: You two assholes have started the apocalypse!!! A part of the city, destroyed; you

        better hope nobody finds out it was you two assholes. Wait a second, the cameras at

        the Art Museum; the cameras at the Art Museum caught everything, this hole shit is

        on tape!!!! (Chino's phone starts ringing; it's their underboss Alberto Locatti.)

(Chino answers his phone)

El Chino: Hey Al, what's going on??

Alberto Locatti: Is your cousin and that skinny little piece of weasel shit there with you??

El Chino: Why what's up??

Alberto Locatti: Chino!! Don't FUCK with me right now, I'm not in the fucking the mood!!

El Chino: Yeah, there here…

Alberto Locatti: Okay, good for you; now put me on the speaker phone!

(Speaker Phone On)

10 Pak: Hey Al, it's us..

Alberto Locatti: YOUS MOTHERFUCKERS YOUS!!!!!!!!!! WHAT THE FUCK DID YOUS MONKEYS DO TO MY BEAUTIFUL CITY!!! THE BOSS IS FURIOUS!! THE MAYOR IS FURIOUS!! THE WHOLE GODDAMN CITY IS FURIOUS!!.......DON'T YOU FUCKING EYEBALL ME YOUS MUTHA FUCKA'S!!!

Flaco: Nobody is eyeballing you Al; you're on speaker phone…

Alberto Locatti: YOU SHUT THE FUCK UP!!!! YOU LITTLE FUCKING ASSHOLE!!! IF IT WEREN'T FOR YOUR FRIENDS 10 PAK AND CHINO; YOU'D BE FLOATING IN THE RIVER, SWIMMING WITH THE FISHES!!!! CAPICHE!! YOUS FUCKING INGRATES!!! GET YOUR ASSES OVER HERE RIGHT FUCKING NOW!! YOU FUCKING HEAR ME!!!!RIGHT FUCKING NOW!!! (hangs up the phone) ☹

(The three of them looking at each other with plenty of worries.)

10 Pak: Oh boy…

El Chino: You better think of something; you need to fix this shit, now.

10 Pak: I hear you cous, I hear you.

Flaco: 10 Pak, what do we do bro?? This one is on me, whatever you want me to do bro.

El Chino: They're gonna hang you by the balls; just keep your mouth shut when we're there. Let 10 Pak do all the talking, hopefully they'll listen to him with a lot more patience than they will us.

10 Pak: We are just going to have to pay our way out of this one; we have to take care of the bosses and their people. Otherwise, we are going to be the escape goats to something much worse if we don't nip this in the butt, right fucking now. Who the hell was that guy that "Leah" was talking too; he didn't look like the rest of the zombies we faced.

(10 Pak was right; there was more to this fashionable zombie than what they thought. If Leah had gone through all that trouble just to wake this guy up; that meant his presence there was of huge significance.)

November 24th 1865 - Port of Wilmington

Pennsylvania/Delaware Stateline

(It was the year the U.S. Civil War ended and the Union Army began sending its soldiers home. The westward expansion was about to begin; Politicians in the government were already fighting over what states would become Republican and what states would become Democrat. Among these soldiers being dispatched back home, Lt. Thomas Cadwallader, better known as "Tommy Bones", along with his brother Jacob; were finally returning to Philadelphia after 3 years of War. They had traveled the Country, all the way to Texas and Louisiana and back. They saw how beautiful the countryside was and how nice and welcoming most of the people were to them. Tommy and his brother came from a Quaker family whose roots ran deep in Philadelphia, since the times of William Penn and the founding of the city. Tommy was a very humble educated man from a middle class family; with so much knowledge gained and with so much to express about, life, religion, and the flaws of man. A group of his fellow Philadelphians accompanied them on their trip back to their beloved city. They were now boarding a U.S Naval Boat carrying supplies up the Delaware River headed to Philadelphia. The Philadelphians among them also hailed from Quaker families such as the Biddle's, Banks, Bailey, Wister, and Sharpless. Men that had been carrying this nostalgic feeling about their city for 3 long years, were only now a few hours away from the "City of Brotherly Love", their home. As the time passed on the river, they finally start seeing familiar landmarks close to the city; they know where they're at now.)

Charlie Banks: You smell that boys…..that's the smell of civilization; no more shit hole towns out in the middle of nowhere for us. I'm never leaving Philadelphia ever again; I was meant to die in Philadelphia.

Jacob Cadwallader: Well, You survived the war; you might prove yourself prophetic.

Thomas Cadwallader: I'm never leaving home ever again either; and I'm definitely never ever going back to that sun blasted shit hole they call Texas.

(tosses a silver dollar coin into the river) So long, you Dixie fuckers!

Peter Biddle: You said it my friend; it's good to be home. (Yells out loud) YEEEAAAHHH!!

I'm gonna drink all the drink, smoke all the smoke; and fuck every whore in

The city!! YES SIIIRRR!!! (The whole group starts laughing together) We are

hitting Broad Street tonight until the sun comes up gentlemen, guaranteed.

(Finally at the Naval Yard, (which was located at the entrance of the city on the banks of the Delaware River) they all disembark and gather up at the end of the docks. They all look at each other and in a moment of silence, they realize how lucky they were to be there. The trials and tribulations they've had to endure seemed insurmountable at the time; making the moment seem very surreal and one of a kind. The men start making their way to where the horse drawn cars for transportation where stationed at. They all make plans together for the next few days, as they all commence boarding different carriages headed in different directions all over Philadelphia.) (Tommy, Charlie, and Jacob board the same carriage because their families happen to live on the same street.)

Thomas Cadwallader: I can't wait to see Mother's face when she sees us.

Charlie Banks: I wonder if any beautiful women moved to our street; that would be nice.

Jacob Cadwallader: What do you say lads; how about we hit Broad Street tonight and enjoy

everything the City has to offer??

Charlie Banks: I'm in.

Thomas Cadwallader: Sounds like a good plan Sergeant; (takes out his "Ellery Model" pocket

watch, a pocket watch very popular among Union Soldiers) let's gather

up at our house, say 6 in the evening.

Charlie Banks: 6 in the evening it is Lieutenant; say hi to your family for me.

Thomas Cadwallader: Likewise Charlie, say hi to your parents on our behalf.

Jacob Cadwallader: Yeah, especially your sister, tell her I said I'm finally home and that I won

that bet we had going.

Charlie Banks: In your dreams Jacob; see you tonight boys.

(They go to their houses and spend the rest of the afternoon with their families; three years away from home seemed more like 100. The reunion between long parted family members was a much welcomed event by everybody. As the night begins to take over, you could sense the energy in the air from being out in the city at night. For the first time in a long time the men did not have to follow orders or live such a stressful life anymore; Freedom felt good. As they walked up Broad Street heading towards City Hall they encountered people from Delaware, New Jersey, New York, and other parts of Pennsylvania. Enjoying the sites, they see how much the city has changed and how much it has expanded. To them this seemed like another world; so much more different than the one they had to suffer through all those years during the War. Thomas being a bit more cultured than his companions decides that he wants to go to the Walnut Theater on Walnut Street for a nice Contemporary Ballet.)

Place: Walnut Theater, Walnut Street

      Center City Philadelphia

Song: Dakini: Movement IV – Adam Crystal (0:00 – 1:00)

(The whole crowd mesmerized and intrigued by the pomposity of the whole event. The music from the orchestra tunes up to the senses, as the lights of the theater radiate a positive adventurous energy. The ballerinas and their male counterparts (danseur, ballerino) wearing some very "Avant-Garde" costumes for their times; all of it put together, gives the stage an even more eye opening presence. Theater is something that you have to be there in order to experience; the magic and the beauty of the cultural arts is food for the soul. It's one of a kind moment and to some it's even a once in a lifetime kind of moment. To the lovers of the Arts, a musical note could inspire even the smallest and weakest of men, with such great might and fearlessness. Enough to rival the likes of Hercules, Sampson, or even the mighty "Rocky Balboa". ☺ As the Ballet progresses, Jacob Cadwallader becomes fixated all of a sudden; one of the beautiful ballerinas is staring straight into his eyes.)

Jacob: By all the stars in heaven….who is she??

Peter Biddle: Uh oh; hey Tommy (pointing at Jacob) here we go again.

(Tommy looks at his brother and sees that look of infatuation in his eyes; Tommy starts shaking his head and laughs. Peter leans in to talk to his friend Jacob.)

Peter: Easy there brother, we just got here; stop and think before you do something reckless.

Don't let your cock do your thinking for you.

Jacob: Hey; it got me through college didn't it..(they start laughing).

(The final act of the Ballet is over and the after party is about to begin; a chance for everybody to mingle, socialize, and do small talk about trivial shit.)

Charlie Banks: Look at all those pretentious bastards; standing there judging everything and everyone. How can they just pretend to be honorable men, when in truth they are nothing but cowards; there's no honor in dodging the draft. Nest of thieving greedy bastards.

Tommy: Easy Charles, we came here to have fun tonight. We'll deal with them at the Congressional hearing; they won't be able to avoid us this time.

(Tommy sees his brother along with Peter Biddle walking over to a group of Ballerinas to introduce themselves. As he browses around the room to see if he can recognize any familiar faces; he stops and sees that a group of gentlemen across the room were looking directly at him and Charlie. Tommy, (loving to piss people off) gives out a smirk and raises his champagne glass to them; giving them something more to talk about. The patronizing, pompous, cowardly assholes across the room; were none other than the younger members of the prestigious families of Philadelphia. Families such as the Burds, the Shippens, Kelly, Lomaxe, Freeman, Perelman, Honickman, Nestel, Wyeth, Haase, Dorrance and Hamiltons. Families that kept their sons from going to the War because they could most certainly afford to do so. Thomas, Charlie, and company were hated and feared by these politicians; Why, because they were war heroes that were huge supporters of President Abraham Lincoln. The former president who had been assassinated a few months earlier on April 14 1865 by John Wilkes Booth; at the Ford Theater in Washington D.C. during a play called, "Our American Cousin". Duly mostly because of their support for Lincoln, being very outspoken, and well versed; certain politicians saw this as a great threat, on top of the fact that they were also very well educated men.)

Several days later…….

Place: Benjamin Franklin Mansion/Independence National Historical Park

   317 Chestnut St, Philadelphia

(At the meeting house for the union patriots, it didn't take long for the newly arrived to see the corruption of the politicians there. It was clear to them that the greedy hands of the Catholic Church and its priests had unleashed misery and poverty upon Philadelphia. A roar of boos erupts; an angry crowd, mostly delegates from the various political groups of Philadelphia. These were the type of people who couldn't agree on anything, not even on the color of shit; they were now at each other's throats. The turn of the century was upon them and new laws and new regulations were going to be introduced into the North, the South, and the expansion out West. The new world was coming and the old bloodlines were making a play to secure their futures. You had the Northern Democrats that were divided into two factions; the War Democrats who supported the military policies of Abraham Lincoln and the Copperheads; who strongly opposed them. The other group, the Federalist National Republicans was a political party that was aiming to get their hands on everything in the country. A group that has always had the mindset of the elitist kind; they want to return to the ways of kings and lords. Having taken the floor, Charlie Banks and Tommy Cadwallader address the room with their final statements.)

Charlie Banks: You disgrace our fore fathers and the freedoms they sought out for us. You

seek to replace them with "Absolutism". (the room goes wild and screams are

heard everywhere. Tommy now takes center spot)

Tommy Cadwallader: You gentlemen mean to set up a monopoly that would benefit only you

and the sycophants that lick your boots. We know about your plans for

the country and the expansion westward; and we know it doesn't end

there. You mean to take over Mexico and Central America and all the

fertile lands they posses; your greed has no bounds. We the people, came

to this land to get away from your wars and your religious prejudices that

do nothing but hold mankind back. Now you seek to use our hard

earned money to conquer other lands and enslave more people; there is

no humanity in you.

Charlie Banks: So, I say that all of you be removed from the charge of protecting this

        country and its many different cultures. Leave it to real educated men

        with scruples and morals to administer. Replace the old deceitful villains

        and the over-righteously pious; who posses only a child's sense of

        morality and only seek out the destruction of the middle class.

(Cheers erupt for Tommy and Charlie)

(Seeing this unfold right before their very own eyes, the members of the Federalist National Republicans Party began exiting the room in pure disbelief. It was clear to them that in order for them to proceed forward with their "New World Order" plans; they would have to remove the heads of the Democratic Party including Charlie Banks and Thomas Cadwallader.)

Back at the Cadwallader household that same evening……

(A worried Jacob Cadwallader walks back and forth looking at Charlie and his brother Tommy with a very vexed look in his face.)

Jacob Cadwallader: Why brother??

Tommy Cadwallader: Jacob…I shall never be tamed or bargained with; that I promise.

Jacob Cadwallader: Brother be calm and be patient; this is not the road to fame and fortune.

Tommy Cadwallader: What should I do then brother?? Seek out a powerful and influential

        patron to pursue?? Cling to him like a vine or a parasite and rise through

        ruse, instead of merit!! Fuck that, no thank you!! Play the fool hoping to

        see some minister give a smile that's not sinister!! Fuck that, no thank

        you!! Find common sense in an imbecile just because he can put my

        name in some gazette or newspaper!! Fuck that, no thank you!! Get

        down on my knees, grovel for money and accept humiliation; forget about

        self respect right?? Fuck that, no thank you!!

Jacob Cadwallader: Brother, calm yourself.

Charlie Banks: Jacob, your brother is right; you can't negotiate with these people at all. They

have no scruples, no human decency, nor any respect for anything that doesn't

belong to their world.   They are so detached from reality that it's actually

frightening to see what people are really capable of; it almost seems like

they're not really human at all. It still baffles my mind that some people can be

so negatively deceitful and poisonous; when we know for a fact that

there are good hearted people in the world.

Jacob Cadwallader: So what is to be done??

Tommy Cadwallader: Brother, the pieces on the board are positioned and on the move already.

What, you think they aren't already planning to takes us out one by one.

Jacob Cadawallder: So what you're really telling me, is that you two jack asses just painted a

target on all our backs; and for what? We just got back from the war and

you two are still looking for a fight!! We can't alter the course of history,

we are but a few mortal men, lucky enough to have survived that hell we

went through. Oh, and if u think you can trust that other nest of scheming

bastards, your Democrat friends; think again because they will sell you out

before you can say "Philadelphia Cream Cheese". ☺

Charlie Banks: Jacob, we know what we are doing; and you're right, we could die.

I'm in Philadelphia and I don't have a problem if I die from this; at least we're

not dying in some ditch out in Texas, Maryland, or Georgia. If I die on these

streets; I'll die a happy man.

 Tommy Cadwallader: I agree with Charlie, brother.

Jacob Cadwallader: Julius Caesar and Napoleon Bonaparte over here; you stupid assholes!!

(storms off)

(There's no denying that certain bloodlines have shaped and are still shaping this city and our lives. Power and influence can also be an addiction (William Burroughs); it's actually amongst the worse because the things rich people do to remain in power; is the stuff nightmares are made out of. It becomes even worse once power and influence fade and are no longer available; symptoms of withdrawals usually become apparent once this happens; the Ego panics and the persons reaction is never a good one..)

Later on that night………

(Peter Biddle appears out of nowhere on his horse riding as fast as the wind; he now approaches the Cadwallader House. He has this look of panic, anxiety, and desperation all over his face while tears run down it. As he arrives to the Cadawallader house, he jumps off his horse almost falling on his face; he regains his balance and composure as he rushes to the front door.)

(Knocking hard on the door yelling at the top of his lungs)

Peter Biddle: Jacob!!!!! Jacob!!!! It's Peter Biddle!!! Jacob!!!!

(After about a minute of yelling, the lights around the house start turning on and Jacob finally comes out.)

Jacob Cadwallader: Peter…what is it!! What's wrong!!

Peter Biddle: We've been betrayed!! Someone in our group betrayed us!!

They knew we were coming!!

Jacob Cadwallader: Peter!! What are you talking about?? Where's my brother??

Peter Biddle: The police; it was the police!! They came out of nowhere and started firing on us.

Charlie, poor Charlie; they grabbed him and opened him up from neck to

stomach. Your brother, he got shot; they took him…..

Jacob Cadwallader: Where did they take him??

Peter Biddle: Washington Square.

Jacob Cadwallader: No no no no no no no

Peter Biddle: Jacob, what do we do??

Jacob Cadwallader: We get the rest of the men from the Philadelphia Veteran Core; and we go kill them all. (Tears of rage start pouring down Jacobs face)

Peter Biddle: What about your brother??

Jacob Cadwallader: Peter; my brother is already dead. What we can do and what we will do is attack them now, when they'll never expect it. Right now at dawn with everything we got!! Let's go get the men!!

Peter Biddle: I'm with you all the way Jacob; we'll make all those bastards pay for what they have done. In the name of the father, the Holy Ghost, and the almighty Christ himself; vengeance will be ours.

(After spending this whole time murdering about half of an entire police precinct and about 27 politicians from the Republican Party; Jacob and his men finally arrive at Washington Square. The Sun is finally coming out as it pushes the night sky away into the far distance. . At the square, a few people are already gathered there looking at the dead corpses lying on the cold ground. Jacob starts looking for his brother amongst the dead, but no luck; Tommy is nowhere to be found. Little did Jacob know that he was standing close to where his brother had been buried, so that no one could ever find him. Jacob falls to his knees and finally breaks down in tears; sharing his feelings in front of his men, his friends, his fellow soldiers, and a few strangers.)

Jacob: Brother, I killed them all; but somehow I feel that will never be enough. I hope you find peace somehow in all this, wherever you may be. You're too stubborn to go to Hell and not much of a saint to enter heaven. (laughs a little) I love you brother; I miss you so much, you stupid asshole.

(Jacob continues his speech; but his words become Lady Crane's words, as she is telling 10-Pak the whole story of Thomas Cadwallader.)

Place: Crane Manor

Kensington, Philadelphia

(Lady Crane Speaking Jacob Cadwallader's last words to his brother)

Lady Crane: To the tune of the repetitive, an "I told you so" would have been in order; but

death is not something you can simply just joke about. Time is something

that is not just simply given, it is earned. If only I had a chance to travel

back in time and fix everything that went wrong, whether it turns into a dream or

into a nightmare; it becomes the greatest gift of all time. Love you; for all times.

10 Pak: No wonder that guy seemed so pissed; I feel sad for him.

Lady Crane: Such a sad story; and by the looks of it a very strong adversary.

10 Pak: I am just a mortal man, with no powers of any kind; unless you count the ability to

bullshit pretty good a superpower, I'm pretty much particularly screwed .

Lady Crane, how am I suppose to help a zombie from the 1800's and defeat a demon

who posses as an Italian hitman, who has the strength of 10 men put together?? Lady

Crane, my word is my oath and I will help you go home to your family; it just seems

that the odds against us are staggering. Yup there it is, I can feel my headache

coming back.

Lady Crane: Awh, you poor lamb. Maybe some ghost bud will lift your spirits up?

10 Pak: (pauses for a second) Sure; I won't say no to that.

Lady Crane: Good, cause I'm all out and we need to go get some more. We can go get some at

my friend Charlie K's place; I've been dying to leave this house, even if it's only

for a few hours.

10 Pak: And how are we going to do that, exactly??

Lady Crane: Open that cabinet drawer up and you'll find a wallet that has a pocket mirror inside

of it. Open it up, I'll jump in the mirror, in which you will then close, put in your

shirt pocket, and then go to this address; I believe it's called Fish-Town.

10 Pak: You want me to take you to Fish-Town; to see your dealer??

Lady Crane: Why, is there a problem??

10 Pak: (looking perplexed)No, no problem at all; I guess we're going to Fish-Town. Let me get

 my keys and the mirror and lets go to Fish-Town. By all means; who doesn't want

 to go to Fish-Town.

Place: Girard Ave. and E. Columbia Ave.

  Fishtown, Philadelphia

Song: Flying – Livid Kittens (0:20 – 2:00)

(10 Pak finds himself driving down the streets of Fishtown on a cloudy rainy day, headed to an old building close to the intersection of Girard Ave. and E. Columbia Ave. He looks out the window and starts seeing all the faces, distorted by the rain. He goes past an intersection where none other than Tommy Bones was standing at on the corner, looking straight at him; yet he goes unnoticed. Finally arriving at his destination, he starts glancing at the landscape looking for known signs or landmarks. Not only did the buildings look old; those things were dilapidated. 10 Pak looks up to the skies and glances at the dark clouds brought in by the wind and rain. The raindrops, feel like small cold punches that keep coming down; as if there were no tomorrow. 10 Pak parks his vehicle in front of the building he was looking for and gets out of the car.)

10 Pak: Let me get this straight, she wants me to go into that old piece of shit building; that

 looks like it could crumble down any minute. God damn it…I bet there's fucking

 crackheads and junkies crashing in there. Fuck this; I'm not going in there empty handed.

(He pops the trunk of the car and gets some of his stuff ready. 10 Pak grabs a bullet proof vest and his desert eagle along with his scorpion knife. Then he grabs a small Uzi with a silencer on it and attaches it onto a holster around his shoulder; last, he puts a jacket over it so it can't be seen. 10 Pak grabs his duffel bag and proceeds into the building; as soon as he walks in the front doors he takes out the pocket mirror. Lady Crane appears before him.)

Lady Crane: I know what you're thinking and before you say anything, know that this building

 is completely abandoned; Charlie K makes sure of it. So there is no need to

 worry.

10 Pak: Lady Crane I didn't make it to where I am because of subtleness and carelessness; trust

can get you killed if you aren't properly prepared for it.

Lady Crane: You really need to smoke; follow me, it's this way.

(As they go down the hallway, they start hearing radio sounds of an Eagles football game accompanied by yelling and crazy laughter. They walk into a room with an old TV and bright neon greenish purplish marijuana plants everywhere; it smelled like heaven ought to smell.) ☺

10 Pak: My pants, just got tighter. (re arranges his junk)

Lady Crane: (laughing) Rafael, allow me to introduce you to Charlie K, the genius

behind the Ghost bud.

10 Pak: Hey Charlie K; I'm a big fan, what's going on.

Charlie K: I'll tell you what's going on!! Viet- God - Damn-Nam!! That's what's going on!!

Don't let anybody tell you any different; the government is up to something. So

believe me when I tell you…..(pauses and then looks puzzled) What was I just

talking about??

Lady Crane: Such the lively character, I like him a lot.

10 Pak: So Charlie, how long have you been down here for?? I only ask, because that Eagles

game you're watching is from a while ago. That's the Eagles against the Houston

Oilers and Warren Moon.

Charlie K: Yeah baby!! Go Eagles!! E!!A!!....

Lady Crane: (puts her hands over Charlie's mouth) Charlie, just listen….

10 Pak: Reggie White, Jerome Brown, and Seth Joyner have one hell of a game on this one.

Our defense is way too much for Warren Moon and his O-line (the announcer calls a

sack by Seth Joyner) The House of Pain game they ended up calling it; fly eagles fly.

Charlie K: Fly Eagles Fly; I like this guy Lady Crane.

Lady Crane: Me too Charlie; he is a trusted friend and that's why we're here. How have you

been Charlie??

(10 Pak puts down his duffel bag and starts bringing some equipment out. He sets up a laptop with a set of speakers and a sub-woofer; he puts on YouTube and plays an Eagles best games highlights since the 90's)

Charlie: I've been okay, taking care of my buddies (pointing to the Marijuana ghost plants) and writing poetry. Would you like to hear some?

10 Pak: Let's see what you got Shakespeare.

Lady Crane: Just as long as there is nothing indecent in your poetry.

Charlie K: Of course not Lady Crane, what do you take me for?? Okay; here it goes.............

    Vibrations of light, resurfacing through the intergalactic

    Jiggle boogie wham bam shizzle of the night.

    When Echoes are gone with the coming of the dawn.

    I gaze away and find nothing trivial to say; Just a crazy beat;

    The bass, the treble, the melody and the harmony.

    The drums, a mix, a bum; the sound, the weed, and the rum.

(both Lady Crane and 10 Pak stare at each other for a couple of seconds.)

Lady Crane: Charlie; that was actually really good.

10 Pak: Very not bad; I like it Charlie.

Charlie: You sure?? You're not just saying that because we're fellow Eagles?? (CaCaaww)

10 Pak: Dude; it was good. Let me guess? You were smoking Ghost bud when you wrote that weren't you?

Charlie K: (with astonished look in his face) How did you know that?? Who told you??

10 Pak: Lucky guess. ☺

Charlie K: It's like my hand was moving on its own, amazing. I'm like a creative genius you know; that's what my bro Bobby Ross always told me; chill like the trees Charlie K and you'll find the way.

10 Pak: Wait a minute?? You knew Bob Ross?? THE Bob Ross??

Charlie K: Where do you think he got his weed from? When he traveled all over the country he always made sure to let me know where he was going to be at. You know, so I could send him his packages stuffed inside his crates, where he had his canvasses and paints. Why do you think his canvasses always smelled like "Happy Trees."☺

10 Pak: That actually explains a lot; so cool. So Charlie listen, do only ghosts come here? Who else knows about the Ghost bud?? Anyone that's still living know about this??

Charlie K: To the extent of my knowledge, no one.

Lady Crane: Rafael, Charlie wants to know if you can help him out; if you do, in return he will help you out. You will become the sole proprietor alive to posses the Ghost Bud Plant.

10 Pak: Wow, that's pretty significant; okay, I'm listening.

Charlie K: Some of my ghost friends informed me that the owner of the building, has plans to have the building demolished for the construction of a new one. If they destroy this building, I will no longer exist and neither will the Ghost Bud.

10 Pak: What!! No more Ghost Bud!!

Lady Crane: So does that mean you'll help??

10 Pak: Not only will I help; we are going to buy this building and keep you safe Charlie; or die trying. (50 Cent quote; Check!! In your face Dante!!)

Lady Crane: Rafael; that's not all; we don't think the owner of the building is the type that is going to want to sell.

10 Pak: What do you mean??

Charlie K: Well; we found out that he's a serial killer.

(brief pause)

10 Pak: Wait…..what?? Did you just say, "Serial Killer"? As in Serial Killer; those two words put together, to form one? Serial and Killer??

Charlie K: What, is there a fucking echo in here; yes "Serial Killer". As in a very bad person; very bad. ARGGghh!!!

Lady Crane: Yes, that's correct; thank you Charlie, I think he got it.

10 Pak: Just making sure; how did you find out??

Charlie K: We're ghosts….remember.

10 Pak: God dam it, duhh Idioto!! Can't believe I keep forgetting. This actually sounds like a challenge; I'm game, let's do this!! Give me the address; I swear that when the sun comes up tomorrow this building is going to belong to us.

Charlie K: Rock, Flag, and Eagle baby!!

Lady Crane: That's right; whatever Charlie said.

(10 Paks phone receives a phone call)

10 Pak: Whats up?

Willis: Yeah, Cookie monster here; we got some asshole driving around every 10 minutes changing parking spots and everything. He seems to be checking for something and he keeps looking towards Lady Cranes mansion.

10 Pak: Can you see the license plate??

Willis: Let me see; yup, New Jersey plates.

10 Pak: God damn fucking Frog!! That punk bitch Hannibal too…

Willis: You guessed it; don't these assholes ever give up??

10 Pak: Apparently not; he makes a move for it, pop him in the ass. Keep me posted.

Willis: Will do; Cookie monster out.

(10 Pak turns his attention back to the matter at hand.)

10 Pak: So Charlie, you were saying??

Charlie K: You get ownership of the building and will be in business; big time.

Lady Crane: Oh and Rafael…if this man really is the monster I think he his; make him pay for his sins because no one else will. That I can guarantee you; this guy has money, property, and plenty of influence with flesh eating lawyers. He is well protected and if it goes to a trial; he will walk.

10 Pak: Lady Crane; consider it done. Damn, that's one more thing on my list.

Charlie K: Damn bro you got a list; putting in the overtime. I can tell you got a lot on your mind too because of the so called "list". Tell me, am I wrong??

10 Pak: No, you are not wrong. Things are starting to pile up, and let me tell you that it won't get any easier from here on out. I'm a chess player; I can see certain pieces already moving, taking up formations that indicate major changes coming. As if dealing with a dangerous demon and an insane looking warlock wasn't enough; sure, ad a serial killer to the list why don't ya.

(Lady Crane drifts over to 10 Pak and starts rubbing his shoulders)

Lady Crane: You've put on too much responsibility on your shoulders. But you have to deal with this man; I do believe you will be saving a life or two if you do this.

Charlie K: Sounds heavy brother…wish I could help.

10 Pak: Appreciate it Charlie, but unless you know how to time travel to the past and change a few things here and there; then there is not much we can do. But it would help me out a ton if I had a time machine; seriously, a ton.

Charlie K: Well, I don't know how to travel through time per say; but I do know some ghosts that do know about that sort of thing. Maybe not a time machine exactly; but they do know where the wormhole here in Philadelphia is located at.

10 Pak: A wormhole; what wormhole?? Where??

Charlie K: Near the Naval yard,

10 Pak: How's this possible?

Charlie K: Yeah, right; the "wormhole" was opened the day of the "Philadelphia Experiment" and truth be told, apparently it wasn't properly closed up.

Lady Crane: They didn't know how too.

Charlie K: Exaclty, these ghosts found a way to travel through time and see everything. They can't change anything in the physical world because they're ghosts; they can just observe, kinda sucks don't it??

10 Pak: Indeed. Charlie, where can I find these ghosts that you mentioned?

Charlie K: The Moshulu on Penns Landing.

10 Pak: Get the fuck out!! The Restaurant Boat on Penns Landing?? How about that shit?

      Im supposed to be having dinner there this weekend; how about that shit.

Charlie K: Alrighty then, we are doing business. Let's hug it out bro, come on.

Place: Independence Hall Market ST.

    Old City Philadelphia

(The day continues on in the busy city of Philadelphia; a city where there's never enough time and where time certainly never waits for anyone. Standing in front of the Liberty Bell at Independence Hall, was a very pale ghostly looking Thomas Cadwallader. Having found clothes to wear that he stole from a Thrift Store, he was all dressed in black, covered up mainly with an old Hoodie that looked pretty bad-ass on him. Some trouble maker wearing a Dallas cowboy's shirt starts approaching Tommy and starts harassing him; but Tommy kept quiet, he just kept looking at the horizon for the sun to set. The trouble maker got closer and became more hostile towards Tommy and actually shoves him against one of the Mural Walls. The Sun at this moment disappears completely; dark storm clouds covered the skies until all light vanishes and then a clash of thunder. Tommy commences to laugh at him.)

Tommy Cadwallader: Hurry to meet death, before your place is taken.

Trouble Maker: Fucking crackhead, what that's supposed to mean??

Tommy Cadwallader: It means that, you're standing in your grave. (starts laughing)

(The man barely says anything else before Tommy rips out his tongue with one quick vicious move and then shows it to him; as his life leaves his body. Tommy throws the tongue at the trouble maker and then starts walking away from the scene as he disappears into thin air.)

Song: The Nobodies – Manson (0:00 – 1:30)

Chapter 6

The
Time We Lost

Song: Four Hills – Dj Day (0:00 – 2:00) (Best intro song ever) ☺

(From up high in the heavens, a Golden Eagle plummets down through the clouds and descends onto the city of Philadelphia. Gliding along with the winds, the Golden Eagle heads towards the Philadelphia Art Museum; always standing proud and looking the part of an old Greek Parthenon. The Eagle descends some more and is now looking to land somewhere; presto, it lands on the Rocky Statue, at the bottom of the steps of the Art Museum. It stares at a car passing by with "El Chino of North Philly, along with Flaco and other associates of a different corporate culture. They go around the circle and start heading over to Broad Street, through Center City. There's a certain type of intimidating presence to some of Center City's old buildings, statues, and monuments; this can't be seen anywhere else but in the North-East. The deeper they go into Broad St., you start seeing what South Philly is all about; they then make their way down to Snyder Ave. After that, to 6th St, where they make a right and go down to the park across the Buddhist Temple on Ritner St.)

Place: Budhist Temple 6th St. & Ritner St.

South Philadelphia

Annual Gathering of the Bulls

(After parking their car a few blocks down the street Ramon, Flaco, and crew start making their way through the crowds. You can hear the loud chatter and the excitement of all the people, young and old. The drums start playing again, signaling the beginning of a new fight. There are many different flags and banners being waved at this event, being hosted by the Buddhist monks. Latin American flags, Asian flags, and African American Banners decorate the landscape of the Park. Secretly, these fighters are representing the different gang-lords of the area; which every year they fight for the right to re-shape the drug territory, without everybody killing each other in a drug war; a war that would weaken them and leave them vulnerable to the groups of N.Y.C. This has kept the peace amongst most of these particular groups since the tournament was initiated about a decade ago. Ramon and Flaco finally make it to the tent where 10 Pak was getting ready at; he was one of the fighters representing the Latino community.)

Flaco: Wuz up wuz up homies!! Damn there's a shitload of fine bitches here today!

El Chino: Looks like a packed house little cousin, you ready for this fight?

10 Pak: Shit, I got this cous. Tell you what, if I lose I'll buy dinner and drinks tonight; but if I

Win, then you fuckers are paying.

El Chino: Who you fighting??

10 Pak: We get the fighter from Cambodia this year, should be interesting….

Flaco: Fuck yeah!!I can't wait to see you in action again bro, fuck him up!!

Rodrigo: You see everybody that's here Chino?? That's Dane over there.

10 Pak: Yeah I see them; let me go say what's up real quick, I'll be right back.

(Present here today were some of the most important people from the Philadelphia Underground. Among them, was Buddha the West of the heart of West Philadelphia; he was there to see his little brother represent the Black Iron Fists of West Philly. Gerry Babula the Bull, of Southwest Philadelphia was there representing the Italians of Perugia. Dane of the North and his crew of North Philadelphia Cats, were representing the United African Nations of Philadelphia.)

(Then there was our group; the Alliance of the Latino Nations of Philadelphia.   Also present there in small numbers were the Black Irish Heathens, led by a man named "Chucky BoBo". Last but not least; a group nobody fucks with, period; the MUNSTER'S of IRELAND of South Philadelphia. Tony the one eye and his Cambodian crews were also there; along with Lady Hue and her Vietnamese fighters. Then there's the group from Thailand and their boss, the most dangerous of them all; a bookie/loan shark by the name of "Sonny Lo". A referee comes in and tells 10 Pak to get ready, that he's coming up on the next fight. 10 Pak's friend and trainer Rodrigo Navarre, does one last walk through concerning their game plan for the fight.)

Rodrigo: Alright you're up next; remember to keep moving away from his left kick. He's

        going to be waiting for you to step into his favorite kick, take that away and

        you should be good. Good luck baby boy, you got this! (manly hug)

El Chino: Good luck cous...be careful…(manly hug)

Flaco: To all the Gods here today; stay out of our fucking way!!!!..Fuck the Gods!!

10 Pak: Fuck the Gods!! (they all start laughing) Here we go. (Starts stepping out of the tent)

(As soon as 10 Pak steps out of the tent, the "Honduran Garifuna" drums start playing their tunes and the Latino crowd goes fucking wild!!! A great roar of cheers for their Honduran fighter erupts through the masses. His name was being shouted by many of his fellow Latinos, fellow countrymen, and fellow countrywomen. They were all there to support one of the descendants of "Florencio Xaltruch"; father of all Hondurans (CATRACHOS). Another huge roar erupts on the other side of the park were the Cambodians cheer on for their fighter. Both fighters start making their way to the center circle, located in the middle of the park. They both enter the circle and start stretching out some more; they keep getting ready for the Buddhist monks to bless and announce the start of the fight. The two fighters finish getting ready and prepare themselves, for a real good bare knuckle martial arts fight. 10 Pak has his people shouting loud and proud, along with the "Garifuna" drum group showing their support for a fellow Honduran countryman. The Cambodians being loud as shit, screaming all kinds of obscenities and laughing their asses off; (must've been something real funny) keep cheering for their fighter. Both fighters square off and come close to each other up to a safe distance; they bow to the monks of the temple and then they bow to each other. They begin walking around in circles slowly measuring each other up. A quick punch thrown by the Cambodian; he misses.)

(The Honduran throws a back spin hook kick to try to catch the Cambodian off guard; but he also misses. The Cambodian dodges another counter attack. They back off each other for a couple of steps; then 10 Pak jumps at the Cambodian with a jumping axe kick as a set up kick. As the Cambodian slides towards 10 Pak's left; 10 Pak attacks right away with a follow up jumping back spin hook kick that catches the Cambodian right in the face. ☹ Lights out, Game Over. 10 Pak easily wins the fight as he starts waving at the Latino crowds. He checks to see if the Cambodian was okay and then starts walking towards the crowds. After he's congratulated by the people from the neighborhood and his "Garifuna" friends; 10 Pak starts heading back to his tent to go get out of his fighting gear. As he sits down on his seat, he opens up his gym bag only to find a letter from Zepi Petri addressed to him. He opens it and sees written, "Tick Tock Tick Tock your time is running out". "Rittenhouse Square 6:00pm.")

10 Pak: This mutha fucka…..(starts looking for his cell-phone in his gym bag)

Place: Old City, Philadelphia

Zepi Petri's Hideout

(Zepi Petri stands in front of a mirror looking at himself in his fine Italian suit and handmade Italian leather shoes. Not only was he talking to himself; but he is also talking to the poor soul tied up to table all bloodied and beaten up. It seems that Zepi Petri was torturing the shit out of this person, just for the simple fact that it was a Saturday; he just felt like doing this to kill some time until his meeting with 10 Pak.)

Place: Wal-Mart Parking Lot

Columbus Blvd. South Philadelphia

(Both Matt and Herbie are meeting a potential buyer for some items; that may or may have not fallen out of a truck near Valley Forge. They are near a parking lot, sitting on some benches at the pier right next to the water by the Wal-Mart. As they've learned from hanging out with 10 Pak, never trust anyone; especially someone who comes to you with a deal to good to be true. They start playing the cat and mouse game with the undercover cop.)

MaTT: So where you from??

Buyer/Cop: I'm from Jersey.

Herbie: NEW Jersey??

Buyer/Cop: That's right.

Matt: Where in Jersey??

Buyer/Cop: Around Freehold, New Jersey.

Herbie: (starts laughing) What exit is that??

Buyer/Cop: What??

Matt: He's a cop.

Buyer/Cop: No I'm not; what makes you say that??

Herbie: Well for starters; someone from New Jersey would've been more defensive
about all the New Jersey sarcasm; but that wasn't where you fucked up.

Matt: Yeah bro; you left your badge hanging out of your shirt pocket.

(The rookie police officer not being able to control his natural reaction to look; reaches for his pocket to check if his badge really was there and gives away his cover. Both Matt and Herbie start laughing as they get up and start walking away, each in a different direction.)

Herbie: Better luck next time, Rookie. (Herbie starts walking away when his phone starts
ringing; it's 10 Pak) Yo! Talk to me..

10 Pak: Yo Herb… we're going to the Moshulu, tonight; before we go there though;
we're gonna have to make a stop at RittenHouse Square.

Herbie: Okay, we bringing back up??

10 Pak: Nothing like that; but bring like about 5 guys, I don't want to get caught completely
off guard at the Moshulu. Remember, we still have those assholes from New Jersey
looking around for us.

Herbie: I know; who do you want on for backup??

10 Pak: You pick them; just make sure they're not complete fucking idiots. Bring Matt
and Damien along as well, he's earned his wings; its time he got some field experience.
Herbie, this is a nice restaurant not a strip club in Delaware; so dress accordingly okay.

Herbie: I'm gonna wear a Hawaiian t-shirt, with shorts, and a cowboy hat; how's that for
accordingly?? (he starts laughing)

10 Pak: (laughing as well) You're such an asshole; see you in a few hours.

Herbie: Later. (Herbie hangs up and sees a sexy young woman walk by in slutty clothes) Yo

baby!! What can I get for a $20 and a pack of smokes!!

Back at the park on 6th and Ritner St.

(10 Pak says his goodbyes to all of his Latino people and starts walking along with Ramon, Flaco, and company to a house he had nearby on 3rd and Daly St. They were getting a shipment of edibles ready for delivery to be sent up to a nursing home in Scranton, PA. Believe it or not, nursing homes are not the happiest of places; for both the staff and the people staying there. Edibles make their time there more tolerable and it definitely helps deal with the arthritis without the actual Marijuana smell.☺ After his crew leaves with the shipment of edibles, 10 Pak starts getting ready for a night that's going to be a lot more interesting that what he realizes☺ Few moments later he walks out of his house and starts walking towards a parking lot on 2nd and Wolf where he had his car. As he is walking, he notices that "Gladys", an older lady that lives on his block, was hesitating whether or not to walk past a group of young teenagers that were sitting on the corner. 10 Pak saw that "Gladys" was afraid that she might get robbed by the young teenagers, so he started walking towards her.)

10 Pak: Nice night isn't' it??

Gladys: Yes it is.

10 Pak: Would you like me to accompany you all the way to the Church?? I can walk with you

past these guys if you wish so?

Gladys: Oh I would really appreciate that; it's like you're my protecting Archangel.

10 Pak: God works in mysterious ways, doesn't he?

Gladys: God bless you; thanks for those space cakes again, by the way. Made Bingo night a lot

more fun; some of those ladies there aren't too nice. One of them is a New York

Giants fan; don't like her at all.

10 Pak: You are welcome Gladys, anytime; and screw those Giants fans, you what I mean.

They're all assholes anyway. ☺

(As they walked by, the teenagers stopped talking and saw that it was 10 Pak himself escorting the Old Lady to the Church half a block away. These teenagers knew who 10 Pak was; shiiiit, they had just seen him fight at the Park earlier that afternoon. They weren't about to try to pick a fight with a trained fighter out of Philadelphia; so nothing was said, just a "head-nod" from all of them acknowledging 10 Pak and then nothing happened.)

Gladys: Wow, there were 6 of them and not one of those little weasels said a word; I'm impressed. I'm guessing you're not scared of them because you probably have seen a lot worse and a lot more dangerous characters than them; am I right??

10 Pak: I find it hard to argue against your observation Gladys; it's mostly true.

Gladys: What did I miss??

10 Pak: The part where you simply have to do what's right and always protect those that can't protect themselves. At the same time being understanding of everyone's point of view, no matter the person.

Gladys: I ought to bring you in there so you can share some of your thoughts with that priest; all he talks about is damnation and all the ugly things in the world. I don't think I like him much; I think secretly he's a Cowboys fan. Imagine if everybody found out that we have a priest who's a Cowboys fan preaching here in the heart of South Philadelphia.

10 Pak: They'd probably water-board him with the holy wine. Besides, I'm not wanted in places like that; I'm not a believer of much anyway, to be honest with you.

Gladys: Screw them!! You have a good heart; that's all that matters, remember I said that.

10 Pak: (finally arriving at the Church) I will, here we go. Try to enjoy the Mass, I guess.

Gladys: Key word being "try" right; god bless you and thank you again, have a good night.

10 Pak: (looks up at the skies as if speaking to God himself) You listening??

(as he walks over to his car)

Place: Camden New Jersey

Hannibal's WareHouse/Hideout

(A group of South Jersey Devils are gathering together at Hannibal's spot; they're there to try to formulate some plan of attack against 10 Pak and company. Their main concern was a major one that had to be very carefully planned out and then executed. It was key, not provoke the rest of the crews of Philadelphia; because if they sensed that the attack was on one of them, then they all stand up and fight you. They take no risks with other groups coming in from Jersey and New York; to them it's Philadelphia for Philadelphians and the South Jersey Devil's knew this all too well. Hannibal is sitting on his desk while his associates sit around bull shitting, playing cards while he answers his cell phone; it's his wife calling.)

Hannibal: Yo, what's up babe? You going grocery shopping, make sure you get everything

          then; oh and don't forget, we need toilet paper. Girl, I don't care what brand you get;

          I'm wiping my ass with it, not taking it out for a date. Okay, love you too. (hangs up)

(Hannibal starts talking to his buddies' playing cards at the table right next to his desk.)

Hannibal: You mutha fucka's didn't deal me in?? Aint this a bitch…

Cory: My bad bruh; I thought you were gonna be all day on the phone with your woman.

Hannibal: Shhiiit. I am Worldly, Un-Godly and profane; as I wonder and I ponder about the

          "what if's" in life.

Teddy B: What you mean by that boss man??

Hannibal: Just imagine for a second if things where flipped around on us; on everybody for that

          matter. Nurses become strippers, strippers become nurses; politicians become

          homeless people and the homeless start ruling the world, that kind of shit.

Cory: I can dig it; if things were different like that, then I would've ended up being a Cop.

Hannibal: There you go, now you're starting to get it.

Cory: Funny idea, me a Cop; I mean sure I would've taken a bribe or two; or three.

          (They all start laughing with Cory) No more than five.

Teddy B: You're an inspiration to us all Cory; you would've made a great Cop. (They keep

          laughing)

(10 Pak walks along the park at RittenHouse Square and sits on a bench. The wind makes its presence felt as the trees start moving back and forth; a moment of peaceful reflection for a very busy person such as 10 Pak. Zepi Petri shows up out of nowhere, just like that out of thin air.)

Zepi Petri: There he is… Honestly I was beginning to have my doubts about you.

10 Pak: Here I am; and why am I here???

Zepi Petri: Any news for me??

10 Pak: How about you give me a phone number or something so I can contact you because this shit; ain't gonna to work.

Zepi Petri: Not a chance in hell. You don't find me; I find you. You want your friend to go home don't you?? It was Rhetorical, so don't feel like you have to answer, okay. Just letting you know that I am waiting for you to make your move; and I don't Like to be kept waiting.

10 Pak: I don't have your special abilities okay; I can't just snap my fingers and have somebody's tongue come out of their asshole, okay. I said I'm working on it; I'm pretty sure that as soon as I know, you'll know.

Zepi Petri: Their tongue through their asshole; I don't even think that's possible. Anyway, hope you're as good as you make yourself out to be. Remember, I'm the professional here, so don't even think about trying to fuck me over on this, your hear me. So chop chop; mutha fucka…

10 Pak: I got one small thing to take care of over the weekend and then I can put my full attention on this come Monday.

Zepi Petri: What the fuck is this?? Since when the fuck do drug dealers not work the weekends; I thought yous were from Philadelphia. Whatever; I'll be seeing you around….

(At a distance you hear a car crash along with people screaming and yelling.   10 Pak turns quick to see what happened and then he turns around again; only to see that Zepi Petri had vanished out in thin air.)

10 Pak: This shit is starting to wear thin; very fucking fast. (turns around and starts making his way back to the S.U.V. where Herbie, Matt, and Damien were waiting for him.)

(10 Pak gets in the Car and Herbie notices that 10 Pak is not looking too happy.)

Herbie: You don't seem to be happy with the arrangement with this guy; I'm guessing we're gonna end up taking him out??

10 Pak: You are 100% correct about that; this guy has no idea how fucking hard I'm gonna hit him. He thinks I'm buying into that bullshit story he told me about himself.

Herbie: So why you putting up with him??

10 Pak: This guy is a clever one; it's going to take a lot more than brute force to deal with this fucker. Let's just hope he doesn't kill us all before we even get a chance to take a shot at him.

Herbie: He's that dangerous??

10 Pak: Herbie, this guy is on a whole other level; we have to plan this right or all of this that we're doing, gone. You understand??

Herbie: Okay I get it, business is business; now how about you cheer the fuck up and let's go have a good time. What do you say pretty boy!! (starts laughing)

10 Pak: Herbie, call me pretty boy one more fucking time and I'm gonna kick you in the balls; now let's get the fuck out of here. I'm hungry and I need a drink; or two.

Matt: That's what I'm talking about bro, fuck all that noise about that asshole. This is another good opportunity for us to find another form of treasure on this old boat. I got the info on it you wanted by the way; you are not going to believe the history of this boat.

(Herbie starts making yawning noises just to piss Matt off.)

Herbie: What's with the lecture??

Matt: Eat a dick Herbie…

10 Pak: Matt give me the short summarized version; and Herbie, pretty please, with sugar on

  top, shut the fuck up I want to hear this. (Herbie starts laughing)

Damien: Is this what it's like to hang-out with you guys?? Can wait to see what's next.

(All three of them at the same time start telling Damien to…)

All 3: Shut the FUck UP Damien!! Little Asshole!!

Herbie: (in a girly voice) Is this what it's going to be like hanging out with you?? You ain't

  seen shit yet rookie; hold on to your balls because at any point anything this can

  go belly up. That's the beauty about this life we choose; death comes at a price.

Matt: The fucking F.N.G got jokes….

Damien: What the HeLL is an F.N.G??

Herbie: Fucking New Guy, get it?? Hey Damien did you hear the news on the radio today??

Damien: I use my phone with Wi-Fi internet, but sure radio, keep going.

Herbie: George Bush Jr. is going to be the new face of the one dollar bill.

Damien: What, I didn't hear anything like that.

Herbie: Yeah, that's right. See, this way when Jr. is doing a line, he can see his own face.

  (They all start laughing hesitantly at Herbie's stupid fucking Joke)

(They take off and start heading over to Penn's Landing off of Columbus Blvd. 10 Pak knew that he had to move quickly and figure out the information he needed about the wormhole located near Penn's Landing. His plan was to find a way to help Tommy Cadwallader go back to his own time period, through the use of the wormhole. So that in return, Tommy could help him deal with Zepi Petri; hopefully by using a spell from the book against him. Thing was, that if Zepi Petri found out that 10 Pak was trying to get rid of him with the help of a Warlock; then Zepi Petri would move fast and kill everybody with no hesitation whatsoever.)

Place: Penns Landing -Moshulu BoAT/Restaurant

Columbus Blvd. South Philadelphia

Song: A Gentle Dissolve – Thievery Corporation (0:00 – 1:10)

(Walking through the area of Penn's Landing, making your way to the Moshulu parking lot; you get to experience one of the more "cooler" chill spots in all of South Philadelphia. As you keep walking through the park, you start seeing all the cool fluorescent lights hanging from all the trees. The colors of the fluorescent lights fade in and out in the dark of the night; making it seem very psychedelic. The ocean winds start blowing in from the east and they make it for an even more comfortable environment to experience; as part of a perfect Philadelphia evening. People are walking everywhere enjoying the park along with its stores and the Independence SeaPort Museum; a place that offers much of the history of this area. The museum includes the checkered History of the Moshulu, a history that brought this Vessel from the pinnacle of sailing success, to the pits of seagoing servitude. This alone would arguably make it the most unusual restaurant in the city, along with the fact that it's HAUNTED.) ☺

(The Moshulu is the world's largest and oldest four-masted sailing ship still afloat. The 3,116 ton vessel was launched in Scotland in 1904 and was named the "Kurt" by her German owners. She sailed the seas with general cargoes until World War I, when the Americans captured her and renamed her "Moshulu", a Seneca word for "Fearless". Her new owners placed her in the lucrative grain trade and she quickly gained status as one of the fastest grain-carrying square-riggers on any ocean. She proved herself in 1939 when she won the Great Grain Race from Australia to England. This race was considered by many maritime historians to be the last dying attempt of the square-rigger era to cling to the relevancy of the times.)

(After that in 1940, the fate that befell the "Moshulu" was one that awaited many of the majestic sailing ships of that time. Her masts and rigging, her 45'000 sq ft of canvas, her very innards were stripped from her hull; the once proud Moshulu became nothing but a barge, a floating warehouse with no direction or purpose. It wasn't until 1970 that the ship was towed to Philadelphia and after a $2 million renovation; it opened as a floating restaurant five years later. Bad luck struck the "Moshulu" once again in the summer of 1989, when a four alarm fire and smoke damage caused the closing of the restaurant. This event ends up sending the vessel to an uncertain fate at a pier across the river in Camden, New Jersey.)

(For an extended amount of time it had seemed that the "Moshulu" might end up in the bottom scrap heap of sailing history. There were plans proposed that would have kept the Vessel in Camden, or moved it to Wilmington, Delaware; which wasn't that far away. Both cities offered millions of dollars in harbor accommodations to the new owners, if they would refurbish it and move it to their waterfronts. But, in the end it was Philadelphia that won the honor to host the Moshulu; Philadelphia had the pier, the parking, Penn's Landing and the developers Michael J. Asbell and Eli Karetny. They opted to return the "Moshulu" to Pier 34, where the ship still remains today, as the centerpiece of a cluster of dining and entertainment facilities. The "Moshulu" wears its $11 million renovation with plenty of pride. It has Central American Mahogany, Victorian etched glass, bright brass-work, a cocktail lounge, and atmospheric dining rooms on the main deck that wrap customers up in luxury. On the upper deck are the restored crew's quarters, the galley, the foc'sle, some displays…..and last but not least; the ghosts of two or possibly three former crew members.)

(Not very many people know about the "special" history of this vessel and how it's haunted; and it's not because they have been hiding it, quite the opposite. The people that work there are quite open about the fact that there are spirits present there. There have been many reports, of all of the lanterns being turned on all fifty-two dining tables; before anyone even gets there during the day. The staff has reported that sometimes when the lantern candles have been completely snuffed out, later on during the course of their shift; they have found the candles flickering in the light of day. Still to this point in time they don't know who's doing it and how. These reports have also been confirmed by the overnight cleaning crews; who have also witnessed for themselves the lantern candles light up, accompanied by strange sounds. According to Eli Karetny, this cleaning crew was so spooked working from midnight to 5am; that they started asking for earlier working hours when other people were on board. Everyone at the Moshulu have come to call it, the"Lantern Ghost; and that's just the first "supernatural entity" on the menu. The second Ghost roams around the upper deck among the masts and superstructures. Eli Karetny believes this to be the spirit of a sea captain or probably that of a sailor. Reports have it, that weird sounds have been heard early in the evening and at closing time; seems to be coming from the rigging, sounds that are like "light whispers". It is important that you remember that this Vessel traveled around Cape Horn 54 times and 28 men lost their lives; it is believed that some of the spirits of those lost souls still remain on its decks.)

(I mean this Vessel is old; so I wouldn't put it past it that it didn't pick up unusual types of passengers, along the tides of time. The "Moshulu" is a veteran of 54 voyages around Cape Horn at the edge of South America where the Atlantic and the Pacific Oceans meet; making it one of the most dangerous places on earth to travel by boat. The waters around Cape Horn are extremely hazardous due to the strong winds, massive waves, very strong currents and icebergs. In 1616 when navigator Willem Schouten discovered Cape Horn, it became very significant because its discovery opened up new trade routes and broke up almost all monopolies. Even though it's not South America's most southernmost island; it's the southernmost point of the "Tierra del Fuego" archipelago of southern Chile. After 1914 the need for boats and ships to travel around Cape Horn was greatly reduced due to opening of the Panama Canal.)

(Some people attribute the strange sounds of the "Moshulu" to the fact that it's a very old boat; a square rigger to be precise. So it wouldn't be unusual if the mind played that trick that had you thinking that the creaking of timbers was actually that of "Spirits" bitching and moaning. ☺ But in this case Eli Karetny explains the difference and actually goes into detail about this; explaining how certain sounds can be "mistaken ghosts". According to Karetny the Moshulu "talks"; and this is one that actually does have an explanation. See, the ship seems to be talking because it's moored (this means "tied") to Pier 34; so when the tide changes, the ship pulls on its mooring and it starts making that sound. Apparently, it is better experienced at night in the dark; giving it that mysterious, unnatural, ghostly sound. Somehow; it would seem that it wants to go back out to sea once again, where it belongs.)

(Having said that, some of the staff are aware of the difference between a "mistaken ghost" sound, to one that actually is a real ghost sound; reassuring everyone that a woman's laughter can't be mistaken with anything else. This is especially true when the woman's hysterical laughing is coming directly from the "ladies room" and nowhere else. In 1998 a "Medium" (Paranormal Investigator) was brought in for dinner and a reading of the ship; stepping on the gangplank was more than enough for her to feel the presence of a strong energy there. She reported that the strongest presence there was not that of a sea captain or a sailor; but that of a middle-aged woman. She didn't go into the specifics of how, when, why, or what; but she speculated that the woman's ghost could be that of a Captain's wife or a crew members.)

(Although, she was leaning more towards the possibility that it could've been a stowaway dressed in Men's clothing; posing as a male sailor for reasons unknown. The Medium also perceived that the circumstances surrounding this woman's presence in the Moshulu were "particularly odd". She sensed that the woman's demise wasn't connected to murder or suicide; but it did feel like confusion and deceit were a factor. The Medium also explained, that she couldn't do much with the few little pieces of information she had; she felt that the woman was secretive and very hard to decipher. She added that "Energies" like this one, were strong enough to spark candles or recapture conversations; but totally harmless. Herbie, 10 Pak, and crew finally make it to the parking lot of the Moshulu restaurant and almost immediately they start exiting the car.)

Matt: God damn it Herbie; my grandmother drives faster than this!!

Herbie: Well go get her then and bring her here, you little asshole!! I'll show her how to drive

"stick"!!

Matt: Herbie, if you keep talking about my grandmother; or something else comes out of your

mouth one more time, I'm gonna cut your legs off at the knees.

Herbie: Oh Yeah!! Well I'll still be taller than you. (they all start laughing)

Matt: Fucking prick…

10 Pak: Will you two fems cut it out!! Alright!! :Listen up!! We are going in here to have a

good time and enjoy ourselves; so no fighting you hear me, no fucking fighting!!

Behave like normal gentlemen please; and for fucks sake, restrain yourselves from

getting too inebriated. Clear!!

Everybody: Crystal….

(They all take a moment to enjoy the view of the Moshulu at night time; this is considered by many in the area to be one of better sites of Philadelphia. They start walking up the boardwalk and then they go inside the "Moshulu"; and let me just say this, "Fucking Top Notch Nice". They are greeted by the Hostess, who then kindly shows them to their table. There that night, were a few recognizable people; and out of all of them the most famous, or infamous I should say, was Jerome Koppel the reporter.)

(He was there having dinner with what seemed to be a very expensive escort; and he wasn't shy about it one bit. 10 Pak and crew now have the privilege to be sitting next to such an eccentric public figure.)

Jerome Koppel: Damn sugar, you looking good tonight!! I wish this was one of those

restaurants were you can eat off a naked bitch and not blink one bit; you feel me.

Escort: Sounds sooooo, classy.

Jerome Koppel: Bitch, you better check your tone.

(Herbie interrupts their conversation, being all loud and annoying as usual.)

Herbie: Holy shit! You're that dude on TV; you guys hiring by any chance?

(everyone in the restaurant turns their heads to them)

Jerome Koppel: That's right stranger, you are correct I am the one and only Big K

Koppel and no I do not do the hiring. Now if you don't mind; my salad is

getting cold. Oh yeah and uhhhh, lower the base on your voice cause

you're one loud mutha fucka…

Damien: (whispering to Matt and 10 Pak) What an asshole…(10 Pak pulls Herbie back)

10 Pak: Herbie, what the fuck I say before we came in here??

Herbie: Relax, I'm not going to spoil your little dinner party okay; although I really wish this

was tittie-bar

10 Pak: I am relaxed, you miserable old prick; don't think I've forgotten about Cheeks in

Baltimore. So you're going to have to excuse my skepticism Herbie, if I don't take you

at your word.

Herbie: You still pissed about that; I said I was sorry. We got out of there in one piece, didn't

we?? (Waitress finally comes up and starts taking their drink orders.)

Matt: Barely..

Herbie: Matt if I remember correctly, you almost cried that night; didn't you??

Matt: I told you assholes, there was something in my eye; uhhh pepper spray, yeah now I

remember, it was the pepper spray.

Herbie: Buuuullshiiit!! We found you behind the juke box all hunched up in the fetal position

crying your ass off, yelling STOP… please STOP.

Matt: I got kicked in the balls!!

Damien: I thought you said you got pepper sprayed??

Matt: (not being able to come up with a lie) How the fuck did this become about me anyway…

(They all start laughing as the waitress is now giving them their respective beverages.)

10 Pak: Excuse me, hi how are you; I was wondering if you know who I can talk to that has

been working here the longest. In other words, someone who knows about the history

of this boat. Where it came from, who were the original owners, when was it renovated?

Waitress: That would be the manager; he knows everything about the "Moshulu". You're in

luck, he's here tonight; I'll go get him for you, Mr.??

10 Pak: Mr. Silver; Thank you, much appreciated.

(The waitress comes back with the manager; he asks 10 Pak if he would rather go outside to the upper deck and discuss the matter at hand. He wasn't sure he wanted the other customers to over-hear their conversation. As they leave, Herbie decides that he wants to play a joke on Matt; by spiking his drink with grinded psychedelic mushrooms. So he gets up and goes over to talk to one of the waitresses and places a couple of $100 bills on her tray.)

Herbie: I need you to do me a favor…(as he laughs)

Waitress: (starts counting the money) What I can do for you?? (Herbie hands her the little bag

with the Shrooms)

(As the waitress is trying to pour the "shroom-dust" into Matt's drink; another waitress accidently bumps into her; she looks back immediately to make sure they didn't catch her in the act. While doing this, she fails to notice that the "shroom-dust" made into two of the drinks, not just Matt's. She straightens herself out; grabs the drinks and then proceeds on to the dining area. Matt quickly grabs his drink and so does Damien; Herbie finally comes back to the table with a huge grin on his face.)

Herbie: Drink up ladies; can't wait to see if there are any ghosts here tonight!!

(Because Herbie is so loud by nature, everything that he said makes its way to Jerome Koppels ears. Now Koppel decides that he wants to pay attention to this conversation; he was one of the few journalists still interested in reporting what had happened the night the dead woke up. The very same night the corpses from Washington Sq. roamed the streets of Center City Philadelphia for about 23 minutes. The very same night 10 Pak, Ant, and company got videotaped at the Art Museum fighting off the dead.)

Damien: Where the hell is 10 Pak??

Matt: Hey guys, I think I'm gonna go to the bathroom real quick, I have to….(he just looks at

them and says) Fuck it….(and just walks off)

Herbie: (with a smug look in his face) Matt, buddy; you okay?? (Matt just keeps walking)

Damien: Hey Herbie, (removes his glasses and starts wiping them off) is it me or are these

lights starting to look a bit fuzzy and distorted??

Herbie: Oh shit….. she must've put the shrooms in your drink too…

Damien: Wait, WHAT??

(Desperetaly trying to find a bathroom, Matt unknowingly goes downstairs and enters the ladies bathroom where the women's laughter comes from at night, when only the cleaning crew is there. He knows that there is something wrong, he's starting to see light trails, and his tongue is starting to go numb.)

Matt: Trails?? I feel like I'm on magic mashruooms; my lips peel phunny. Why my lips peel

phunny?? Why ca't I say mashhroom..What the pluck?? I flacking tripping!! Fluhh..cking

He-bie!!!

(As soon as Matt turns around to try to leave to go whoop Herbie's ass; the ghost of the stowaway woman in the bathroom appears right before him. Matt freezes up because he can't believe the situation he's in; tripping balls while bumping into a ghost… that's uncharted waters for him; lol. The Ghost quickly reaches out with her hand and touches Matt right in the forehead; where his "Third Eye" is located at. Immediately she starts showing Matt the past, present, and the future. Like a giant TV screen in front of him, he starts seeing all these images of all the places the Moshulu had been too; places like Africa, Australia, Asia, America, Great Britain, and Europe.)

Song: Teknology- Mountain Dub feat-Ras Chidy (1:05 – 2:25)

(On the Upper Deck, 10 Pak was done with his conversation with the manager and had remained outside for a while longer; he wanted to hear the sounds the Moshulu makes at night for himself. 10 Pak looks out into the Delaware River, as he tries to imagine where the "Wormhole" could be located at; he also knows that he must figure out how the ghosts travel through it. He takes a deep breath and exhales slowly, as if the weight on his shoulders was starting to take a toll on him. He starts heading back downstairs when he all of a sudden stops, he feels that someone is watching him; he pauses only for a moment before he continues down stairs.)

(10 Pak comes back to the dining room area just to find Damien on the floor calling out for help while Herbie is trying to calm him down. 10 Pak rushes over to them and starts making his way through the crowd of people; finally making it to where Damien was at. 10 Pak leans over Damien to see what was wrong with him.)

Herbie: Dude, your back!!

Damien: Talk....me…down.. MaN!! Talk…me…down!!!

10 Pak: Herbie what the fuck is going on?? Please tell me you didn't start anything.

Herbie: I…I…I..uhhhh..I…

10 Pak: I can't believe this, I'm not even gone for ten fucking minutes and this shit happens.

Where the fuck is Matt.??

Herbie: Matt's in the bathroom; he ain't feeling well neither.

10 Pak: Bathroom, what bathroom?? Shit!! I hope he's not in the one bathroom I think he's in.

Fuck!!

(The Manager and some of the waitresses come over to help 10 Pak and Damien; one of the Waitresses puts a wet towel on Damien's forehead and starts holding his hand.)

Herbie: I'm sorry, I didn't mean for this to happen.

10 Pak: God damn it Herbie!! Seriously, what fucking language I gotta speak in; because I

know you don't speak fucking Spanish.

(Right away, as soon as he says that, 10 Pak realizes that he had figured out the mystery of women in the bathroom. He had also figured out why nobody, not even the "Medium" could decipher what she was all about; 10 Pak turns around and puts the pieces together real quick. The "Moshulu" had traveled so many times around the tip of South America; this meant that the stowaway either spoke Spanish, Portuguese, or maybe French.)

Herbie: Wait, what's the matter; you got that look in your eyes again.

10 Pak: Herbie, I just figured it out; son of a bitch, I just figured it out. Shit really does happen for a reason; had you not done your usual dumb shit, I would've never of reacted and said that to you. Holy shiiit this is fucking weird!! Matt!! I gotta go help Matt…Herbie stay with Damien I'll be right back.

Herbie: So, are we cool??

10 Pak: Herbie; you're still my lucky charm, you mean old prick.

(10 Pak along with the Manager, start making their way to help Matt. On the way there, 10 Pak explains to the Manager his theory on why the ghost only laughed and never said anything; because she didn't know how too.)

Manager: You sure this will work?? It's a bit of a stretch, don't you think??

10 Pak: There is only one way to find out. (starts knocking on the bathroom door.)

(They start hearing the women's laughter come from inside the bathroom and they start trying to open the door forcefully, but the latch won't open.)

Manager: What now??

10 Pak: Let's try my theory out?? I'm going to try Portuguese first, maybe she's Brazilian.

  Senhora, fala Portugess?? (Miss, do you speak Portuguese) Damn, nothing.

Manager: Let me try French; Madame, parlez-vous francais?? (Madam, do you speak French?)

  I don't think this is going to work…

10 Pak: Here's one last try, Spanish. "Disculpe Senorita" (Excuse me miss)

(The laughter stops immediately)

Manager: No way, it worked. I don't believe this.

10 Pak: Neither can I; okay here goes nothing. " Senorita, yo queria saber si mi amigo Matt se

    encuentra bien; El es una muy Buena persona. Yo le dije a la mama de el, de que yo

    lo cuidaria. Como usted puede ver; hecho un trabajo bien mierda. Usted cree que me

    pueda ayudar??" {Miss, I wanted to know if my friend Matt was okay?? He's a good

    person and I told his mom that I would take care of him; and as you can see, I'm doing

    a real shitty job. Do you think you can help me out??}

(The door opens and Matt collapses before them; as they're pulling him out of the bathroom the door shuts behind them, almost immediately. The Manager decides to go get help and calls the paramedics. 10 Pak lays Matt on the floor and tries talking to him; but Matt is still under the influence of the mushrooms and his trip isn't done yet. 10 Pak takes off his jacket and bundles it up like a pillow under Matt's head.)

10 Pak: There you go buddy; just relax and it'll all be over soon. I'm right here I'm not going

    anywhere; I got you buddy. I'm now going to try to have a conversation with the lady,

    so don't mind what you hear okay. You might think it's the shrooms, but this is gonna

    fuck with your head; so I suggest you just look away and ignore everything you hear.

    "Senorita, mi nombre es Rafael Bertrand de la Plata; descendiente de Florencio Xaltruch;

    padre de los Catrachos y protector del pueblo Hondureno y del pueblo Nicaraguense.

    Un hombre de gran valentia y honor, que gano el respeto de la gente del pueblo; despues

    de salvarlos de las manos malvadas de el Admiral ex-confederado William Walker.

Translation – Miss, my name is Rafael Bertrand de la Plata; and I am a descendent of General

    Florencio Xaltruch; father of the Catrachos (Hondurans) and protector of

    the Honduran people and the Nicaraguan people. He was a man of great honor

    and fierce courage, who won the respect of his people when he defeated the evil

    Ex-Confederate Admiral William Walker; in a battle at Nicaragua.

10 Pak: La verdad, es de que para mi es una obligacion como ser humano decente, el poder

    expresar estas palabras de "El Che", Ernesto Guevera de la Serna. Digo esto, para que

    su espiritu viva para siempre entre los corazones, las mentes, y las sonrisas de la raza

    latina. A mi solo me queda como recurso efectivo, la palabra; asi que con mi voz ,

    enciendo las llamas de hermandad de la gran patria de Latino America. Que ahora mas

    que nunca, tenemos que entender.. que la division de Latino America y nacionalidades

    inciertas e ilusorias, son completamente fictisias. Constituimos una sola raza mestiza

    desde Mexico, hasta el Estrecho de Magallanes. Asi que tratando de librarme de

    cualquier carga de provencialismo; reso por Honduras y por una Latino America unida.

    Quiero que usted sepa que es este mensaje, el que yo llevo imprimido en el Corazon.

Translation- Truth is, that to me it is an obligation as a decent human being, to be able to

    express these words of "El Che" Ernesto Guevera de la Serna. I say this, so that

    his spirit can live on forever in the hearts, minds, and smiles of the Latin American

    people. My words are my only effective resource; so with my voice, let me light

    the spark of brotherhood of the Great Latin American Nation. Now more than ever,

    we have to understand that the division of Latin America, with its uncertain and

    illusionary nationalities; are completely fictitious. We constitute ONE mixed race,

    from Mexico all the way the down to the Strait of Magellan in South America. So

    therefore, as I try to rid myself of any charge of provincialism; I pray for Honduras

    and a united Latin America. I want you to know, that it's this message that I have

    imprinted in my heart.

(A few moments of silence go by when…………)

Lady Ghost: Puedo ver que usted es una persona educada con Buenos valores morales.

Tambien es algo obvio que le han ensenado a usted a como ser un caballero, pero

valentia es algo que no muchos tienen; y eso es algo que no se puede ensenar.

Puedo ver de que usted no le tiene miedo a nada ni a nadie, ni siquiera a la muerte.

Translation: I can see that you're an educated person with good moral values. It's also pretty

clear that you have been taught how to be a gentleman; but courage, is something

that can't be taught. I can definitely see that you fear nothing; not even death.

10 Pak: My father was an Agricultural Engineer and also a teacher at the University back home.

My mother is still a nurse with a tough right hook and a huge noble heart.

Lady Ghost: A humble household I see. You on the other hand, seem to have adventure and

danger written all over you; there's a different aura emanating, I can sense it all

over you. If you knew to speak different languages; then that means you knew I

was here. How long have you known??

10 Pak: Not till very recently; and it wasn't a living person that told me about you. Believe it or

Not, it was other ghosts by the name of Charlie; he himself and a proper Aristocratic

Lady Crane, set me on this path.

(He then proceeds to tell the Lady Ghost everything; all the way from the start. How he was approached with this idea by his two friends; then all the fun, adventure, and treasure that followed. More importantly, he pulls out some of the ghost bud and says the magic words.)

10 Pak: From start to finish. Turn wind to mist. Reverberate and diminish.

(and they begin to get stoned.)

Song: Ciudad de la Furia (Unplugged) – Soda Stereo (1:15 – 2:25)

(10 Pak walks into the bathroom and closes the door behind him. As the moments evaporate into the air, instead of laughter now all you hear is coughing coming from inside the bathroom; while Matt was still on the floor passed out. Not completely aware of his surroundings, 10 Pak didn't realize that there was someone watching them the whole time; recording with audio and video. The person watching everything unravel before him, was none other than Jerome Koppel, the reporter.)

Lady Ghost: Why were you looking for me in the first place??

10 Pak: Finding you was just the first part of my plan; the second part all depends on your

        willingness to help me out.

Lady Ghost: Let me smoke some more of that Ghost Bud and I'll see how I can help you.

(10 Pak goes ahead and grabs some more Ghost Bud out of his pocket and says the magic words one more time; and they both start inhaling the magical mist. As they keep smoking, Jerome gets closer and closer to the bathroom door. What he didn't realize, was that the Sticky Icky Ghost Bud was specifically designed to spread throughout a room for the sole purpose of the contact high. Jerome starts feeling the weed quickly and his eyes are starting to get red; he takes a deep breath.)

Jerome Koppel: God damn I'm getting lit!! This is some good shit…(starts dancing a little bit)

(He hears someone coming; he puts his recorder and camera away and starts heading back up stairs. Even though he didn't have much evidence; the evidence he did have, was absolutely paramount.   He had seen and heard more than enough to convince the people he worked for that he had found what he was looking for; he had hit the jackpot.)

10 Pak: So where is it that you come from??

Lady Ghost: Chile.

10 Pak: Chilena, I see; I can't say I've ever met anyone from Chile before. You my dear lady,

        are the first.

Lady Ghost: Good way to celebrate; you got any more of that Ghost Bud??

10 Pak: Of Course I do, but first I need you tell me something. It is rumored, that around here there is a wormhole that acts as a bridge to the past and to the future. I've been told that some ghosts have actually traveled through the hole as they please.

Lady Ghost: This is true, but the ones on this boat have only seen it from a distance; we don't know where it's exact location is at, if we did we wouldn't be here. But we are very close, that I can tell you with certainty. Also, we did hear that there was a new kind of Ghost-Warlock looking for it also; be careful with him, I hear he is very dangerous.

10 Pak: So I was right about him; I came here thinking that I would leave empty handed. You have no idea how much you have already helped me; is there anything I can do for you??

Lady Ghost: You can most certainly leave me the rest of that Ghost Bud; I'm going to smoke later with the other two ghosts that live here.

10 Pak: Don't you want to be freed from this place?? Ghost bud; that's it??

Lady Ghost: Myself and the others have come to accept our fate here with this boat; we are a part of it and we actually like it here. And now with this Ghost Bud; I'll enjoy being here even more in the restaurant. Believe me, we're going to be okay; don't worry about us; and definitely don't forget to visit and when you do…

10 Pak: I know I know; Ill bring a lot more Ghost Bud for you and your friends, I promise.

Lady Ghost: You are the best; I still can't believe you figured out the whole language puzzle.

10 Pak: Luck is on my side, apparently; I am fortune's fool.

Lady Ghost: I hope you find what you're looking for; even if you don't know what it is yet.

10 Pak: I appreciate that, I really do.

(They hear someone coming; 10 Pak gives the Lady ghost a hug, or at least tries too as they both start laughing. The manager finally makes it back to the bathroom and sees Matt laying there, still unconscious. He starts knocking on the door; 10 Pak comes out after a few seconds of him calling out.)

Manager: Well?? What Happened?? Is that weed I smell??

10 Pak: Yes it is…regarding the Ghosts here, I was right. As to how it happened; they didn't share that with me, but just know that they like it here and they mean no harm. From now on they are going to be cooperative happy ghosts here. Who's to know what really happened and why their soul's just withered away with time; but the sadness and bitterness that remained, no longer exists. They actually enjoy your company and the rest of the staff's; but you are going to have to let them smoke their "Ghost Bud".

Manager: Mmmhhh….Weed smell in the boat, not exactly what I was hoping for; but if it keeps them happy, then that makes me happy. We'll just bring some extra ventilators to suck the smoke out before it reaches the main areas; I'll make it work.

10 Pak: There you go; glass half full kind of guy; that's good. Oh yeah I almost forgot, the lady told me that she has a present for you, hidden underneath the floor boards in the Captains Quarters. She said that when the ship was being renovated, all three ghosts made sure that the workers never got to it; they kept scaring them off. I believe she said that they are gold doubloons from the late 1600's found there.

Manager: You kidding me; this has definitely got to be the weirdest night I've had here in this boat. That's good news; those things are worth a lot of money; I'm flabbergasted.

10 Pak: Best kind of news there is. Now that we have solved the mystery of the Lady in the

Bathroom; I think it's time to take my friends and call it a night.

Manager: I agree, I think it would be for the best; and if it's at all possible don't bring your

friends again. Drinks are on the house for you, within limit okay. Another thing,

Jerome Koppel was here tonight at the Moshulu. Just saying, with everything that

happened, all the commotion; there is a chance he might of overheard something. That

guy is a Fox in a hen house; don't let the silly look fool you, that guy is amongst the

most clever of hustlers around here.

(Man oh man, was that Manager right. Now that Koppel knew about 10 Pak and crew, plus the ghosts, and their involvement with the destruction of parts of Center City; it was only a matter of time before the story hit the local news.)

10 Pak: No way?? Cool shit, thanks a many. (starts picking Matt up) Come on Matt, time to go.

(Grabs Matt by the arms, picks him up and throws him over his shoulder like a sack of potatoes. They start exiting the Restaurant; the outside crew that Herbie had on security detail had also started gathering up in front of the Moshulu's parking lot. Without being too subtle, they secure the perimeter as the people from inside the restaurant gaze curiously at them. 10 Pak walks off to the sidewalk by the main road; he sees some homeless people and heads over there because he wants to give money to them.)

(As he starts walking on the cobble stones, the winds from the ocean breeze start picking up; a reminder that the "Fall Season" was here. If you have never visited the Northeast part of the country, it is always best to go either in the Fall or the Spring. The Landscape is completely decorated with all the different colors of the rainbow. The foliage of the trees turns into a vibrant orange and red, as the warm weather no longer embraces us with its presence. Somehow, it would seem that the days are shorter and that the night takes over a lot quicker. With the Fall, the sense of the unknown and the mysterious always looms in the air in the old cities of the NorthEast; it's what some of us love about it.)

Place: 2nd and Moore 11:00pm

South Philadelphia, PA

(It's like if the city itself knew what we were up too, sending us strange weather and even stranger days; as if it was warning us of the rough road ahead. An ominous feeling just keeps looming around; waiting for that other foot to drop. A young well dressed well groomed lady walks down 2nd street, after having parked her car a few blocks away. She turns into an alleyway that leads up to her house; as she goes past several houses, she starts feeling a sharp numbing sensation on her ass. Her eyes start getting heavier while her footsteps become erratic and discombobulated. The young woman looks over and she sees a "dart", stuck to her right butt cheek as she looks up and she falls down; a shadow approaches her. The dark figure picks her up and takes her to the trunk of his car, which had been parked on the street right behind her all ready to go. He places her inside the trunk, shuts it, and heads out of there in a flash; then nothing, no sound, no people, no help. Or so he thought….A small "drone" was making its way behind the mystery car with the kidnapper and his victim. The Drone's purpose there was to keep following the kidnapper all the way to its intended destination. This kidnapper was the owner of the building where Charlie and the Ghost Bud were located at in FishTown. Little did this kidnapper know, that he was being followed by a drone belonging to the one and only hacker, "Paul the FireWall"; a good friend of 10 Pak's. Paul was running surveillance on this guy as a favor for 10 Pak, in exchange for a free year's supply of top of the line THC edibles. He calls 10 Pak's contact to give him an update on the present situation.)

Place: Moshulu Parking Lot

Penns Landing

(Willis comes up to Herbie asking for 10 Pak, telling him he's got a phone call from Paul. Herbie starts looking around, till he sees…..)

Herbie: Yo Dizzy!! Where's 10 Pak??

Dizzy Rane: He's over here by the cobbles; pissing his money away on some homeless assholes.

(cobble stone-streets still found all over Philadelphia)

(Herbie walks up to 10 Pak and hands him the phone.)

Herbie: Here pretty boy; it's Paul. (Hands him the phone) (10 Pak answers…)

10 Pak: Talk to me…

Paul the FireWall: Okay, I found your serial killer and he's not alone. You were right about this asshole.; I guess I owe you a $20. He's on the move and I'm on his tail. (smoking a vape pen as he eats a THC lollipop)

10 Pak: Good shit Paul, told you not to bet against me; I never lose.

Paul: (exhaling smoke) Don't worry, I'm not losing any sleep over it; I'll live. So what's the plan with this piece of shit, you're not letting this guy get away with this are you??

10 Pak: What do you suggest??

Paul: Save the girl and maybe, call the cops.

10 Pak: That's exactly what I was thinking Paul; get me inside his house so I can talk to him first. Give me 10 minutes with him and then you can call the cops; I want to talk some sense into him first.

Paul: And if you don't like what you hear??

10 Pak: Then, I'll switch to lead poisoning.

Paul: You're not going to let the cops take him?

10 Pak: Not this one; he'll find a way to weasel out of it and he'll go free. Besides, I have my Orders; but we will save the girl that I promise.

Paul: Somehow, I'm ok with that.

10 Pak: Good man; let me know the second you find out exactly where he lives. Oh and Paul, we are against the clock on this one, Serial Killers don't keep their pray around for long; so we don't have much time if we want to save her.

Paul: Understood, I'll call you as soon as I get something.

10 Pak: Appreciate it Paul. (they both hang up) Herbie; round them up, we're leaving. Have Willis go drop off Matt and Damien. Tell Dizzy that the rest of us are headed for Old City.

Herbie: If that's where we are going, then why don't we just go wait at Delilah's??

10 Pak: We got to be ready to go on the fly; an order from up above says this guy is top priority.

Herbie: Alright, let's get them moving. Yo Willis!!!

(They all start mobilizing and start heading out in two separate groups with separate destinations. Willis takes about 5 guys with him, along with Matt and Damien. They take Columbus Boulevard all the way the down to Oregon Ave.; down the road, they make a left turn on Front St. so that they can get on the I-95 ramp heading south towards the town of Chester . In the meantime Herbie, 10 Pak, and the rest of the crew go the opposite way on Columbus Boulevard. They drive further down the road as they go past Morgan's Pier, Dave and Buster's, and also Cavanaugh's; they finally make a left turn onto Spring Garden. They park on 7th street, close to the "Edgar Allan Poe Natural Historic Site".)

Herbie: Okay, it's 3:30; Dizzy hand me that phone again, time to call Paul.

(phone starts ringing on Paul's end)

 Paul: Okay, here's the game plan. 10 Pak, go to 4th and Brown St., from there, walk over to

Café La Maude. The house you're looking for is right next to the Café. I'll place the

drone on top of the house as a beacon for you; don't want you walking in the wrong

house. As an exit, you've got Leithgow Street at the back; from there you go to Reno St.

Tell Ritchie to place the car on the corner of Lawrence and Reno St; that'll be your pick up

point. Send Dizzy and two other guys to the corners of 5th and Poplar St and then on 3rd

and Poplar. Send the rest of the guys to do the same on the intersections of 5th and 3rd on

Brown St. Everything is ready to go; just say the word and we're on.

Herbie: Message received; waiting on the green light..

(Herbie turns to 10 Pak)

10 Pak: (gives Herbie the Ok nod) Game on boys.

Herbie: Okay, green light is a go everybody; I repeat, green light is a go.

Inside the Serial Killer's house……..

(The layout of the house was in such perfect alignment; it seemed flawless. The paintings, the murals, the carpets, the furniture, the sculptures, and the mementos of past images of people that he once knew; lifetime ago it would seem. It is precision and the utmost cleanliness; two characteristics that often point to a particular type of proclivity that can only be found in Serial Killers. This particular Serial killer now finds himself in his secret room, with no worries looming about; he seems to be getting ready to do some gruesome shit. His victim (who he had locked up in a giant dog cage) wakes up and starts crying because of the predicament she finds herself in. The serial killer starts laughing at her as he walks over to the living room and turns on his music on loud. He starts walking back towards the girl when all of a sudden, the music stops playing; the serial killer goes and checks.)

Serial K: God damn it!! (Looks at his phone) These fucking messages are always interrupting
> my songs.

(He glances around real quick and sees nothing; he turns the music back on. As he turns around, 10 Pak appears out of nowhere and knocks him the fuck out with a head butt. A couple of minutes go by when 10 Pak throws a glass of water into the serial killers face. As he finally wakes up, the Serial Killer sees that he's all tied up and wearing a ball-gag so he can't scream. He sees 10 Pak changing the music on the phone and then walks over to the table, to sort out his knives and a hatchet (small axe); he also sees the guns that he's carrying on him. 10 Pak looks at him directly and walks over to him.)

10 Pak: You finally wake up; not really sorry for the ….you know. (points at his face) Alrighty
> then, let's get started. I can see that you're a busy man so I'll make this quick. But first,
> I need you to know that I'm not playing around; and that, much like you, I'm the real
> deal; so….

(10 Pak grabs a knife and throws it at the serial killer's foot and pins it to the floor. The Serial Killer yells in agony, but it's all for nothing because the music drowns out his screams; plus....you know…the ball-gag. 10 Pak starts looking around the room and sees the girl in the cage staring back at him.)

(He can see the tears in her face as she stretches her arms out as if asking for help. Enraged, 10 Pak directs his attention once more at the Serial Killer as he grabs another knife.)

10 Pak: You fucking piece of shit!! What do you think happens with all the families you've hurt; the false hope dad's and mom's suffer, still waiting for their kids to come home. The happiness and the light of joy; you took that from them you….fucking parasite. (throws the other knife and pins the other foot) Hey asshole!! (grabs him by the face) You're lucky I don't have all night and I'm sure you don't feel like getting hacked into to pieces. SO!! I want you to sign these papers and give me complete control of these properties you own. I'm going to untie you now; so shut the fuck up and sign.

(10 Pak proceeds as he said and unties the Serial Killer and takes the ball-gag off; he puts some papers and a pen in front of him.)

Serial K: Whatever you want; please let me live. I got money, a lot of it… I'm very rich I could hand you over a small fortune, if you let me go.

(The girl in the cage starts crying; in her heart she believes that she is not being saved anymore. She thinks that the mysterious man will take the money, look the other way; and then just leave her there to her fate. Suddenly she hears laughing and she looks up at 10 Pak to see what was going on; she sees that he just keeps laughing.)

10 Pak: You don't get it, do you? I am the vengeful hand of god, sent here to make sure you pay for your crimes against those that cannot help themselves. So just sign the fucking papers before I shove your ass up your ass, because if I have to say it one more fucking time….I'm going to go all Samuel L. Jackson on your ass. I'm still debating whether to let you live or not; so you just sign, you hear me!!

(The Serial Killer starts signing the papers and he is now thinking that if he keeps talking, trying to get 10 Pak to feel sorry for him; eventually he'll let him go.)

Serial K: I'm signing I'm signing; I got some Bearer-Bonds in my safe, million dollars, all yours if you just let me go. She's nothing…you've got properties and money; what do you care about her? Come on man!! I'm talking about a lot of money here, more than you can dream of. (Finishes signing all the papers and puts them back in the folder and hands them to 10 Pak) What do you say, do we have a deal??

10 Pak: More than I can dream of huh??? (10 Pak starts laughing)

Serial K: Yes… more than you can dream of…do we have a deal???

10 Pak: Thing is snowflake, and this might come as a shock to you; but I actually have more money than you do. As for my dreams; well let's just say that they aren't limited to something as trivial like money. Therefore you see; my answer is going to have to be a big fat NO. Oh yeah, almost forgot; Lady Crane sends her regards. I promised her I would say it.

Serial K: What…But…you said…

10 Pak: I LIED…

(10 Pak Starts laughing again because he sees the Serial Killer actually pissing himself. That feeling of hopelessness along with helplessness was starting to finally sink in the Serial Killer's psyche; he was starting to feel what all his victims had felt.)

(10 Pak was making damn sure that he learned his lesson before he sent him on his way to the fiery pits of HELL…10 Pak starts reciting some lines off of "Dante's Inferno".)

10 Pak: Through me you enter into eternal pain, through me you enter the population of loss.

Abandon all hope ye who enter here. (The serial killers cries become louder)

Serial K: Dante's Inferno??? (with a terrified look in his face) Who are you??

(10 Pak then grabs thc Serial Killer and throws him against the wall. In a very quick motion he starts grabbing all the knives and starts throwing them at him; pinning the Serial Killer onto the wall. Finally, 10 Pak throws the hatchet that ends up splitting the Serial Killer's face in half.)

Song: Sacrilege-Yeah Yeah Yeahs (0:00 – 2:00)

(The girl, staring at 10 Pak in pure disbelief; falls in love head over heels with him. A guy, who fell down from the sky (fallen Angel) for her; 10 Pak scoots down to talk to the girl…)

10 Pak: The cops are on their way; you're safe now. Oh yeah and uh….you never saw me.

      (winks at her)

Caged Girl: (in a soft spoken voice) Thank you…thank you.

(As 10 Pak gets back up; one of his business cards falls out of his inside jacket pocket and lands right in front of the girl without 10 Pak noticing. The sounds of the police cars start making their presence noticed, outside of the house; Paul had already contacted them, giving 10 Pak enough time to get out of there. The Cops finally make it to the top floor of the house; they break down the door and start searching the place with their flashlights and guns out. The girl sees the business card and she quickly grabs it and puts it in her mouth; hiding it from the police to protect 10 Pak. She knows that she can get in a shit load of trouble for concealing evidence from the police; but she didn't care one bit, she would never turn in the man that saved her from a horrible death. The Cops finally come up to her flashing their lights and seeing her in the cage.)

Cops: Hey lady you okay; (shouts at the other officer by the door) We need the Paramedics

      here!!! Guys help me out, let's get this cage open. You're safe now miss; it's okay..

Cop #2: Hey guys, look at this; oh my god, what sick son of a bitch did this??

(The cops are looking at the dead corpse of the serial killer, pinned up against the wall like a pin cushion with his face split open by a small axe; the scene was pretty gruesome. All the noises start drowning out in the girls head; all she can keep thinking about is the mysterious man that had saved her. Now she was determined to find him, no matter what. The cops open the cage up and get her a blanket to cover her up as they wait for the paramedics to arrive. The girl, for the time being was now safe again.)

Chapter 7

Strange Days Have Found Us

Song: The Sense of Me – Mud Flow (0:00 – 2:00)

Place: Jefferson Hospital

     Center City, Philadelphia

(Another rainy cloudy day in Philadelphia; Fall is now here and life goes on the same. The girl that 10 Pak had saved is at the Jefferson Hospital trauma section, getting ready to be discharged. All her wounds were healing up nice and she is now ready to leave. Looking through her window, as if it were a moving picture catching all the colors of the sunlight melting through the scene projected; she can see her reflection up close. As its mankind's nature to stare, to look around, dream, and imagine; she ponders again about her mysterious anti-hero.   The television in the corner of her room had the news on; strangely enough it was Jerome Koppel with his segment called, "That Some Weird Shit". He started mentioning everything and I mean everything; including the description of the culprits responsible for all the destruction caused by the unexplained supernatural events of that "phucked up" night.)

(On the TV)

Jerome Koppel: (turns to the other camera) Big K Koppel here ladies and gentleman

        and whooooh; do I have something to tell ya'll. The weirdest, the craaaziest,

        and the most Phucked Philadelphia Ghost Story you have ever heard. ☺

(As she is listening, she hears the very same description of the man who saved her. She thought to herself that this was no coincidence. To her, this was a major sign; she had now made up her mind to go find her savior. She leaves the hospital in Center City and heads home to her apartment; after about a 35 minute cab ride she finally arrives. The girl enters her apartment and she gets an eerie sensation of loneliness and sadness. She goes to her room and drops her bag from the hospital and chills there for a moment. She pulls out 10 Pak's business card and as she is looking at it, she notices that there is no phone number on it. This was to be the first obstacle in her path to find 10 Pak.   Later on that night, she starts getting ready to go to work; it just so happens that this beautiful girl is a "stripper" at one of the clubs in South Philadelphia. As it turns out, our damsel in distress was by no means a "Snow White"; but she definitely qualifies for the sleeping beauty category.)

Meanwhile…..all the way on the other side of town…..

Song: Ghost Town – The Specials (0:00 – 1:20)

Place: Corner Store on Durfor St. and 4th St.

South Philadelphia

(Herbie and company are at a corner store on 4th St and Durfor St. in South Philly. Herbie wins a scratch off; again, $1000. Reporter nearby at the corner half a block away, was reporting on the frequent weird shit going on in the area. She sees that Herbie's reaction to the "Scratch Off" he was holding was a very positive one; so she goes over to Herbie with her camera man.)

Reporter: Sir Sir, now that you won what are you going to do? What is the first thing you're going to go get??

Herbie: Oh, that's easy; Cocaine and Hookers..(lol)

(The reporter, in pure disgust starts stepping away from Herbie and makes her way to her van along with her Camera man.)

Reporter: Disgusting asshole!! Let's get the fuck out of here before I catch something.

(Everybody in Herbie's crew that was with him at that moment started laughing at the reporter and her camera man. That's one of the reasons why most of the crews loved Herbie; because he definitely kept it really funny.)

Herbie: Hey Asshole!! Watch where you blow that weed smoke; and go get the sandwiches will ya.

Dizzy Rane: The wind is blowing everywhere around here; stop busting my balls, I'm going.

Willis: Hey guys, look sharp; here he comes.

(Herbie was meeting with an important South Philly Irishman by the name of Chucky BoBo; they were there to discuss details of a different type of corporate culture, dealing with commodities of very high profit margins. ☺ They were also there waiting for 10 Pak and Flaco so that they could head over to Fairmont, to go see the "Eastern State Penitentiary Prison"; a very Haunted place indeed.)

(In the Fairmont section of Philadelphia you can find a stabilized old ruin, which is considered to be the "Alcatraz" of the east; the magnificent Gothic Monstrosity of "Eastern State Penitentiary". It opened in 1829; this massive building was so advanced for its time, that it had running water when the rest of the city did not. It had a flush toilet in every cell, when even the President of the country was still using an outhouse. This place ran so efficiently, that 300 other prisons around the world were built on plans based on architect John Haviland's design. Hard places breed hard men, breaking them to the point of insanity; and this 30 ft high, 12ft thick walled building was no exception. Due to its design, the walls would amplify the sounds and make them reverberate throughout the whole entire place. Screams of agony and anguish will forever remain present through these hallways and its dusty crusty old cellblocks. It is obviously evident that this system, established by the Quakers, is the reason why there are pissed off spirits still wandering about; too enraged to move on. The inhumanity they had to endure here, to a bunch of pious self righteous assholes, was horrifying. These Quakers that built the prison, believed that everybody should live their lives' according to what they thought was proper. As we say here in South Philly, Phuuuuck That!! Even though we pay an insane amount of taxes here as it is; again, it's the rich families and their sycophants that still get their share of the money that we pay taxes on; silly world isn't it??) (Rhetorical) ☹ This simple system of strict solitary confinement was drawn up in 1787, by a committee which met in Benjamin Franklin's home. The main topic of discussion among these fine gentlemen was the concept of isolation for punishment; and therefore putting the word "Penitence" in "Penitentiary". The Law around here back then, as it still is now, is a very fickle thing; it phucks over whoever it wants too, whenever it wants too. It is a certainty, that for some reason, "Lady Justice" is always praying on those less educated and less fortunate. As if it wasn't enough being locked up, these fuckers really knew how to twist the knife on you. The inmates cells were only equipped with a toilet, table, bunk bed and a bible. In addition, the prisoners were locked up in there all but 30 minutes in the morning and 30 minutes in the evening. To add insult to injury, those 30 minute breaks were also spent in isolated exercise plots outside the cells; with no visitations or interaction with other prisoners. There were these opened slots in the ceiling were only one beam of daylight managed to get through; these were known as the "The Eye of God". The TEMERITY of these assholes!!! For a group of people to be so presumptuous and arrogant; to think that their own beliefs in God over exceed the basic human rights of others. That's mankind for you. ☹)

(This place had been criticized by many prominent people; including the one and only Charles Dickens on his visit to the U.S. Claiming that the harsh conditions in this place were just too inhumane. It is registered that Al Capone himself spent a year here in 1929; also, a man by the name of Willie Sutton escaped from it in 1945. Finally, in 1971 the prison was completely closed; leaving behind a plethora of negative energy in its wake. There is evidence of such negative energies being manifested as spirits of past inmates that suffered greatly and died in this "shit-hole". Maintenance crews and visitors have all reported the distant sound of evil itself, along with the sound of a psychotic women's voice echoing throughout the cells; shadowy forms gliding along the walls as faces appear and disappear on the walls. Today, Eastern State Penitentiary is a haunted tourist attraction in the Philadelphia Area; people from all over come to the prison to experience the gruesome history and insanity of this place. The silly twisted shit mankind perceives as entertainment.)

Song: Walking Jerusalem – Dub Syndicate (1:00 – 2:55)

....On the road to Eastern State Penitentiary

(On the way there, 10 Pak starts going through his notes, records, and accounts; he has written down a list and bio of people who've worked there throughout the years. He was mostly interested in the very graphic report of ghostly activity made by a Locksmith. His report entailed a very specific list of details that didn't seem like they could've been made up just for the hell of it. Let's just say that this guy pretty much encountered the "Mother-ship" of all ghost activities in this area. The Locksmith recalls that at one particular moment, while performing routine restoration work, he was removing a 140yr old lock when..... a very powerful energy set itself upon him. The ghastly phantoms that dwelled in those cells introduced the locksmith to their phucked up tortured past; faces in the walls, a glowing floating rock, and the voices coming from all over. The most interesting part was when he claims that he was physically transported into a nether-world by a tidal wave of energy, made by like 100 ghosts; they were drawing him into this horrible supernatural nightmare that didn't end there. A dominant spirit rises above all others in the form of a man with three rings of mist swirling around it; seconds later many other forms seem to come out and make him feel like as if he was inside a microwave. Moments later, he recalls that it felt like as if he was naked in the North Pole, freezing his ass off in the middle of a snowstorm; so confused and scared, unable to move standing there petrified.)

Herbie: There she is!! ……. Look at that mean old bitch….

(At last, they arrive to the haunted ghost attraction of the once infamous Eastern State Penitentiary Prison. It is only half past noon; they got plenty of daytime to work with before the tourist attraction opens its doors for business to the public. In the hopes of finding something that would be helpful to them, they make their way into the Prison with boxes full of cigarettes, Fireball Whiskey and of course, many copies of "Hustler Magazine". The manager walks up to them to say "what's up"; as he escorts them to "Cell Block #4", which supposedly is the area with the biggest paranormal activity. He then begins explaining to them the do's and don'ts about this place.)

Manager: So what's going on with all the cigarettes and booze?? You guys throwing a party in
      here??

10 Pak: We are here to communicate, in our own way, with those of our kind; such enmity
      merits a friendly ear, an understanding ear; to listen to the injustices they endured and
      old stories they may want to take off their chests.

Manager: (looks at them as if they were crazy) Riiiight….Sounds interesting; you paid me a lot
      of money to be here, so make yourselves at home fellas. Oh yeah; try not to venture
      outside this designated area without a guide, you don't want to get lost down those
      dark corridors when the sun goes down. Take that very seriously guys okay….

Flaco: Will do sir

(The manager leaves the area to go back outside.)

Herbie: So where do we set up??

Dizzy: Right here I imagine.

10 Pak: Right here is fine.

Herbie: You sure about this??

10 Pak: Of course I am NOT sure; there are no guarantees with any of this shit, you kidding me.

Herbie: Just checking….

Flaco: (going through his notes) Yo, check it out; fucking Al Capone stayed here for a bit.

That's crazy that he was here inside these walls; makes you think, doesn't it??

Herbie: Yes it does. I wonder which of his mob buddies ever came to visit him??

(10 Pak pauses for a second, a light bulb goes off in his head; there was only one gangster still alive today that had stuck around this area since the end of the 1700's. Fucking Zepi Petri. That meant that Al Capone must've met Zepi Petri one way or another the year he stayed here. 10 Pak knew he was on the right track now; all he had to do now was to try to make contact with the ghosts and see if they knew anything about the subject at hand.)

10 Pak: (without saying his name for fear of summoning him) I can think of a few.

(Some of the other men bring in a table and a chair for 10 Pak to sit on; they set it up as if he were interviewing people for a job.)

10 Pak: Herbie; get them going; and get Flaco up here.

Herbie: Alright boys, let's get this show on the road; start opening up all the cartons and bottles

and put the fan on them to spread the smell. Dizzy, where's the little weasel at?? Tell

him we need him up here, like yesterday.

Dizzy: Got you. (starts making his way back through the rest of the crew)

(Everybody starts setting themselves up behind lines of salt carefully drawn out throughout the floor. Flaco comes up to 10 Pak and Herbie smoking a joint; 10 Pak pulls out a piece of paper from one his folders and gives it to Flaco to read out loud.)

10 Pak: Need you to read this out loud, if you please.

Herbie: What's that??

10 Pak: A quote from the group "Outkast"; its one hell of a powerful message that just might

get us in good with whatever roams around here.

Herbie: Alright, let's see what happens.

Flaco: Sure thing bruh…(clears his throat) Operating under the crooked American system too long; OUtKAST!!! Pronounced Out-Kast; adjective meaning homeless or unaccepted in society. Are you an outcast?? If you understand and feel the basic principles and fundamental truths contained within this message, then you probably are. An outcast is someone who is not considered to be part of the normal world; he's looked at differently, he's not accepted because of his clothes, his hair, his occupation, his beliefs or his skin color. Now look at yourselves, are you an Outcast?? I know I am; as a matter of fact "PHUCK" being anything else.   (Andre 3000 and Big Boi)

(10 Pak steps in and puts his two cents in.)

10 Pak: I stand before you accepting that I am nobody; I am but a grain of sand in the grand scheme of things. My life will come and go in a blink of an eye, like the rain and the wind; but my name will remain. I will die a pauper and my bones will turn to dust; but my name will remain. Without any fear left in my heart, let death take me to whatever destination I'm bound for; because when the time comes for me to join the line of my people, I'll die a happy man because my name will remain. I'm here to tell you that the law has its foot on our throats still to this day and we are being treated worse now more than ever; but we have the numbers and we are determined. Freedom is just an illusion, we can't really vote, there's systemic poisoning of the food and water; and the suppression of our rights and the desecration of the constitution. We are being dumbed down at an alarming level; to be reduced to the intellect of a sardine, so we can act like mere sheep .

(distorted sounds start echoing around them)

 (As he ceases his speech, out of nowhere a breeze starts picking up. Suddenly, noises are being heard and figures are starting to lurk out from the darkness as if being awakened.)

10 Pak: Here we go.

Flaco: Ohh, I fucking hate this part.

(One spirit comes forward, taking the form of a very dangerous looking individual and breaks the ice and starts talking to them.)

Ghost-Spirit: What do you want here?? Why do you want to talk with us??

10 Pak: We are here to see if we can benefit mutually from each other's help. We seek

information; what is it that you seek??

Ghost-Spirit: That's…that's…..uhh you're putting me in the spot over here. What do we want;

oh yeah, how about some fucking freedom!! You are going to have to spring us

outta here my friend. All of us at the same time; and we will tell you were Al

Capone hid his last Journal. It contains information about the Italian Mafia

from here to Chicago; Dates, places, and names of cops and politicians under

Capone's payroll.

Herbie: How the fuck you break a ghost out of jail??

Flaco: Can I get a lifeline for this question; call a friend perhaps?

Dizzy: You were watching re-runs of who wants to be a millionaire again, weren't you??

Flaco: Psst, please. (asks the ghosts) You don't like the haunted attractions here??

Ghost-Spirit: (turns to Flaco and with a deep voice) No.

Herbie: You guys see the girls in the bathrooms taking a shit; that must get old huh??

Ghost-Spirit: Okay assholes, enough with the 20 fucking questions. Promise to liberate us from

this hell on Earth and we will tell you where the Diary is.

Herbie: Al Capone's Diary would be worth a lot of money if we sold it to the right person.

10 Pak this is pretty big, you need to make this deal.

10 Pak: Herbie, you know how to break a ghost out of jail?? I'm all phucking ears because I

have no clue how to go about it.

Herbie: Phucking easy; we blow up a bunch of holes on half of the walls. Do it the same

way they would back in the day.

Flaco: What if you bring the whole building down??

Herbie: Then no more prison; problem solved.

10 Pak: There for no more ghosts; (whispering to himself) just like Charlie and the ghost bud.

Herbie: Speaking of which, I'd start smoking-out all this crazy looking fuckers before they

decide to put us on the dinner menu.

Flaco: I concur doctor; do something because they really are starting to look at me as dinner.

Spirit-Ghost: Well then friend; Speak of the mutual benefits of this partnership of yours??

10 Pak: Well; for starters…

(He pulls out the ghost bud and says the magic words; then he slowly blows the mist in the direction of the ghost-spirit and company. The smell envelops everybody in the room including the ghosts; right away they know what they've been missing out on and they want more.)

Song: Human Fly – The Cramps (0:00 – 2:00)

(A creepy fog starts pouring out from the walls, the floor, and the ceiling; everybody starts taking a couple of steps back. You can see faces in the walls and you could hear the voices coming from all over; figures and shadows walking about in the fog.)

Herbie: I wonder if I have any relatives in there; check that out.

(Herbie starts opening up some beers and some bottles of "Fireball" and pours them all over the floor and the walls. Flaco keeps hitting a weed-bubbler full of ghost bud, as he makes buzzing noises pretending to be the "human fly"; in the meantime everybody else is partying it up heavy duty. 10 Pak starts opening up 3 huge duffel bags filled with Ghost Bud that are stanking up the room nicely. He places a big fan on the duffel bags to start spreading out that beautiful wonderful smell, evenly and heavily; he recites the magic words, turning the room into a giant hot-box.. He rolls a big fat "ghost bud spliff" and lights it up; puff puff puff in front of the fan.)

(About ten ghosts stand in front of the fan and start inhaling and exhaling to the beat of the music. 10 Pak starts looking around and sees how cool it is to see a bunch of ghosts exhaling weed with them; at Eastern State Penitentiary of all places. Through the intoxicating chemical interaction of the booze and smoke, it seemed pretty clear that for once in their miserable existence. The ghosts actually felt some resemblance of human decency again with these so called "misfits" of society. To remind myself that once again it proves my theory; {No matter what happens in life, the same matter always gravitates towards itself.} This means that the people that are the same in pretty much everything; always tend to hang out with each other, no matter what spectrum of reality. 10 Pak engages in several conversations with a bunch of different ghosts, asking them about their pasts and asking them about Al Capone. They tell him about Al Capone's look on life and where he stood on the difference between fear and respect; quoting the one and only Nicolo Machiavelli: "It is far safer to be feared, than loved.")

(Finally after a few hours of getting it in pretty good, the spirit with the three rings of mist shows 10 Pak, Al Capone's cell. He breaks through the wall inside the cell, thus revealing a hole covered with soft plaster; in it, the last Journal of Al Capone. This small notebook held enough information within its pages to alter the course of the "Cosa-Nostra's" future generations and their outlook on the "old ways". It is needless to say that this priceless item could catch a very hefty sum, auctioning it off among the right people. It is now almost opening time and the group has to start packing it up; it's time to leave the haunted attraction. Some customers start showing up at the parking lot; only to find Herbie's drunken ass taking a piss on a trash can, with his pants down to his ankles. As they leave the grounds of Eastern State Penitentiary in Fairmont; they all start getting on their phones and begin contacting people about their find. Their mob bosses want to buy it right away, aware of what a find of this magnitude meant and how much it could cost in an "open auction".)

(It took only three days of negotiating to come up with a very favorable deal. In the end, the person who acquired it was a cousin of the Carrafa's; a man by the name of Gian-Luca Tinnelli of Staten Island, New York. Alberto Locatti comes out with his bodyguards and starts walking over to 10 Pak and Herbie. He hands them over a briefcase full of bearer bonds in the amount of a full $15-million$.)

Al Locatti: Here you go boys; don't spend it all at once; you lucky fuckers. How in the world

did you guys get a hold of something as big as Al Capone's last journal?

How did you know where to look??

Herbie: What are you, a cop?? What's with the 20 fucking questions?? We are not telling you

shit, you mean old bastard.

Al Locatti: Watch your mouth, asshole; I was talking to the brains of the group.

Herbie: Fuck you, short ass.

Al Locatti: Keep it up asshole; I'll chop your legs off!!

Herbie: Yeah, well I'll still be taller than you. Wait, I think I just had Déjà vu…

(Everyone starts laughing, including Locatti's body guards; 10 Pak is now trying to make sure that the laughing stops and diffuse the situation as he talks directly to Locatti.)

10 Pak: Wish I could tell you it was some grand scheme Al; but it wasn't. All it was, was

a lucky hunch that's all; sheer dumb luck on our part.

Herbie: There, you happy. (keeps laughing at Al Locatti)

(Locatti looks back at 10 Pak and shakes his hand.)

Al Locatti: If you ever put out a hit on this asshole, call me first; I'll gladly do it for free.

Herbie: Yeah whatever, Al.

(Locatti heads back inside the building and 10 Pak is now showing off the bonds in the briefcase off to Herbie.)

10 Pak: (smelling the bearer bonds) Smells like a fun night out tonight; what do you say boys??

(Matt, Flaco, Damien, Herbie, Dizzy, Danny, and 10 Pak; all start yelling like a bunch of crazy assholes on Game-Day. Why, you ask; because the boys are going out to party hard tonight, starting out at their favorite casino in Philadelphia. They all start making their way out of the parking lot; completely unaware of an undetected person within their proximity.)

(They keep going on about their business as the one and only Tommy Cadwallader is watching their every move. He is waiting for the perfect opportunity to try to take the book of the dead from their hands. Tommy has a feeling that they keep the book with them at all times, hidden within one of their cars; he yet has to figure out which one.)

(Later on that night)

Song: Marching the Hate Machines (Into the Sun) – Thievery Corporation (0:30 – 2:00)

(The girl that 10 Pak had saved from the clutches of death is presently on her way back to work at one of the clubs in South Philadelphia. On the way there time seems to sort of slowdown for her; as she prepares herself mentally before going into an atmosphere like that. {*Believe me; I worked as a bouncer for more than 15 years at bars and night-clubs.}* For some reason the lights on the streets seemed to be glowing in a whole new different way for her; even the way everything moved around her appeared different. It's hard to imagine, after having been through such a traumatic experience; who could blame her for her whole new perspective on life.   The cab driver drops her off at the club off Columbus Blvd. across from the Home Depot and Wal-Mart.)

Place: Club Risky S. Columbus Blvd

      South Philadelphia

(As the girl enters the club, the music gets louder and the neon lights become brighter. She makes her way pass some of the security guys and carries on to the dressing room. She starts getting undressed and strips down to her thong; laying out her makeup and outfit on her chair. After about 30 minutes, her makeup was now complete and she changes into her work dress that leaves little to the imagination. The dancing entertainer makes her way to the Dj booth to announce her availability. The Dj proceeds and calls out our dancer on standby; she is now waiting for the current song to be over, so she can jump on the main stage and start performing with her first set of songs.)

Song: Down (Sunday Girl) – Stone Temple Pilots (0:00 – 1:30)

Dj: Alright Philadelphia, welcome once again to the one and only "Palace" of pleasure; best

place to be, only place to be. Let's keep the good vibes rolling into the night with

the Beautiful "Candy". Take it away sexy, tasty, Candy!!

(Candy takes over the stage; right away it becomes very evident that this girl doesn't lack any confidence at all. Taking full command of the stage, she attracts the many glaring eyes that are now set upon her beautiful thighs, lips, and "sighs". Why "sighs" of relief, you ask?? Believe it or not, that strip-club is the safest place for her at this point in time. Not feeling vulnerable because of the huge fucking bouncers that work there; she and the other girls feel well protected there. Not one of the bouncers is under "6.4" ft tall, they're all battle tested and with plenty of experience. The quickest of "Cats" in the worse of situations, know what I mean; that's the kind of guys you want working security for your club. That's if you want it well run of course; an efficient security team actually makes for a safe location. There was no doubt that this girl was strong; both mentally and physically. Beautiful smile, golden hair, perfect tits and a body that could make even blind men say "holy shit.")

(not too far away)

Place: Live! Casino N. Delaware Ave.

Philadelphia, PA

(The night starts out at the poker table and it doesn't take long for them to start hustling their money quick.)

Herbie: Yo!! That girl looks like Halle Berry; check that out. (Flaco and Dizzy turn their heads)

Dizzy: Nice, but isn't the real Halle Berry old now?? She's gotta be getting up there in age bruh.

After all those years living in Hollywood, her shit probably looks like roast beef by

now….(they start laughing)

Herbie: Mmhhh Roast beef; my favorite. (they keep laughing like the assholes that they are)

(It's Matt as usual with the luck of the Irish that hits for a "royal flush"; the whole fucking group goes "berserk" as they celebrate. Everyone is ecstatic because Matt just doubled their money and now they have more money than what they started out with. Seeing though as they have a shit load of money to party with, the group decides to go to the nearest strip club in South Philadelphia; take a guess at which strip club they end up at?? ☺)

Song: You on the Run – Black Angels (0:00 – 2:00)

Place: Club Risky S. Columbus Blvd

South Philadelphia

(The guys arrive at the club and they join in with the Tri State Area's finest. Men and women from South Jersey, North Delaware and Eastern Pennsylvania all gathered in Philadelphia for the night life and the adventures. Feeling comfortable in their own atmosphere; our anti-heroes navigate their way through the gamblers, thieves, hooligans, strippers, Doctors, drug-dealers, lawyers, tourists, celebrities, and just about anything you can fucking think of. The boys go directly to the main bar with the stage in the middle; drinks start flowing as they keep pouring into the unknown of the night once more. The guys are partying hard looking at the beautiful women, getting lap-dances, and champagne rooms back to back. Strangely enough; Candy, the girl that 10Pak had saved from the serial killer walks right by him in the Champagne Room. She sees him and tries to get his attention, but can't; other dancers already in front of her are trying hard to get to the guys spending real money. Plus, the really hot blonde that 10 Pak is getting a champagne room with; well let's just say that she isn't about to let him out of her sights. In the champagne room, the sexy little blonde Swedish devil takes off her outfit and keeps only her thong on. She reaches towards his crotch area with her mouth and starts blowing hot air on it; then, like a slutty little ninja she climbs on him and starts riding him.)

10 Pak: What is your name, sexy??

Dancer: Lena.

10 Pak: Ok Lena, I gotta say I'm loving your Swedish accent.

Lena: How can you tell my accent is specifically from Sweden??

10 Pak: I had two roommates in college, who were also my soccer teammates that where from

Vaxjo, Sweden. Niklas Runbert and a drunken asshole by the name of Per Johnsson. ☺

Lena: No way; Vaxjo is in the south, I'm from the northern part of Sweden; a city called Lulea.

10 Pak: Lulea; I bet it's beautiful up there.

Lena: Best place on Earth; especially in the summer.

10 Pak: That's not like that Mid-Sommar fucked up movie; with the shit going on??

Lena: Don't be an asshole; of course not. (they both start laughing) Although, a tall tanned

sexy Spaniard like you; you'd make all the men jealous, they'd probably want to fight

you or maybe kill you. They'll think you are there to steal all their women.

10 Pak: Well, if all the women in Lulea are just as smart and beautiful as you; then they

SHOULD, be worried. Besides, I've never lost a fight as a grown up; got my

ass kicked plenty as a kid . But nowadays, I usually tend to win whatever fight I involve

myself into. (starts laughing at the idea)

Lena: You laugh, but this I know to be true; it's happened in history before actually, believe it or

not. (starts kissing his neck and lips, as she covers his face with her hair)

10 Pak: Ok, I'm listening, getting a lap-dance and a history lecture; it's like dinner and a show.

Lena: (laughingly) Shut the fuck up; obviously you know the story of the Spanish Armada sent

against England?

10 Pak: Yes, I know this story.

Lena: The part they never talk about is the part where all the Spanish soldiers that where

shipwrecked or driven away by the storm, survived. They washed ashore on the coasts of

Eastern Ireland. These marooned Spanish men didn't panic at all; they thought they were

in some special land related to Heaven. They encountered beautiful blonde and red

headed women of both Celtic and Scandinavian descent. Mesmerized by their beauty

they quickly forgot about their motherland Spain and their asshole King. Forever

remaining in Ireland; some of them actually making it back to Scandinavia to settle

there for the rest of their lives.

10 Pak: So you already want to take me home with you back to your country.

Lena: The idea may have slipped my mind; there's something about you. It's special like that;

and I want you all to myself.

10 Pak: Yup; my pants just got tighter.

(She takes a marijuana lollipop out from his shirt pocket; slowly takes it out of the wrapper and starts licking it; nice and sexy. They both keep laughing and enjoying each other's company; they keep talking some more as they start exchanging phone numbers. Outside the Champagne Rooms, Candy is still waiting for 10 Pak or one of his friends to come out; unfortunately for her, the DJ is calling her on standby to go perform up on stage. She fears that once up there 10 Pak might come out and leave or go with another dancer to get more lap-dances. Her Anxiety was starting to climb through the roof, when she decides to take a seat at the bar. A bouncer approaches her to see if she is ok.)

Bouncer: Candy, you okay??

Candy: The whole room is spinning, I'm getting nauseas; I can't.

(The bouncer helps her up and calls out on the Radio to the DJ, to skip on to the next dancer. The bouncer takes her to the dressing room so she can lay down on the couch for a bit. The house mom goes over to her and puts her hand on her forehead.)

House Mom: You're feeling a bit warm, not to be concerned though. Just stay here and relax,

> I'll get you some water. I can't believe you decided to come back so soon after

> what happened to you girl; you should've taken your time coming back.

> (As she turns around she sees Candy crying) I'll call you a cab, I'm sending you

> home; I can't let you do this to yourself.

Candy: I just ….okay. Okay.

(A few minutes go by when 10 Pak, Flaco, and Dizzy decide to go outside for a smoke break. Dizzy takes out a medium sized blunt and lights it up; as he puffs puffs puffs and passes it to the left. Flaco is looking around, scoping the area to see if he catches anything interesting when….)

Flaco: Ears up boys; we got company. (points straight over to the street)

(The one and only Jerome Koppel and his sound guy where there; just, chilling there on the hood of his car with a camera in hand and one of those audio listening antennas on the other.)

10 Pak: You believe the balls on this crazy asshole; never seizes to amaze.

Flaco: Take a picture of this!! (gives him the middle finger)

Dizzy: What's Up!!

(screaming from across the street)

Jerome Koppel: Oh Yeah..well fuck you too then!!.

Sound Guy: Please don't piss these guys off; these are not wanna-be gangsters with plastic guns.

> They are not known for their sense of humor, okay; so just for tonight keep it at a

> minimum.

Jerome Koppel: Oh hell nawh; you did not just tell me what the fuck to do. I'm paying you; you

> little shit. But I get your point; I ain't trying to get my ass kicked out here.

> Just don't get it wrong; it doesn't mean we gonna start acting like scared little

> bitches either, know what I mean.

(As all of this is going on, the house mom and a Bouncer are walking Candy out to the street in front of the club. The bouncer walks back inside to go get some cab-fare and Candy is left with the house mom. Candy gives the house mom a huge hug and then places her bags on the sidewalk.)

HouseMom: Oh my, it's getting chilly out here; my fucking tits.

Candy: You don't have to wait out here, I'll be fine; there's some people right there.

Besides, the cab will be here any minute now; don't worry I'll be fine.

HouseMom: Okay; I'll send the bouncer back out to wait with you. Love you girl, call me

when you get home, I mean it.

Candy: Love you too, I will; I promise.

(The house mom goes back inside and about a moment goes by and Candy starts smelling marijuana in the air. Unknowingly, she starts shaking her head at the audacity of the person that is smoking right out in the open. She turns and looks to see where it was coming from; she sees that it is 10 Pak himself smoking a joint with Flaco and Dizzy. Not believing what she is seeing and how quickly her luck had changed; she wastes no time and walks over to 10 Pak and company.)

Candy: (looking at 10 Pak) Excuse me, can I talk to you for a second??

Dizzy: It's just weed smoke lady; ain't gonna kill you.

Flaco: Damn bro, looks like Matt isn't the only lucky one tonight.

10 Pak: (exhales smoke) Why would you want to talk to me??

Candy: Please; it's important.

Dizzy: Bit persistent aren't you?? You sound dangerous honey; don't think my man trusts you,

and to tell you the truth neither do I; you might want to shoot him or something.

Candy: Oh my god; why would you say that!! Wait, are you fucking with me??

(They all start laughing)

Flaco: Dangerous times you know; this is how scary movies start.

10 Pak: Okay. But if by any chance you are a vampire; just know that these gentlemen

will gun you down before you can even blink.

(Staring straight into his eyes and remembering that this was the guy that pinned a freaking "serial killer" to the wall; she knew that every word coming out of his mouth was probably very true. She calmly tells him to give her a second of his time; that it is of the utmost importance.)

Candy: Okay; I am not an assassin, I'm not a bad person; I'm not even a Republican. (lol)

Please, just a minute of your time.

10 Pak: Okay miss, you got my attention….

(They walk off to a safe distance)

10 Pak: Okay lady, what's up??

Candy: Okay; just hear me out because I'm just going to come out and say it. (She shows him

his business card that he dropped at the serial killer's place) You dropped this after

putting 7 knives into the man that abducted me and was getting ready to kill me. (she

starts crying) You saved my life that night and somehow I found you or you found me

here tonight; I just wanted to thank you for saving me. I hid this from the cops when

they came in right after you left; you told me the police were coming, remember??

(she steps in closer to him and looks him straight in the eye) You saved my life;

Remember???

10 Pak: (takes a moment) Ohhhh shiit. (he immediately looks over to Jerome Koppel)

(Koppel, in a state of amazement can't believe what he had just heard. He had his camera on the whole time and recorded the whole conversation; this was now evidence that could put 10 Pak in front of a jury; or make Koppel very rich. Koppel realized right away that he now had 10 Pak by the balls; as he looks back at 10 Pak with a huge smile on his face.)

Jerome Koppel: I GOT YOU!!! (starts laughing)

10 Pak: Fuuuuuck...

(Koppel and his camera man get in the car immediately and get out of there quick; they know what's at stake and who it is that they are dealing with. 10 Pak couldn't believe what the hell just happened; and to make matters worse, the girl starts crying. ☹)

Song: Strange Days Have Found Us (The Doors) – Thievery Corporation Mix (0:25 – 2:00)

Chapter 8

Who is the

Enemy Here??

Song: Siberie – Manu Chao (Intro) (0:00 – 0:40)

(It is November 2nd here in Philadelphia; the day of the dead has finally arrived. There will be a great big gathering, midnight at Penn's Landing. Full moon on for tonight; expect energy of the greatest kind emanating out onto the whole area. Some gatherings like concerts are quite the thing to see; but a gathering of the craziest most eccentric people wearing skulls, celebrating the life of our deceased; well, that is something else all on its own. For those of us that believe purely in the Angel of Death; this day marks the holiest of days because it's when we show our respect for the dead. Why?? Some of you may be asking; and the answer is simple. Of all the known things in this world, be it religion, science, math, or medicine; there's never any certainty about them because they are not "constant". Time reveals new applicable methods to improve said fields; new things are always popping up that are being discovered that contradict theories we thought to be actual facts before. But with the discovery of the high speed internet, new phone technology, and the evolution of pathogens, I've come to the conclusion that there is only one constant truth in the universe; everything has an end. The end, Death, rebirth, whatever you want to call it; you can always count on it. Death cannot be reasoned with, doesn't discriminate, doesn't judge, and doesn't show mercy nor compassion. It's the one thing that will happen to all of us; and as usual, time will go on without us when our "Deaths" finally catch up with us. Some of us have accepted the fact that death will come for us one day; it's inevitable. To think otherwise would be considered to be a child's idea of morality and truth is that until you've accepted this in your heart; then you will never be truly free.)

Place: Queens Village

South Philadelphia

(The weather seems to be just as fickle as the politicians around here; can't seem to make up its mind at all. As the sun sets into the west, few people are still outside enjoying of what remains of the day. Matt finds himself walking along the streets of the Neighborhood; with no destination in particular. He walks with his son enjoying the scenic views of a once vibrant and noisy neighborhood. These uncertain times have taken a toll on all of us; life will never be the same for us "the people". Politics and current social events have driven a wedge between the citizens of this nation who once called themselves, "United".)

(Matt's cell phone starts ringing; it's Flaco calling)

Matt: Yo, what's up??

Flaco: What's popping bro; you ready for tonight? It's going to be fucking wild. Make sure you

     have your mask and wear all black; Herbie is bringing extra masks in case we need them.

Matt: Sounds good; I'm going to go drop my son off to his moms and then I'll go meet you guys

     at Penns Landing.

Flaco: Sounds like a plan; see you later.

(Matt walks back to his apartment and starts getting ready to go drop off his kid. He gathers up his son's belongings and gives him a great big hug. They both start walking down the block where Matt had his car; then they start making their way to his baby mama's house a few streets away from his place. On the way there, he notices that there are a lot more cops than usual in the area. Apparently they were mobilizing to protect the Broad Street area around the City that protestors and looters had been trying to destroy; as retaliation for the murder of "Walter Wallace Jr." by the Police here in Philadelphia. Matt turns on the radio to see if he can listen in to what's going on around the city, since the riots started all over again.)

Matt: (as they arrive) Alright buddy we're here; remember, anything bad that mommy and

     grandmom have to say about daddy is complete bullshit. Okay Buddy.

Little Matt: Okay daddy; I love you daddy.

Matt: Love you too buddy.

(His son walks up to his mom's house as the mom comes out to meet him. She gives him a hug and grabs his little bag. She gives Matt the finger, turns around, and heads back in her house. Matt waits until their inside the house and then leaves to go meet his friends. As he's driving he starts talking to himself.

Matt (to himself): Live life, just live and enjoy the positive and the beautiful places still left.

     There are good people out there, there is a tomorrow, be positive.

(There's been quite a bit of uncertainty in the air in Philadelphia for the moment, tomorrow is Election Day and it looks like it's going to be a tough one to call. A lot of us here hope that "Biden" wins the presidential election so we can finally get rid of that piece of shit tyrant asshole, "Trump". He is the worst kind of hypocrite that has brought out the worse in a lot of people just to soothe his fragile "EGO". He sleazed his way into the presidency; it's not like it hasn't been done before, but this asshole takes the prize. Not only is he from New York, but he's also from the Upper East Side of New York City; where all the rich assholes are gathered up at. As we all wait for the other foot to drop, on stuff we have absolutely no control over; we keep on going with our lives as much as we can. Defying an order from the City and our mayor, the meeting is set for tonight to celebrate once again the "Day of the Dead"; with all of those who believe in many things normal people couldn't understand.)

Place: Gathering of the Dead

Spruce Street Harbor Park –Concert Area

Columbus Blvd. South Philadelphia

Song: Poison – Mountain Dub (Feat. Amira Lacrima) (0:30 – 2:00)

(They all gather up by the parking lot that is used for the Seaport Museum and also for the people taking the ferry across the river to New Jersey. On the other side of the river on the New Jersey side, you have Adventure Aquarium and the 76'ers practice facility; among many other things. With a very full moon in the skies to bless this night; the unknown takes shape in the deepest darkest of the shadows in the night. Death walks among us once more, disguised to feel mortal as a way of self amusement and self fulfillment. The group starts making their way to the Gathering of the dead; on their way there, they encounter a good number of people that were ready to celebrate with them as well.   There was another large group coming in out of nowhere, starts walking right behind them; heading to the concert area where the main groups of people were gathered at. The people behind the boys kept walking slowly not making a sound, making it a bit creepy and suspicious. They carried on with their really cool outfits and costumes, staring at them with their big yellow eyes that seem so really real and a bit intimidating. But hey, if they're there to celebrate the day of dead and have some fun; then fuck it, right.)

(We make our way uphill on the ramp, looking at all the different cool stations and little shops that people had set up all around the location. The place looked more like a small maze that was actually more like a small troll market, filled with vendors from all over the Tri-State area. Everybody really into the whole concept of the "Day of the Dead", dressed up to the fullest. They start seeing all the cool decorations and designs. One of the coolest things there, were the choreographed dances up on the main stage done by artists that also appreciated this Holy day. People from all ages, from all parts of the city, from different ethnic backgrounds, and different walks of life; didn't matter, they were all Philadelphia.   The guys keep making their way around the area, finally linking up with the rest of their main group.)

(At a short distance away, the wormhole portal commences to reverberate energy from a different world, one parallel to our own plane of existence. It starts emanating a weird type of light that seems to merge with all the lights from the concert; like a rainbow going along with the music. 10 Pak sees it and knows that they are really close to the location of the wormhole. He was following the coordinates given to him by the Lady Ghost from the "Moshulu"; from his point of view, he had now narrowed down the location to two possibilities. Now, so close to finding out the location of the wormhole; the time had come to set up his meeting with Tommy Cadwallader. Help him help himself and in the process help 10 Pak by getting rid of Zepi Petri; there for releasing Lady Crane from her eternal confinement. It wasn't going to be easy for him to convince someone like Tommy Cadwallader, to help him join a fight that had nothing to do with him. After all that Tommy Cadwallader had been through; all he wanted was a ticket back home. Speaking of which; Tommy was right across the street watching them and waiting for the right moment for him to strike. As Tommy the Warlock waited; he starts walking around looking for something to do. He walks over to one of those yellow donation bins that look like giant trash cans; you know, the ones you donate clothes for the people in need. Tommy breaks the latch with the lock on it and grabs a handful of clothes and lays them out in front of him; he starts going through them one by one.)

(Grabs a Dallas cowboys jersey)

Tommy: Awful colors, just hideous; must be a girl's team.

(Grabs a New York Giants Jersey)

Tommy: No way; I would much rather eat a bowl of horse shiiit.

(He looks around some more and then grabs a Philadelphia eagles "All Black" jersey)

Tommy: I like this; this is nice. I am definitely sporting this green and black; it's so manly.

(Sorry…NO Washington Red Jerseys here ☹ We don't give that shit to people around these parts; not even for free. Lol. Much love D.C. ☺)

(A few more hours go by; Tommy finally sees the crew getting in their cars. He senses the dark energy being put out by the book and feels it coming from their direction. All of a sudden, a homeless beggar appears out from the side street, walking towards him looking to make conversation.)

Tommy: There are clothes here, if you'd like to help yourself out to some.

Homeless Beggar: Are you Thomas Cadwallader??

Tommy: How do you know my name?? Speak man!!

Homeless Beggar: I was paid to deliver a message to you; a parlay, the young man said.

(Tommy was looking a bit confused and a bit relieved also; things just got much easier for him.)

Tommy: How much did he pay you?? Did he treat you well??

Homeless Beggar: He gave me enough money to turn my life around Sir. A gift sent from the

Heavens; don't know how this luck landed upon me, but I sure appreciate it.

Tommy: What kind of man would you say he is?? His character and demeanor; what's he like??

Homeless Beggar: He said you would ask that. He's sharp and educated; well mannered also.

He doesn't seem to have bad intentions about anything, to tell you the truth.

I will tell you one thing though; he also has this dangerous feel about him;

I wouldn't want to piss him off

Tommy: How so??

Homeless Beggar: I see a lot of sadness behind his eyes and his smile. The type of sadness that can quickly turn into rage; the type of rage that can consume everything in its wake.

Next morning………

Place: 10th St. and South St.

South Philadelphia

Song: Te para Tres (Unplugged) – Soda Stereo (2:00 – 3:58)

(10 Pak is at a friend's studio, playing the drums to a song that he dedicates every year to his father that had passed away. He smokes his joint as he plays the drums along to the slow beautiful song that brings joy to his heart; remembering that he had a good person for a father. He also remembers clearly how the forces of the world conspired against a good man and kept him from doing great things; a reason for his hate of the world. One of "this" writer's greatest fears is that in the end when everything is finally over; he shall have accomplished nothing. His name will finally be forgotten, when the few that know it follow along in their deaths as well. Life is cruel like that, when it withers you away slowly with time; it waits for you to get old and weak so it can start playing fucking mind games with you. Never live in regret and treat every day as if it was your last; this is pretty much what I've come to accept as the recipe for a happy life. From a young age he had been involved with the school band, marching band, and a couple of reggae, ska, and rock bands growing up. As a drummer he always used to quote another drummer by the name of "Beano". "Men are from Mars, Women are from Venus; but drummers, are from Pluto. 10 Pak keeps playing along to the song with the slow rhythm and melody. Outside the room were a couple of his people talking to Jerome Koppel; who had just arrived with his bodyguards to talk business with 10 Pak. Koppel was there to cut a deal with 10 Pak and find out what was really going on with the whole ghost's drama around the city. He said that it was his obligation to report on this because of his journalistic integrity; but I think it was mostly to feed his ego and curiosity. Flaco, Ramon, and Smoak were the ones there talking to Koppel and company.)

Jerome Koppel: Wuuz up; JOmies?? (Flaco and Ramon start laughing)

Ramon: This mutha-fucka..

Flaco: Jerome Koppel just called us, "Homies" with a J; how about that shit??

Smoak: He's in there; but only you can go in and I need to check you for weapons.

Koppel: You serious right now, bruh??

Smoak: The person you're about to talk business with is of great importance to some

very dangerous very prominent business people; these Cats are on a whole other level.

I'm here to make sure that their golden goose remains safe; you feel me brother.

Koppel: (looking up at Smoak) Damn you're a tall mutha fucka…Alright brother, I'm cool; do

your thing. I'm not here to start shit, just wanna talk to the man, that's all.

Smoak: Okay, right through there; love your show by the way.

(Koppel walks into the studio and sits down to talk business with 10 Pak. Being a very smart negotiator himself, Koppel knew that all the cards where on his side. But he also knew that he if he overplayed his cards; he could end up dead, floating in the Delaware River. He sits down as he keeps his eyes focused on 10 Pak.)

Jerome Koppel: You're a hard man to find; and I hear you come well recommended by people

that actually matter. Don't worry I'm not here to make your life any harder

than it is; I just want to be the one to tell the story that's all. With access to

your story, I can make it back on top of the News World here in this particular

corner of the world.

10 Pak: If it's the story of the century you're looking for; then you've come to the right place.

I believe that we have mutual interests that could benefit from a partnership between

us. Also, we can actually help out a lot of people around the city as we carry out my

plan.. There's plenty of money for you here; just as long as you help me expose the

real monsters in this city; the one's that keep stealing everybody's hard earned money.

Jerome Koppel: You really are something else you know that; not what I expected at all.

10 Pak: Disappointed??

Jerome Koppel: On the contrary my brotha; I'm pleased to know that I'm not the only crusader in this god forsaken city. Keep talking brotha, I'm listening. Tell me about this plan of yours, lay it all out for me.

(10 Pak continues to tell Jerome Koppel everything and I mean everything; including how they've been helping poor people around the city with Lady Crane's hidden treasure. He also tells him about the families that are stealing tax money directly from the city's treasury with the help of certain key city officials. As he keeps listening to 10 Pak, he realizes that this story is getting more and more dangerous; with implications that could put a lot of top people behind bars. This was the kind of shit that Jerome Koppel had been waiting for his whole life; a chance for him to finally stick it to the system and do something legendary for the people. The bargain has been struck and now these two men are on a mission to do the unheard of, the impossible, and the clinically insane bat-shit crazy plan that no one would see coming. As they end their meeting, they shake hands and Koppel exits the building. 10 Pak wants to play a while longer on the drum-set, so he grabs his phone and through Bluetooth to his headphones; he plays "Lateralus" from the band "Tool" before he decides to call it a day. He sets the song at minute 6:00 because it happens to be his favorite part of the song to play along; plus the fact that 10 Pak is a huge Danny Carey fan. In case you were wondering, which I'm sure you were; Danny Carey is the drummer for the band "Tool".)

Song: Lateralus – Tool (6:00 – 9:05)

"There is no avoiding War; it can only be postponed to the advantage of your enemy."

Nicolo Machiavelli

Place: F.B.I. / Treasury Department Field Office

       Center City, Philadelphia

(A middle aged man walking in haste heads over to the regional director's office, with a bunch of folders in hand. He has an urgent message that must be dealt with immediately. He walks up to the secretary and she immediately buzzes him into the office. As he walks into the office he sees an older gentleman staring out the window looking at the city landscape.)

Regional Director: What is it now??

Messenger: Sir, we have a problem; apparently a group of nobodies have been inquiring about the Philadelphia Experiment. It seems that they have been given very good intel about the location of the anomaly.

Regional Director: Is that so??

Messenger: Yes Sir; how should we proceed??

Regional Director: Do we know who's been feeding them this information.

Messenger: No Sir; we have no idea how they've been doing it. These guys came out of Nowhere; we're completely in the dark on this one.

Regional Director: How interesting; let's find out more about these nobodies, before we make any rash decisions. Keep me informed.

Messenger: Yes sir.

A couple of blocks away and a few streets over………

Place: Love Park, Center City

      Philadelphia, PA

Song: The Trip – Kim Fowley (0:00 – 2:00)

(Flaco had grabbed a few of the boys and camera crew to go to Center City for the day; they went to film a prank show that involved, you guessed it; pranking people. They started out at Love Park and it didn't take long at all for this idea to take a "shit" sideways. Right from the start the prank goes horribly wrong and a fight breaks out; and it gets bad. Flaco and the boys end up getting chased by a bunch of pissed off people all the way down to the parkway. They ended up over by the Art Museum, where most of the area had been completely occupied by protesters. Tent city was an understatement, the area used to look so beautiful and these geniuses ruined it all; and for what?? For nothing; because in the end their protest will change nothing just like the million other times people have protested. Protesting is just another word for complaining, bitching, and whining; and what does all that get you?? Absolutely nothing; change can only occur through force and violence; to think otherwise would be nothing else but a child's idea of morality. Flaco grabs his phone and calls 10 Pak for help.)

Place: Black Frog's Super Secret Hide-Out

    Camden, New Jersey

(Meeting of the South Jersey Devils is in full session and their leader does not look happy at all.)

Black Frog: How is it possible that with all the men and all the money I've invested; and this is the result you guys give me.?? You know what I am?? …. Put your hand down Raheem; that shit was Rhetorical. I'm a mutha fucking cliché; big black boss man acting like Cab fucking Calloway!!!! Nah mutha fucka's; this shit ends now! We are going to hit them one more time and this time were doing it the right way; with full force. We'll come in from the south through Delaware so that they're look outs don't catch us coming in through the bridges. I expect all of you to be ready to go the moment I fucking call you; you mutha fuckas better buck up cause these are real gangsters we're going up against. Get your heads in the game brothas; and you'll come out so fucking rich you're going to be able to set yourselves up for life.

Place: Chi-Chester, PA

    Herbie's House

(Herbie sits outside one of his spots he uses for lying low, in times of doubt and paranoia. He is hanging out with a couple of strippers that have a bit of a particular proclivity for the consumption of harder drugs. Herbie is talking to a friend of his over the phone; currently telling him a joke.)

Herbie: You listening?? Okay, so an Eagles fan, a Giants fan, and a Cowboys fan are all sitting up high on top of a building. The Giant fan says, we're the toughest ones and the baddest! This one is for my team!! and he jumps off. Then the Eagle's fan, quick to speak, says; I love my team and this one is for you BIRDS!!! The Eagle fan grabs the Cowboy's fan and pushes him off the building. (Herbie starts laughing his ass off over the phone.) Alright, I'll talk to you later.

Stripper #1: Hey Herbie, you going to hook us up or what??

Herbie: No problem; Cash or Ass??

Stripper #2: Come on, you got be kidding me.

Herbie: Look honey, this ain't called let's make a deal; if you don't like it, then BYE.

Stripper #2: Such an asshole.

Herbie: That's my middle name sweetie; don't take it personal. Not my fault you're broke.

Place: Club Risky S Columbus Blvd

    South Philadelphia

(In the dressing room of the club, Lena was finishing up getting ready and finally steps out on to the floor to go meet 10 Pak. As she is walking out she decides to walk around the area where 10 Pak was sitting at. She wanted to take a look at him from different angles and at the same time check out the atmosphere of the crowd. As Lena walks past the bar, she notices that there was a certain dancer staring at 10 Pak from a couple of seats back. She sees that 10 Pak is on his Phone, so Lena walks over and sits right behind the dancer and engages in a conversation with her.)

Lena: Dangerous thing; staring at someone else's man??

Candy: Your MAN?? Didn't know guys came in here looking to be faithful.

Lena: I imagine it must be hard for you; after what happened. Regardless of that, this guy is

       special and I don't plan on sharing him with any of you bitches, you hear me.

Candy: Loud and clear; but believe me when I tell you that I don't have to chase him.

       He'll come to me; by his own choice.

Lena: Funny; don't push me bitch.

Candy: Whatever…

(Lena starts walking away towards 10 Pak and as she reaches him she gives him a great big French kiss, just to piss Candy off. As Lena keeps kissing 10 Pak, she turns around and opens her eyes up to look straight at Candy. Candy gives her the middle finger then gets up and walks over to the bar to get a drink.)

Candy: (talking to herself) Fucking little blonde bimbo bitch; think Candy, think. Don't let this

      Swedish meatball fuck with you.

(Lena starts giving 10 Pak a great big hug and massaging his arms and hands.)

Lena: You see that girl over there; she desperately wants to talk to you.

10 Pak: That obvious?? She's been sitting behind me since I got here; not sure why she won't

      come over and talk, I don't bite.

Lena: Well, it's pretty clear to me what it is that she wants.

10 Pak: Didn't take you for the jealous type.

Lena: On the contrary, I wouldn't mind a little threesome action to tell you the truth.

10 Pak: Not going to lie to you; she might know me from somewhere else. Maybe she knows

      someone from one of the old clubs I used to work for; who knows. I doubt that a

      bit because she looks younger; and I'm not looking for young. I got what I want right in

      front of me.

Lena: And what's that??

10 Pak: A full blossomed woman.

Lena: Well said.

10 Pak: Listen, I got to get going; one of my friends just called me and he needs me to go bail

      him out of a ridiculous situation he got himself in.

Lena: When will I see you again??

10 Pak: Tonight, tomorrow, whenever you want; call me and if I'm not busy you can come over

      or I'll come over.

Lena: Sounds good to me; what about the girl??

10 Pak: I'm going to leave that up to you; in a couple of days I'll be at this address helping out

      some friends for a charity they have going on. (writes down an address and time) If you

      want her to come talk to me, then give her this paper; if not then fuck it I'll talk to her

      now then. Although I must say that I really don't like my business being put out there;

      there are too many ears in this place.

Lena: I understand; and don't worry, I'll give her the paper.

10 Pak: Thanks for being understanding.

Lena: You can pay me back later by eating my pussy out all night long.

10 Pak: Sounds like a plan. (they give each other a kiss and a hug)

(Lena starts making her way to the bar to go talk to Candy. Candy was talking to one of the bartenders when she sees Lena approaching her.)

Candy: What now??

Lena: (hands her the piece of paper) I'm going to give you a chance to prove to yourself that you're NOT better than me. Here, I got you a date with him so give it your best try; although it won't matter because in the end he'll still choose me over you. Besides, we already fucked like animals; and he loved it. So, let me know what my pussy tastes like, bitch. He's got to go for now; so don't bother him okay. (starts walking away)

(Candy talking to herself again)

Candy: What the fuck just happened; was not expecting that. That cocky fucking bitch; thinks her pussy smells better than everybody else's.

(She opens up the note and sees a time and location for her to meet 10 Pak at. She looks up and sees that 10 Pak was already headed out the door. She didn't know what to make of it; but in any case, she got what she wished for.)

Place: Center City Philadelphia

Song: Keep the streets Empty for Me – Fever Ray (0:00 – 2:00)

(The streets are empty and as of now; the Covid-19 Pandemic has altered all of our lives in one way or another. This sucks on so many levels because for those of us who are ahead of the curve and can see things coming that others can't; well it sucks for us even more. We can see how the majority of the people have been "dumbed down" to become nothing else but a subservient culture. The middle class has been long gone for some time now because the "rich elite" and their sycophant politicians made sure of it. They got rid of the one group of people who was educated and strong enough to set them straight and put them back in their place.)

(The fact that people can't see that a two party system is a rigged system; is mind-blowing. Before you start yapping about how there are more than two political parties in this country; let me remind you that those political parties you're thinking about, never get air time on TV. They're never present for the Presidential debates; automatically assuming that the winning candidate will come from one of the two major parties. And why is that?? Tell me; why is that?? The Republican Party and the Democratic Party are two in one, playing as Good Cop and Bad Cop; they own all the Radio stations and TV stations around the country and the security systems that over see them. It would be nice to see members of the Libertarian Party, The Green Party, and the Constitution Party debating amongst the two main parties for the President's chair. The Democratic and Republican Parties have taken over the country ever since the end of the Civil War; and they will not relinquish that kind of power and influence without a fight. This ladies and gentleman, was what Tommy Cadwallader and his friends saw coming, they spoke against it; and it got them killed.)

Place: Washington Square, Center City

       Philadelphia, PA

(The day is coming to an end; the sun starts hiding behind the tree lines to the horizon. The air starts getting a bit chillier and blows in all directions as if it knows where it's going. 10 Pak arrives to the meeting place before Tommy. As he walks around the park remembering everything he and his friends had been through; he feels the end is coming for them, fast. 10 Pak senses that something is a bit wrong; he realizes he's being watched not by one, but by several people in the park. He knows it can't be the cops; not yet at least; it finally clicks.)

10 Pak: South Jersey Dickheads; just what I needed. There's no way I was followed; these

       fuckers must have been waiting here the whole time for one of us to come back.

(10 Pak heads over to the center of the park and sits down on a bench. He takes out his phone and texts some of the guys in his crew, over at a restaurant about three blocks away. He's crossing his fingers, hoping they can arrive on time. But in the meantime, some of the south jersey devils start moving in; positioning themselves as pieces on a chessboard. There are a lot of pedestrians walking by; it's that time of day where the 9-5 crowd starts making their way back to their homes. The traffic dies down considerably and the same people that he saw earlier staring at him have stayed put this whole time.)

(He's counted five men so far that he's sure of and about 2 more that seem doubtful. He looks at his watch to see what time it was, when all of a sudden he notices that there are no more pedestrians. Shit just got real and he decides to duck down to pretend to tie his shoes when a gunshot goes off onto the bench. You can see the birds leaving the trees in the park from the noise being made. A couple more bullets ricochet off the bench as 10 Pak is on the ground taking cover behind the bench and the big trash can next to it.)

Song: 100 Main St - Dat Adam (1:35 – 2:03)

(The noise of the guns and the shouting of the men suddenly stop; no more noise at all. Tommy Cadwallader had arrived just at the perfect moment to save 10 Paks ass from an early grave. Tommy comes out from the ground right behind one of the south jersey devils and decapitates him instantly. The other five men turn around and see Tommy making some weird move with his hands; a wicked spell, which renders them completely helpless. As they fall to their knees, blood starts spilling out from their noses, their ears, their eyes, and their mouths as they cough and cough and cough. 10 Pak gets hit with a piece of the spell and he starts bleeding out as well and passes out right there in the middle of Washington Square; experiencing a quick encounter with death and the thousands of people that had been buried there throughout time.)

Place: Herbie's Apartment

    Marcus Hook, PA

(A very beautiful woman, who's incredibly deceiving looks hid the fact that she was a stripper/escort; she comes up to Herbie's apartment to pick up some party accessories. This particular beauty went by the code-name, "Sugar". She had arrived there with her mom, an older woman whom which through the course of the years had developed throat cancer; due to her five pack a day habit. She had one of those tubes coming out from a hole in her throat; and yes, she did have that little machine that looks like a small electric shaver. You know, the ones that you press to the side of your throat and make you sound like a robot on shrooms. Yeah you know the ones I'm talking about☺. Anyway, they go in Herbie's apartment and he gets introduced to Sugar's Mom and after all the pleasantries; Herbie and Sugar go to his bedroom and close the door behind them to do some catching up.)

(After about an hour they both come back out laughing and hugging each other and they see Sugar's mom sitting there on the couch; carrying a silly grin on her face. Out of nowhere, Sugar brings out the craziest of ideas and suggests to Herbie, if he'd like to try something different? Before he could say anything she tells him that he was more than welcome to stick his dick down her mom's hole in her throat. As soon as she says that, Herbie's phone rings; he picks up.)

Herbie: Not now….

Damien: We got a problem.

Herbie: You fucking kidding me right now!!

Damien: We can't find 10 Pak. There were gunshots at Washington Square, by the time we got there; there was nothing there but like five corpses. Looked like a hit.

Herbie: You guys weren't with him??

Damien: He wanted to meet that crazy fucker by himself; his orders.

Herbie: God dam it!! Ok give me like 20 minutes; no, you know what…make it an hour.

(hangs up phone)

(All you hear in the background is Sugar's mom laughing robotically through her machine.)

Sugars Mom: Ha Ha Ha Hnn Hnnn Hnnnnn

About an hour later……..

166

Place: Kelly Dr. / Boathouse Row

(10 Pak wakes up on a bench near Boathouse Row off of Kelly Dr, facing the river. He sees Tommy Cadwallader staring at the river, reminiscing about the times he had spent here in the past with his friends and family.)

Tommy: I remember this area, like if it was yesterday; the sound of the river hasn't changed.

10 Pak: A lot of things must have been different; the city was quite the site to see I imagine.

Not exactly paradise city these days; but it's where we live.

Tommy: Is this what our city becomes, so many homeless people; so many parts left
unattended and all those people suffering. The rich have taken everything; even the
good quality of life that everybody should have had, no matter the color of the skin or
religious background. That's one of the reasons why we fought in that ungodly war; to
erase the mistakes of the past. Now I see that we are the most dreadful group
of hypocrites.

10 Pak: You mean the civil war??

Tommy: Is that what they ended up calling it; how befitting

10 Pak: In some weird way, I'm a bit tied into the aftermath of this war; well my great great
grandfather. He defeated a confederate Admiral down in Central America. The
confederate Admirals name was William Walker; and my great great grandfathers name
was Florencio Xaltruch, father of the Catrachos.

Tommy: I sensed something different about you when I first saw you guys that night in the
park. So Xaltruch fought against confederate forces; that makes us natural allies
young man.

10 Pak: I guess it does; how about that??

Tommy: I knew this country's greed was making other places suffer. I guess in the end our
dream died and our efforts failed to make a difference. Don't mind me, words
of a dreamer.

10 Pak: I'm a dreamer as well; can't say that it's done me much good. But, somehow I refuse

to lose that part of me; the world and the people in it will not change my mind. There is

too much suffering going on out there for me to give up hope.

(10 Pak tells Tommy Cadwallader that he was avenged by his brother and that he didn't miss much since he was gone. A number of wars here and there; wars that ended up claiming the lives of millions of people. Everything became monopolized and both the democrats and republicans joined forces to take complete and total control of the country.)

Tommy: Well said; by any chance, do you know what the "Rules of the Game" are??

Have you ever heard that expression before??

10 Pak: As a matter of fact, I have. "The greatest enemy will hide in the last place you

would ever look." – Julius Caesar

Tommy: I'm impressed; I'm speaking to an educated man. "First rule of business, protect

your investment."-Etiquette of the Banker 1775

10 Pak: "The only way to get smarter is by playing a smarter opponent."

–Fundamentals of Chess 1883

Tommy: It is far safer to be feared, than loved."-Niccolo Machiavelli

10 Pak: How about that, I'm speaking to an educated man. Shit, almost forgot; I have to contact

my friends and let them know I'm alright. I'm sending them a text. Speaking of which;

I know a way to get you back to your own time; I know the location of the wormhole

you'd been looking for.

Tommy: Impressive these "phones" is what you call it. Amazing, I guess some things do get

better in the future. The wormhole; how on Earth did you ever manage that??

10 Pak: Luck I guess and the fact that I speak to ghosts; well, I was allowed to speak to them

through the help of one ghost I call friend. This friend is in need of my help; and

honestly I could use your help on this matter. It involves a very dangerous Demon

who doesn't need an excuse to kill someone. I've been buying time trying to figure out

how to eliminate him; and so far I have nothing.

Tommy: A demon?？ Sounds like a challenge; worry not, I will help you. Tell me, I sensed a special aura coming from you when I was brought back to life that night at the park. Your friends seem to follow you wherever you go; they're loyal to you, why is that??

10 Pak: It all started with my old Boss, a bookie from Philadelphia who dealt with all kinds of bets in New Castle County. He is a huge Philadelphia Eagles fan and he is very superstitious and to him I was a lucky omen. See, a long time ago there was a great player for the Eagles by the name of Steve Van Buren and he was born in La Ceiba, Honduras; the same city I was born in. He said it was good luck to have me around and from that point on I got involved with different aspects of the business. From there on I've managed to make money for everybody around me. I'm like King Midas, without the magical touch.

Tommy: So your ties with the City do have some sort of legitimacy.

10 Pak: I'd like to think that, yes.

Tommy: Well then, I think we have an understanding; the price of my ticket back home is the head of a demon, how poetic. I think I know how to help you with this problem of yours; but there are a few things I need for the spell. More specifically; Nordic Runes.

10 Pak: There's a museum at the FDR park across from the Nova Care center; it's called the American Swedish Historical Museum. You're more than likely to find what you're looking for there; meet me at this address after you get what you need. Don't be late please; or you'll find my head on a spike along side with Lady Crane's.

Tommy: I shall be there to help you my friend; I promise.

10 Pak: Thank you; Thomas Cadwallader.

(10 Pak writes down the address to Lady Crane's Mansion and the coordinates for the "worm hole". He tells Tommy that he trusts him and to meet him there right before the break of dawn. They shake hands and start making their separate ways, as 10 Pak turns around to say thanks again; he sees that Tommy had disappeared with the wind into the darkness of the night. 10 Pak turns around again and sees a couple of S.U.V's heading his way, it was his people.)

Damien: We've been looking everywhere for you; we thought the worst at one point.

I knew you were ok; you're too stubborn to die.

10 Pak: Well, were about to put that to the test. I have to go face death itself right now; you

guys are taking me there right now.

Damien: This doesn't sound good; I thought you were going to call it a day. Don't you need to

rest?? You got a message from Chuckie Bobo; he says the FEDS are on the

move. They're coming for us all for questioning; they know about the spot he said.

10 Pak: It's now or never.

"The Most Precious light; is the one that visits you in your darkest hour." –

Mehmet Murat Ildan

Place: Lady Crane's Mansion

Old City, Philadelphia

(Silent is the night on the street of Lady Crane's Mansion. Silent is the moment that a monster awaits, within the darkness of the shadows surrounding the house. Silent is Death, which lingers in the air, the mist, and the night sky. Zepi Petri waits at the mansion; his patience pretty much non-existent by this point in time. A couple of S.U.V's shine their lights around the corner as they make their way to the front of the house. They stop right in front of the house and wait about half a minute and they continue on. Zepi Petri shows himself and comes out from a shadow on the front Lawn. Just for a second, before he even blinks; a barrage of bullets start coming in from the side followed by a couple of hatchets being thrusted onto his back and face. He drops down on to his knees; couple of seconds go by when the laughing begins. Zepi Petri, slowly removing the hatchets from his body just laughs and laughs; he stares directly into 10 Paks eyes as he comes out from the bushes behind him.)

Zepi Petri: WELL....I didn't think you had the balls to betray me. Very not bad, but not strong enough; okay, let's see where this takes us.

(He stomps his foot on the ground and 10 Pak falls to his knees and starts bleeding out from everywhere. Zepi Petri slowly gets up and starts turning into his demon form; setting everything around him into a blaze of fire. As he takes a couple of steps towards 10 Pak, laughter comes out from behind him lurking out from the shadows of the street.   Tommy Cadwallader had arrived to join the fight, as he quickly throws a spell on Zepi Petri and renders him immovable.) (Tommy grabs the Viking Runes (rocks with marks) and throws them in front of 10 Pak and starts chanting the words to summon a"Berserker".)

Song: Thousand Years of Oppression – Amon Amarth (1:45 – 2:00)

Tommy: Skeggold!!, Skalmold!!, Skildir ro Klofnir!!

(Axe time!! Sword Time!! Shields shall be Splintered!!!!)

(Tommy then proceeds to cut his arm and pours his blood onto the Runes. The spell makes 10 Pak turn into a "Raging Berserker"; unable to control the rage of a thousand storms within him, he starts spinning in circles around Zepi Petri. The spinning makes the illusion of more berserkers being present at the moment, then suddenly; one berserker rushes out to Zepi Petri and tears off his head from his body. Lady Crane Emerges from the house onto the front steps and looks around among the flames. She sees the berserker slowly transforming back into 10 Pak, as he walks slowly towards the house with Zepi Petri's head in his hand.)

Song: Thousand Years of Oppression – Amon Amarth (4:45 – 5:30)

(He lifts it up in the air and shows Lady Crane her captors decapitated head; her curse is now over. Lady Crane's ghostly form slowly starts disappearing into the thin air. She waves a kiss goodbye to 10 Pak and places her hand on her heart as she says Thank You; she then vanishes completely and ceases to exist. Tommy turns to 10 Pak and also says goodbye, he is now on his way to find the "wormhole" so he can travel back in time to his Philadelphia at the end of the 1800's.)

Song: Siberie (ending) – Manu Chao (3:45 – 4:20) ☺

Place: The Lakes/FDR Park

    South Philadelphia

(The light of the morning finally makes its presence felt; they finally leave and 10 Pak decides they should make their way to "the Lakes" FDR Park. He wants to say goodbye to his friend in his own way. 10 Pak sits at the edge of the stones right by the water under an old temple; he plays his guitar to the tune of the song as he contemplates life and death. He plays his song out in the open under the storm clouds for Lady Crane to hear; wherever she may be.)

Chapter 9

Last

of

the 79's

Song: For the Damaged Coda – Blonde Redhead (2:00 – 4:00)

Place: Rawle and Henderson LLP

16th and Chestnut St. - Center City, Philadelphia

(The day starts a new at the law firm; some lawyers and the rest of the employees at the office are gathering up around the break-room in orderly fashion. It would appear that some of them are putting money down, making last minute bets; today is the day that they decide who the winner of the "Back to the Future" bet is going to be. There was a package being held here in this particular place since Jan, 1st 1866 belonging to the Cadwallader Estate; the oldest of customers of the firm, Rawle and Henderson LLP. Headquartered in Philadelphia; this is the oldest Law Firm in continuous practice in the United States. The Law Firm had strict instructions for the package to be delivered at a precise time and place; sound familiar?? Yup, when Marty gets the package on the second movie; well that was the bet, to see if this was real or just bullshit. Everybody finishes up putting their money down on the bet as their mail courier, or "package boy" if you want to be a dick about it (lol); is getting ready to depart with the package. As the mail person exits the room everybody goes back to whatever they were doing before. One person in particular, decides to go out for a smoke break out of nowhere; he sends a text to an unknown number, "package is on the move." He closes his phone and tosses his cigarette that was never even lit in the first place and goes back inside. Moments later the delivery man arrives at the package's intended destination; 10 Pak's house. Accompanied at that moment by Herbie and Flaco, 10 Pak takes the package and sees the last name Cadwallader on the paper and the date it was sent on. 10 Pak looks up and sees the delivery man staring at him. It seemed like the delivery man had something on his mind and had a question coming up.)

10 Pak: (looks back at the delivery guy) What is it??

Delivery Guy: Hey bro, there's a bet going on at work, back at the law firm; lots of money

                involved because some people didn't think this to be real. I got money on this

                too bro; I just need to know if it's Legit??

(10 Pak looks at the envelope in awe; he couldn't believe that Tommy actually kept his promise to write to him. The letter contained the magic password to open up the "wormhole doorway".)

10 Pak: This is more than legit; this is my Ace in the hole.

Song: Treasures - Thievery Corporation (0:00 – 1:00)

Place: Rittenhouse Square – Koppel's Residence

   Center City, Philadelphia

(Matt and Flaco arrive at a small park in front of the Luxury apartments at the Rittenhouse Square area. They see that Jerome Koppel is sitting there waiting for them drinking his cup of coffee; he's got like five body-guards spread out about 10 – 15ft from our spot.)

Jerome Koppel: What's up boys; nice day isn't it??

Flaco: Nah Mr. Famous, my bitch got Covid; I ain't had pussy in like a week. Do you know what's that like??

Jerome Koppel: As a matter of fact; no I don't. I'm just saying, I'd go mutha fucking crazy without pussy for a whole week. Now seeing as I couldn't give a shit about your vagina problem; what's the word from the general?? Is this going down or what?? Is he going to walk the walk; or just talk the talk.

Matt: (places a briefcase next to him) See for yourself.

(Koppel opens up the briefcase and sees a couple of letters made out to him and about 10 million dollars in Bearer Bonds. He starts laughing, he can't believe that there is someone that is actually true to his word; especially when it's about money and going against "The Man".)

Flaco: Our friend hopes that this is enough to convince you that this shit is for real. He wants you to be "the noise that interrupts the signal"; fuck the Philadelphia Status Quo.

Matt: Come on Koppel; let's take down these rich crooked righteous arrogant assholes. Here is our chance; we won't get a better opportunity than now to stick it to these motherfuckers. All the people that had suffered all throughout the city because of these assholes and their fucking laws. North, West, and South, we all pay these Tyrant assholes our hard earned money; it's a viscous never ending cycle that has to come to a stop.

Jerome Koppel: I've been fighting these dirty rotten mutha fuckers since the 80's. A lot of people have tried to expose them in the past; without any positive results. We've tried to show the world that this secret society is real. We are the ones that give a damn; we are the ones that care about the Welfare of everybody, not just the privileged few. Oh I'm game, mutha fuckers…It's on.

Song: Weight of love – The Black Keys (1:30 – 3:00)

Place :   Corner of 3rd and Wolf

       South Philadelphia

(On the corner of 3rd and Ritner, there is a small restaurant situated right there. On the side of the building there are some steps that lead up to an apartment on the second level. A girl approaches the bottom of those steps; it's Candy and she is getting ready to make her way up to go meet 10Pak. Candy double checks the address given to her by Lena; she seemed a bit nervous, anxious, and cheerful all rolled up in one. She checks her hair, her breathe, and her boobs; she makes sure she's looking good. As she slowly walks up the steps you can fully appreciate how fit she is; as most strippers are. The heels she was wearing really accentuated her calf muscles; nice compliment to the very sexy top she was wearing. I'm talking classy sexy; not hood rat sexy, big fucking difference. At the top of the steps she sees all these cool lights, signs, and decorations; over by the ledge on the balcony smoking a joint stood 10 Pak. She walks over to him as he exhales the weed smoke towards the moonlit sky; doing that trick that catches some back with his nose. She takes the joint from his hand and takes a puff and inhales and then exhales slowly to the tune of the song.)

10 Pak: So what did you want to talk about??

Candy: I finally get to talk to you all by myself; still can't believe it.

10 Pak: Not just a pretty face; you're smart as well.

Candy: I wouldn't be here if it weren't for you; and don't worry, I'll never tell another soul what happened that night.

10 Pak: Ok; much appreciated. So what do you want?

Candy: I want you, I want to thank you properly; the way you defeated that evil person with neither hesitation nor remorse. It had an effect on me, you don't understand, I thought I was done for; you rescued me from my death. (she leans in and starts kissing him)

(They go inside the apartment into the bedroom and they spend the night together engaging in all kind of sexual depravities. Later on that night as they both lay in bed asleep, 10 Pak starts having weird dreams. He had about a million things going through this head right now and whether it was out of stress, anxiety, or sadness; a solution was about to manifest itself in the coolest of forms.)

Song: I'd rather be with you – Bootsy Collins (0:00 – 1:20)

Place: Inside 10 Pak's Dream

(10 Pak finds himself alone, up on an empty stage. A bright shinny funkadelic light approaches him from up above; moving along to the beat and the rhythm of the song. Finally as the glare dissipates, it becomes clear as to who it is that is there to visit; the great "Bootsy Collins".)

10 Pak: Bootsy Collins!! I must be tripping..

Bootsy: What's happening baby..

10 Pak: Where the hell am I??

Bootsy: Chiilin in your head; relaxing, hanging out in your dreams.

10 Pak: Are you like, my fairy god father or something highly unlikely like that??

Bootsy: Ain't no faeries here player; just a smooth cool brotha, with the need to lay down some truth on you.

10 Pak: Oh shit; it's one of those dreams..

Bootsy: What's the matter pimp daddy?? You got everything in the world a man could Want; and you got a fine naked white woman by your side. Damn brotha, you look like you just came in from the rain. What's bringing you down baby??

10 Pak: That's just it, I wish I really knew; or perhaps I'm over thinking this a bit too much and maybe I should just let things fall where they may. You know, just say fuck it. I'm the only one putting in the effort and I'm the only one thinking this all the way through. I keep thinking about the future and what stresses tomorrow will bring; I'm trying to stay five steps ahead of everybody and it is exhausting. Shit, I wish I had a pen; how bout I get your autograph, nobody is going to believe this.

Bootsy: Quick, what's your favorite Bootsy Collin's song??

10 Pak: Shiiit; that's easy. Munchies for your Love, of course.

Bootsy: That's groovy baby. Check this out young blood; you don't have to put the weight of the world on your shoulders anymore. You've done more than enough for your friends and your people; I'm here to tell you that the light at the end of the tunnel is here. Checkmate young brotha, your plan works; you got them right where you want them. Enjoy yourself and from this point on, all you have to do is watch the dominoes fall and go with the flow; Power to the People baby.

10 Pak: Power to the mutha-fucking People.

(And just like that, he wakes up from his dream realizing how important this sign was. Sign of all signs, meant no more stress; a good omen, at last.)

Song: The Hardest – Gasoline (0:00 – 1:30)

Place: Buddha the West's Mechanic Shop/Office

Cedar Park, West Philadelphia

(A couple of Feds walk up to the shop and they start asking around for "Buddha". A couple of big mutha fuckas walk out in front; behind them comes out "Buddha the West".)

Buddha: Feds in my house, in West Philly; this is interesting. You sure you guys not lost; your Maps App going all funky on your phone.

Fed 1: We need information on an associate of yours from down in South Philly; we'll make sure your well compensated for your troubles. Here's our card, don't hesitate to call.

(The Feds end up leaving the shop and as they drive off in their cars Buddha and his bodyguards walk out onto the sidewalk.)

Buddha: 10 Pak was right about these fuckers; he called it, I'm impressed.

BodyGuard1: What'd he say??

Buddha: That they would come for us all, "Divide and Conquer". It's an old Roman strategy.

Place: Dane's Real Estate Agency – N. 2nd St. and Grange Ave.

   Olney Section, North Philadelphia

(Another group of Feds approach "Dane of the North" at his place of business. Some of the customers that were there were people from the neighborhood. They start whispering to each other as the Feds walk past them in the lobby and head over to the Secretary.)

Secretary: Gentlemen; how can I help you??

Fed #1: We are looking for Daniel Rodrigo Valentine.

(Dane comes out and tells the agents to step into his office, he tells his secretary to hold all his calls and to make sure not to be interrupted by anyone.)

Dane: Feds in North Philly??…You guys get lost off of 95 or something?? (starts laughing)

Fed #2: Funny; no we are not lost. We are here because we need you to tell us about one of

   your buddies down from South Philly; his businesses, contacts, associates, etc, etc.

   You know the drill, if you don't help us; I'm sure if we dig deep enough we'll find out

   how much dirty shit you've got going on. Trust me when I tell you that we'll lock you

   up and throw away the key; and nobody is going to do shit about it.

Dane: I see; well leave me your card and if I find out anything helpful, I will give you a call.

(The one Fed throws his business card on the table in a very rude kind of manner. Dane starts smiling and laughing as they exit the door; he starts ripping the Feds card in half and throws it in the trash and calls his secretary.)

Dane: Yo Juanita!!

Secretary: What's up boss??

Dane: Call your cousin; we need to send a message to Ramon and friends. Fuck the Feds, they

can eat a dick! They don't know how vulnerable they really are in a city like Philadelphia.

Secretary: What password should I use??

Dane: Tell them; "Jimmy Rollins #11 is up to bat."

Secretary: Will do boss.

Dane: The dominoes are in place; like our friend predicted. This is going to be fun; can't wait.

Place: 5th St. and Jackson St. Chuckie BoBo's Place

   South Philadelphia

(As the Feds walk up to Chuckie Bobo's place; Chuckie Bobo himself walks out in front of his men and straight out tells the Feds where they can go.)

Chuckie Bobo: Go fuck yourself JR!! Grab that business card and shove it up your ass

you fucking piece of shit. Now get the fuck off my block!!

(The Feds, knowing how well connected this guy was with the Irish Politicians and Union Leaders; they just drop the business card in front of him as they turn right around and walk back to their cars and drive off.)

McLaren: What are these assholes up to now??

Chuckie Bobo: I know who they want…..ain't fucking happening!!

McLaren: They want our number one money maker for themselves; the balls on these fuckers.

Chuckie Bobo: Not a fucking chance in hell. Call the Candy-Man; tell him we're good to go.

(On the other end of that phone call with Rob McLaren is the Candy-Man, also known as 10 Pak. He was on his way to Brighton Beach, New York City; closing out an important deal that would make people like Chuckie Bobo among others a lot more money.)

10 Pak: Once I get to Little Odessa I'm meeting them right away; I don't plan on staying for too

long. We're almost there; I'll send you a text when it's all done.

McLaren: Be careful with those Ruskies up there; Happy Hunting, talk to you later.

Song: Muzika dlya fil'ma – Persephone's Bees (0:00 – 1:20)

Place: Brighton Beach/Little Odessa, New York City

(More often referred to as Brighton Beach; Little Odessa is well known for having a substantial number of Russian and Ukrainian inhabitants. It feels like its own little world separated from the rest of the City. Presently, 10 Pak is on his way to meet an old friend of his from college that lives there. This person has business connections with people from very different types of corporate cultures going back to Mother Russia. As soon as 10 Pak arrives at his friends Viktor's bar, they start with the introductions as they all start drinking some good Vodka. 10 Pak's entourage, along with his friend Viktor's, start celebrating the good old days; as they look towards the future. They also celebrate because 10 Pak is giving Viktor sole access to the Ghost Bud north of Philadelphia. Viktor was going to be the only one in New York City selling Ghost Bud; if he agreed to 10 Pak's terms of alliance with the Philadelphia groups.)

10 Pak: You still dating that Hippie chick involved in that whole "Occupy Wall

Street" mess.

Viktor: Not anymore; I still contribute to the cause as much as I can. You know, fuck the man!!

10 Pak: You're still banging her aren't you??

Viktor: Keep it down asshole….my new girlfriend is around here somewhere, I think.

10 Pak: Remember those waitresses from Kahunaville??

(They both start laughing as they keep drinking and reminiscing about the early 2000's and the lack of technology there was back then in those days. 10 Pak starts talking to Viktor about the "Ghost Bud" he got his hands on and how he is the only person on this side of the planet that has it. He tells him that this particular "commodity" can turn things belly up in the underground Black Market here in New York. He explains to Viktor that he wants to put everybody in New York out of the weed business for good; and Viktor would be the only one with access to it. Viktor knows that a strong partnership with the groups of Philadelphia meant that he had reinforcements in the south; against the groups in New York and from North New Jersey. Both of them attended a small business school in Delaware; so both of them had a sharp eye for business deals that would generate more money than the usual commodities.)

(10 Pak also sold the idea to Viktor, that in these crazy times of uncertainty with the whole "Covid" pandemic; it would be better for them, to find an item that can over-sell anything easily in times of recession. Viktor in return gives 10 Pak information about the illegal things Wall Street had been involved in and why the whole "Occupy Wall Street" was formed. Viktor goes on and tells 10 Pak that this whole fucking mess started with the smartest group of crooks in the western world; the fuckers at Wall Street. The story starts when these "Wall Street fuckers" paid a pretty good penny to have the movement "Occupy Wall Street" slowly go away through the years. After October 9th of that same year the movement had spread out to 951 cities across 82 countries and in over 600 communities in the United States. Due to this, the leaders at Wall Street started setting things in motion as they manufactured events, that as they trickled down; it redirected the media's focus away from them at Wall Street and on to someone else. "Occupy Wall Street" began in September of 2011 in New York City's Zuccotti Park. Having taken over part of the Financial District, they started focusing on the topics of the Wealth Inequality, political corruption, and corporate influence of government; protesters were guilty of occupying private property, picketing, holding demonstrations inciting civil disobedience and Internet Activism. I hate to say this, but it's no coincidence that once Wall Street was put under a microscope, Barrack Obama then gets re-elected at the end of 2012; remember "too big to fail" and the corporate bail outs?? That same year a gunman kills 26, including 20 children at the sandy hook elementary school in Newtown, Connecticut. Obama starts with the weapons ban talks; the gun industry shoots through the roof with profits as an effect of this. Everybody's buying more guns as a direct result of Obama's new weapons ban.)

(Hurricane Sandy strikes the eastern seaboard, many people lose everything because of loop holes in the housing market; Wall Street makes a killing on this. 2013 Out of nowhere, Edward Snowden leaks highly classified documents from the National Security Agency. Later that same year 2013, terrorists attack the Boston Marathon by detonating two bombs at the finish line of the race; killing three and injuring 283 runners and spectators. Still on 2013, the Supreme Court strikes down the Defense of Marriage Act, which banned the Federal recognition of same-sex marriages and refused to recognize the legal standing of proponents of "Proposition 8"; which resulted in the re-legalization of same-sex marriage in California. That same year in 2013 "Black Lives Matter" emerges and begins protesting against the systemic widespread racial profiling, police brutality, and racial inequality in the United States justice system.)

(Is it such a coincidence that right after technology becomes more advanced, more and more black people were being killed, which is nothing new; except that this time around, it was done so that it would be visible to the world, very visible. These were the people whose deaths at the hands of police were reported across the country in a matter of minutes. Eric Garner July 17th 2014, Michael Brown August 9th 2014, 12 year old Tamir Rice Nov.22 2014, Walter Scott April 4th 2015, Alton Sterling July 5th 2016, Philando Castile July 6th 2016, Stephon Clark March 18th 2018, Breonna Taylor March 13th 2020, George Floyd May 25th 2020.   By this point in time with everything that's going on plus the CoviD pandemic; I don't think the world gives a shit about "Occupy Wall Street" anymore. ☹ I wouldn't be surprised at all; if one day we were to find out that the Wall Street paid the Chinese government for the pandemic to hit at a global level.)

(Viktor, 10 Pak, and friends continue drinking and bullshitting; they finally get down to business and they start smoking the ghost Bud that 10 Pak had brought along. Everyone was impressed; and high as shiiit of course. 10 Pak takes a picture with Viktor on his phone, he sends it to McLaren to show him the good news that the deal went through. The picture shows Viktor and 10 Pak with their thumbs up, giving McLaren the okay.)

Viktor: So, have you talked to any of our college classmates??

10 Pak: Not really; I think about them just about as much as they think about me. Except you

   Viktor; you're the only one worth talking too. (raises his drink to make a toast) To the

   good old days.

Viktor: To the good old days. To our wives and sweethearts; may they never meet.

   (they both start laughing as they pour themselves another Vodka drink)

10 Pak: Ill drink to that and I will also drink to a successful venture between our organizations.

Viktor: Yes. This will make us an enormous amount of money; on behalf of Mother Russia, I

   say thank you my friend. (raises his drink once more) Cuba Libre!

10 Pak: Cuba Libre!! my friend.

Next Day…..

(Herbie is Calling 10 Pak early in the morning; 10 Pak half asleep answers his cell phone.)

10 Pak: What's up??

Herbie: You sound like shit; wake up pretty boy we got a lot of shit to do today.

10 Pak: You fucking prick; I came in late last night from New York, everyone is happy.

Herbie: That's good news; I got more good news for you.

10 Pak: Are you being sarcastic?

Herbie: Yes I am; Dizzy Rane gave me the bad news; they're coming for us.

10 Pak: Everything in place??

Herbie: Everybody knows about them now; we are set to go.

Place: Girard Ave. and E. Columbia Ave.

   Fishtown, Philadelphia

(Flaco along with Matt, Ramon and some of Ramon's men are loading up the ghost bud that's getting ready to get sent to Little Odessa in New York. Flaco is drinking his coffee when all of a sudden his coffee cup gets tipped towards him and it spills on his jacket; you hear Charlie the ghost laughing his ass off.)

Flaco: You fucking prick, asshole, ghost shit, monkey fucker!!!

Charlie: Whatever you little bitch!!! Get to work, if you got time to lean; you got time to
      clean!!

Flaco: What the fuck!! Ohhh no you don't!! You don't want to fuck with me buddy!!

Charlie: Oh I'm sorry, did I spill coffee on your jacket; nice jacket by the way, does it
      come in Men's size.

Flaco: Mutha fucker!! I'll kill you!! (Charlie laughing while he smokes some ghost bud)
(Ramon comes in the room)

Charlie: Yo Ramon, my man!! What's up bro you ready for this; pretty fucking cool aint it??

Ramon: I still can't believe I'm talking to a ghost; yes Charlie, pretty cool.

Charlie: That's right baby.

Ramon: Come on Flaco we got to get going; we got to send the real trucks on 95 now and send
the decoy trucks along 76. Remember not to put up any resistance when we get
arrested; then we're home free.

Charlie: Yeah Flaco; what you need directions or something?? Ha Ha…You better not fuck this
Up, you hear me!!

Flaco: Seriously, do we have to put up with this asshole??

Ramon: What the fuck you think??

Flaco: God damn it!!

(matt comes in the room)

Matt: Guys we're ready; let's get going.

Charlie: Hey!! Who let the little leprechaun out of his cage!! Show me the rainbow little man!!

Matt: Eat a dick, you fucking hippie!! Guys, let's go.

(They head out and continue on with their part of the plan; it looks and feels like it is going to
somehow end up working for everybody. Well, almost everybody; depends on your objective
point of view and whose side your on. ☺)

Place: F.B.I. / Treasury Department Field Office

Center City, Philadelphia

(It is now midnight and down at the federal building, all the final orders are going out for the
arrests of 10 Pak and known associates. Calls are being made out to local police precincts for
cooperation with the capturing of said individuals; the Agent in charge gets a phone-call from
one of his higher ups. This is one of the family members from the secret society that own the
city; he is giving him instructions on how to proceed with the matter at hand. At the same time,
the local cops that were called to assist; well, they start making calls of their own to the people
that take care of "their" best interests.)

(A cop walks up to the Agent in Charge)

Cop #1: Sir, we got a message from Chuckie Bobo, it's the location of the Anomaly; that's

where 10 Pak is going to be at. That's not all Sir, here. (hands him the note)

To The Asshole in Charge,

He's going to be at the site mostly affected by the Philadelphia Experiment; before the first light of the day. This still won't help you in the end; you're trying to catch the wind with your bare hands. Luckily, you can only get smarter by playing a smarter opponent; so, guess what?? It's time to play a smarter opponent.

Sincerely,   GO FUCK YOURSELF

Agent in Charge: (Talking to himself) Prick till the end; I'll deal with you later. So he knows

the location of the wormhole; I wonder if he found out how to open it?? Well

either way, it is said that it can only be open at the break of dawn.

(Speaks out loud to all cops and all Agents)

Gentleman get ready, we got the place and time; as of now the Chess pieces are

on the board and we are on the move. I want checkpoints between the areas

of Penns Landing all the way to Naval Yard. Tell the Officers assisting us to

meet us here and as soon as everybody is ready to go , we mobilize.

Place: 3rd Street and Tree St

10 Paks House - South Philadelphia

(10 Pak is at his place chilling one last time before everything goes down. He is smoking some good "juicy fruit weed" as he finishes watching the movie "Revolver" by Guy Ritchie. This is one of the most brilliant underrated movies ever made; it was so deep-thinking, intricate, and clever that it just went over the majority of people's heads. The irony is that the film went unnoticed, under the radar so to speak; exactly the same way that voice inside your head goes unnoticed and under the radar for most of your lives.)

(The whole movie is a clever sign for how our ego controls us.   Making us second guess our every decision as it prevents us from doing what's righteous; rather than what feels right. All in all, it's one of the best movies ever; no bullshit. At this point in time, 10 Pak is paying attention to the end credits, which go into detail about the true nature of the ego. As he hears what they are saying; he listens carefully to everyone's opinion loud and clear.)

Dr. Yoav Dattilo, PhD.-The ego is the worst confidence trickster we could ever figure, we could ever imagine…cause…you don't see it.

Dr.Steven C. Hayes PhD. – And the single biggest con is.."I am you."

Dr. Peter Fonagy PhD..FBA - The problem with the ego is that it hides in the last place that you'd ever look, within itself.

Leonard Jacobson - It disguises its thoughts as your thoughts; it's feelings as your feelings, *(founder of the Conscious* you think it's you. People have no clue that they're imprisoned; *Living Foundation)* they don't know that there's an EGO, they don't know the distinction.

Andrew Samuels PhD – Peoples' need to protect their own egos knows no bounds. They will lie, cheat, steal, kill, do whatever it takes to maintain what we call "ego boundaries."

Dr. David Hawkins MD., PhD – At first it's difficult for the mind to accept that there's something beyond itself; that there's something of greater value and greater capacity for discerning truth than itself.

Dr. Deepak Chopra MD. – In religion, the EGO manifests itself as the Devil and of course no one realizes how smart the ego is because it created the devil so you could blame someone else.

Dr. Peter Fonagy PhD..FBA – In creating this imaginary external enemy, it usually makes for a real enemy for ourselves and that becomes a real danger to the ego; but that's also the Ego's creation.

Dr. Deepak Chopra MD.–There is no such thing as an external enemy, no matter what that
voice in your head is telling you. All perception of an enemy is
a projection of the ego as the enemy.

Dr. Peter Fonagy PhD..FBA –In that sense, you could say that a 100% of our external enemies
are of our own creation.

Dr. Obadiah S. Harris PhD – Your greatest enemy; is your own inner perception, your own
ignorance, is your own Ego

(From the Movie "Revolver")

(10 Pak's focus was also on another subject mentioned in the movie; Chess and Cons. This is
described as a dangerous combination of chess moves and concepts of the Con; with the sol
ambition to execute the ultimate Con and score the ultimate prize. 10 Pak knew that he always
needed to be thinking quicker and thinking bigger; he goes to the bathroom and stares at himself
in the mirror.)

10 Pak: Where's the best place an opponent should hide? In the very last place you would ever
look. You can't see what's right in front of you, can you? So now that the opponent
is challenged, it means that his intelligence is questioned, he won't be able to accept
that; no one can accept that..not even to themselves. They will come at you with
everything; these agents will protect the rich elite with everything they've got
because they think that they are best friends.

(In chess there is no enemy, there is no good or bad; that's the elegance of the game. 10 Pak,
being an astute chess player and a fan of "The Art of War" by "SUN TZU", uses a chess strategy
to lure in the Feds into a trap. The strategy is simple; it's for me to feed pieces to you and make
you believe that you took those pieces because you're smarter and I'm dumber ….. if you change
the rules on what controls you; you will change the rules on what you can control..Fear is an
illusion and arrogance is the ego; let the chips fall where they may.)

Song: The Darkness – Hippie Sabotage (0:00 – 2:30)

(10 Pak smokes his joint as he stares out the window; everything is normal outside, people going about their own business, mailman delivering everybody's mail, and kids playing on the sidewalk. He takes a deep breath and exhales as if shedding some weight off his shoulders. He starts putting a few things into a small backpack; he grabs a picture of his daughter and slides it in his shirt's front pocket close to his heart. 10 Pak also grabs the letter from Tommy Cadwallader, which remember, contains the password to open up the wormhole. The password sent by Tommy was the Latin Phrase, "Vi Veri Universum Vivus Vici"; which in English translates to – "By the Power of Truth, I, a mortal, have conquered the Universe." 10 Pak looks around his apartment and thinks about the memories made here; he knows he's going to miss this place. Home is where the heart is; the sounds, the memories, the smiles, and the people who really cared about you. Without this, then what's left in life? An empty emotionless shell of a person filled with doubt and regret dwelling in darkness. That's not living; not sure what that is to tell you the truth. In the wall in his bedroom, he had a quote from one of his favorite movies written on it. From the Movie "Johnny Was".)

"Question is?? What would you do if you had to make a decision between being loyal to the past; and trying to make a future?? -

"-If a man ain't got no roots, he don't have no future; you got to have roots to hold on to."

(Johnny Doyle and King Raz)

(This quote is the beginning dialogue from the movie Johnny Was; he reads it to himself one more time as he leaves his place without looking back. He carries with him a tear in his eye and a joint on his ear, to accompany him into the next chapter of his life. Everything is about to change for him and "goodbye" is inevitable if he wants his plan to succeed.)

Place: Newstation Forum Headquarters

    Bala Cynwyd, Philadlephia

(Jerome Koppel sits patiently waiting for a call; the signal to go on with his part of the plan.)

Co-Worker: You're here early as shit; what, did you pull an all-nighter

Jerome Koppel: I have a good feeling about today; I can't wait.

Co-Worker: You seem different; you look determined and awake today.

Jerome Koppel: Oh I am, my brother; I am.

(Other co workers walk in and start talking about the elections and the pandemics, more and more of the current social issues than anyone wants to hear. At this point in time it has been a brutal year for most of the people and nothing comes as a surprise anymore.)

Other Co-Worker: Hey guys, does anybody know why there's a lot of cops' gathering up in a

        two block radius from here. It feels like their surrounding our building.

(Everybody rushes to the window and starts looking outside being all nosey and shit.   But it is no coincidence that the cops are there and that Koppel is getting ready to make his move; those Cops have all been given a chance to retire rich by simply protecting Koppel.   For them, comprehension is not a requisite for cooperation; just as long as they are all well compensated for it. Koppel realizes that this is the point of no return; it's now or never.)

Place: Philadelphia Southern Police

    Hideout House

  8th St and Mifflin St.

(Police officer on the phone with FBI Agent.)

Cop: Yeah we got them; they're here detained behind bars and in cuffs Sir. We have about

      a dozen men watching them Sir; we have it all under control. (Hangs the phone up)

(The cop turns around and all he sees is everybody playing cards drinking and smoking, watching the game on the big screen TV; oh yeah and Flaco ordering pizzas. There were only three and one of them looked like Jerry Garcia, no bullshit.)

Song: Runaway – Yeah Yeah Yeahs (1:35 – 4:00)

Place: Location of the "WormHole"

Empty Pier off Columbus Blvd.

(It is almost morning and the dawn still lingers waiting for the sun to rise. 10 Pak arrives at the right coordinates of the Wormhole location. He turns around and looks at the city skyline and realizes how much he is going to miss the City of brotherly love. At this very moment, there are a lot people in need of help because of the corona virus pandemic an poverty; he knows he must go through with this. He remembers Tommy's letter telling him to live free, find peace, and forget about trying to save the world; to just save yourself before you are consumed by the forces of the "Unknown Fates". 10 Pak knows he is being watched by the feds and the local cops; this is the moment that determines not only his life but the fate of many others.)

(He takes a deep breath and recites the words)

10 Pak: "Vi Veri Universum Vivus Vici"

(The wormhole appears right in front of him; like a giant TV screen. It emanates this light blue and white color in waves of liquid, so calming and peaceful; everyone including 10 Pak were looking at it in awe and amazement. 10 Pak turns around with a huge smile on his face; as he raises his middle finger at the Agents and screams the words.)

10 Pak: "Check Mate"!!

(The lead Agent just now realizes that he is in a trap; as he turns around, the local cops are pointing their guns at him and his agents.)

Lead Agent: You crooked pieces of shit!!!

Sergeant Cop: You're the only piece of shit here!!

(The cops blast them all away in a matter of seconds; not leaving anybody alive. After checking the bodies, then they make it appear as if it was 10 Pak that did the shooting. This was all part of the plan that 10 Pak had laid out; everybody would get rich and nobody would be found guilty because 10 Pak would take all the blame. You can't arrest a man that disappears into a "wormhole" or "time portal"; whatever "sy-fy" term sits best with you.)

(So in their report, they would say that after 10 Pak killed the FBI agents; he was then gunned downed by the local cops and fell into the river where he couldn't be found. That's what was going to be reported as the actual facts of the event that night; in which case, nobody looks for a dead man. The one Cop flashes his light towards 10 Pak three times, letting him know that they are with him.10 Pak turns around and walks into the wormhole without any worries in the world; he knows that the plan will be executed to the very last detail as he instructed. One of the local cops gets on the phone with Chuckie Bobo and tells him that it's done, to proceed along with his part of the plan. Another Cop calls Jerome Koppel and tells him to proceed as wel,l with his part of the plan.)

Place: Newstation Forum Headquarters

   Bala Cynwyd, Philadlephia

(Jerome Koppel is now live on the news exposing a bunch of groups and organizations involved in the embezzlement of the people's money in the City of Brotherly Love. These local groups and individuals are being arrested at their own homes and places of business by local authorities now aware of the situation. Some of the money that 10 Pak donated was to pay off the higher ranking officers along with the Judges; this was to ensure the capture of the secret group that had been feeding off the money of the people like parasites. Koppel was also reporting about the huge donations made by the same anonymous source to all the youth groups, single mother help groups, homeless shelters, boys club, Medical Centers, Red Cross, local schools, middle schools, and high schools.)

Koppel: This event changes tomorrow and everybody in it; the streets and alley ways will now

remain free from the despair of the homeless people living there. The flow of heroin

has been reduced to a minimum; along with its dealers that feed off the ruined lives

like leaches and vultures. Families will experience a better quality of life; a life

without having to spend all their hard earned money just on bills, taxes, and

medical expenses. Teachers will be able to do their work without having to worry

about their own financial security; easier for the kids. The very essence and sentiment

of brotherhood will now be shared by most in the city. Except that is, for the

mutha fucka's getting bit in the ass now. Got you now bitches; that's right, I don't give

a damn; Koppel out!!

(The truth had finally been exposed; but yet I doubt it will make the National News; at least we achieved our goal on a local level. Jerome Koppel was still addressing the audience through the news with his message of unity and hope.)

Jerome Koppel: To the Philadelphia of tomorrow; stay united because you're not alone. There are still good people left in this world, in this country, and in this city. My mind won't stop through the motions and don't give it any thought; I will fight on with you.   The time is now to get caught up in the moment; don't breathe alone the emptiness and don't let the darkness feel like home. Come on Philadelphia; smoke with me and go with me, we need to keep on moving now.

(As Koppel keeps reporting the news; a camera shows in the background trailer trucks full of food and clothes being given out to the people of the poorer areas of the city. It is such a conundrum this life we live in, especially during these times that seem to have us all wondering about what the future will bring. There's more to life than just the bullshit we've been fed all this time. Now that the moves are made and 10 Pak is gone; the city will be able to heal itself into a better place for everybody.)

Chapter 10

The Food Court

Song: Babylon Too Tough – Gregory Isaacs (0:00 – 1:30)

Place: The Lakes FDR Park

South Philadelphia

(Everybody is gathered up at 10 Pak's old favorite spot today; they're there to say good bye in their own way and in their own words. It turned out to be a real nice day today; Flaco lights up a joint and takes a couple of puffs and passes it to his left to Matt. You could hear the wind flowing through the trees; the clouds were covering up the sun as they smother everything with a calming shade. Even though 10 Pak hadn't died, only a few people knew what had really happened; everybody else in the group was meant to be miss-directed; so that the deception could seem real enough. Nevertheless, everybody missed their good friend and the security he provided for those around him. After a few people had already spoken, Flaco starts expressing his words and there were a lot of them; a couple of minutes into his speech.)

Ramon: Jesus Christ, you almost done??

Herbie: Seriously, the rest of us want to talk too before the sun goes down, you know.

Flaco: How much time do you think it took to eulogize a great man like Benjamin Franklin or

Burt Reynolds?? or Bob Ross? Huh, how long?? Now shut the fuck up and let me

say goodbye to my boy. (lights up another joint)

Herbie: Oh great, Stoner Smurf is taking his sweet ass time; I gotta piss you little shit!!

Flaco: Go piss next to the building assHOLE, I'm Talking here!!

Matt: Don't be shy, you can crouch down if you want and don't forget; you gotta wipe front to

back. (They all start laughing at Herbie as he tip-toes his way to the side of the building.)

Herbie: Very funny; you little piece of weasel shiit.

(After all the events that had transpired up to this point, no one had really been blamed for any of it and with the authorities unable to make any arrests; the group knew they weren't going to get in any serious trouble. Their day in Court had come; they now had to face the music in order to finish the deception that 10 Pak had planned. As they finish their eulogies', the group starts getting ready to go down to the Court House in Center City.)

Place: Main Circuit Court-House

> **Center City Philadelphia**

(Almost the whole group is present at the court house this day, along with their attorneys and a few family members. The Judge has entered the courtroom and the Bailiff announces that the court was now in session. As the Judge sits down and acknowledges everybody in the courtroom; he looks around and sees that one person had fallen asleep. He starts clearing his throat.)

Judge: I'm going to need someone to wake that young man up for me, so we can get this show

> on the road.

(Matt gets up and goes over to Damien and slaps him on the face. As Damien wakes up he makes a funny strange noise as he comes to.)

Damien: What the fuck??

(Everybody in the courtroom starts laughing at Damien.)

Judge: Young man, this is not a Motel 6; I need you to wake up, get up, and go to the bathroom

> and wash your face. When you're done, then you can come back in here.

Damien: Yes your Honor; sorry your Honor.

(As Damien gets up and goes to the bathroom you can hear everybody talking and laughing in the background. A brief moment goes by when the Judge clears his throat again.)

Judge: Okay, comedy time is now over; let's get serious. Let's discuss the matter at hand here;

> this is a hell of a story. Lots of people involved; prominent people that seem to have

> been caught with their hands in the cookie jar; we'll see what transpires with that.

> Now, can anybody tell me; what's the difference between a Cop and a Criminal??

(Flaco, still a bit inebriated from the night before and stoned from only moments ago; gets up and just blurts out.)

Flaco: That's what I'm saying; what's the fucking difference??

> (the whole courtroom starts laughing)

Matt: God damn it dude!! You trying to get us the chair??!!

(The Judge starts laughing and starts writing on his book as he keeps laughing.)

Judge: Very Funny; let's see who gets the last laugh. (judge keeps laughing)

A year later……………

Song: Barbie and Ken – Jesse (0:10 – 1:00)

Place: King Century Mall

Philadelphia Out-Skirts

(Out in the distance on I-95 a nice sports car speeds its way off the highway ramp and makes it into the mall parking lot. Mall opening time is in a few minutes and even though he's almost late, Matt takes his sweet ass time getting his stuff out of his car. As he walks up to a side entrance, he sees the overweight security guard cleaning off the cigarette-butts from the floor with a broom and dust pan.)

Matt: Hey Kenny what's up? You lose weight bro??

Kenny: Fuck off Matt!!

(Matt continues to walk along as he passes a few stores and a few kiosks on his way to his job. Strangely enough, as he continues on his way; it seems that several women have taken an issue with Matt and have no problem letting him know how they feel.)

Matt: Hey Girlie girl…

Girl in Kiosk: Go fuck yourself, asshole!!

Matt: That's why you're still single.

(Matt starts laughing and continues on past the Pretzel shop and the Shoe store)

Shoe-Store Clerk: Fucking Douche-bag

Matt: Nice to see you too beautiful; how's your sister??

Shoe Store Clerk: Go to HELL!!!

(He passes the Chocolate Store and a very sexy girl comes out.)

Matt: Debbie how come you never called me back??

Debbie: Because of you I can't get an orgasm unless I use Alka -Seltzers, you asshole!!

Matt: Hey, I just put the idea out there; not my fault you're a sex-freak..

Debbie: Don't ever talk to me again; Asshole!

(Debbie just turns around and goes back to work as Matt walks away laughing. Still walking along with no care in the world, Matt turns the corner making his way finally to the food court; where himself, Flaco, and Damien now worked at. The pizza shop they worked at was owned by Herbie; which at this point, had more money than he knew what to do with. He never got caught and nobody ever seized any of his stuff. Plus his shares of the Sticky Icky Ghost Bud where off the roof, making him filthy rich. As Matt arrives at the pizza shop, Flaco and Damien are already there talking to a not so happy looking Herbie.)

Flaco: Yo Herbie cut the bullshit; when we getting our checks??

Herbie: Fuck your checks!! Don't stand around here not doing anything you little assholes; go clean something, what the fuck am I paying you for. Don't you fucking eye-ball me!

(Danny walks over to Herbie with like an 8-ball bag of coke in his hand.)

Danny: Hey Mr. Herbie, you forgot your flour in the bathroom again.

(They all start laughing at him because it's not the first time this has happened.)

Herbie: Give me that; now get back to work, you lazy fucking no good cheeba monkeys.

(A few hours go by and everybody's anxiety level starts going up because its payday and Herbie doesn't seem to give two shits about it. Another reason why the boys are a bit agitated is because they are waiting on Matt's little brother, John; to come over with the weed they ordered. Since 10 Pak wasn't around anymore, their main weed connection was no longer available; thus the dependence on other providers of said commodity. The Judge had ordered them to two years of part time community service on a regular basis thanks to Flaco; on top of the level one probation. Level one probation, I believe is just a phone call once a month; you don't even have to go in and get pissed tested. Working under Herbie was the only way they could get a bit of freedom; simply by not being tied down to some regular shitty paying job, even though they had money as well.)

Flaco: Yo Matt, why is your brother taking forever?? I need to smoke now bro; you have any

lollipops left??

Matt: I got 2 green apples and 4 orange creams left; I'm saving those for later.

Flaco: I still can't believe it bro, no more lollipops for us.   Where the fuck is John!!??

Damien: I still can't believe you two trust that genius to do anything right.

Matt: What are you saying??

Damien: I wouldn't trust your brother to tell me what time it is; let alone handle the money

and drugs.

Song: Purple Pills – D-12 (0:00 - 0:25)

Place : Media Suburbs

    Outside Philadelphia, PA

(Matt's younger brother John walks up to their friend Steve's house; Steve was their dealer who had fresh shipments of Colorado products on a monthly basis. Steve's place was like a 24/7 convenient store for marijuana products; edibles, bud, tinctures, butter, you fucking name it. John walks up to the house, smiles at the surveillance camera and gets buzzed in. As he walks in, he gets hit with a huge wave of weed odor strong enough to knock out an elephant; John sees Steve and a few of his friends smoking and drinking, high as shiiiit.)

John: Hey wuuz up fellas?? What's going on with you all?? Yo Liam, Jeff says that if you go

back to Wicks, he'll name a crab-cake after you.

(Everybody present there starts laughing at John's shenanigans)

Steve: What do you want John?? Make it quick we got to head out to the mall.

John: Oh that's cool; give me two ounces of the Maui Wowie and one ounce of the

Coco Kush, 5 bags of the Berry Gummies, and that will be all for today.

Liam: Hey John, what time does the mall open??

John: (very indecisively) I don't know; not sure 10 maybe, 11ish.

Pete: Dude, you don't know what time the mall opens?? Don't you work there??

John: Well, uh….

(Everybody stops doing whatever they were doing and silence takes over the room for a few seconds. Everyone is staring at John; slowly but surely the laughter starts creeping in big time. They all start laughing so hard at John for something so stupid and simple that only stoners would find hilarious.)

Liam: You are too much; okay your total comes to $1100.

John: You guys take cash app??

(Everyone starts laughing at him; ripping into him, hard.)

Steve: Your brother called ahead; so just give me the cash and stop fucking around fat boy.

Place: King Century Mall

     Philadelphia Out-Skirts

(Back at the mall, the whole place is getting ready for their Centennial Anniversary coming up on the weekend. Banners and signs are starting to decorate the walls on the inside and on the outside of the mall. Pretty big deal around here because all the stores are not obligated to participate; but it is frowned upon if you don't. And by frowned upon, I mean that you'll lose business, money, and favors; Capiche. ☺ The stores had to be involved with the promotion of the centennial anniversary; they had to make sure that at least two employees acted as representatives for their stores at the Variety show. Matt looks at his watch and is starting to get pissed at his brother because he should have been there about an hour ago. Flaco realizes that Herbie hasn't been around for a couple of minutes and decides to look for some trouble. Flaco, Matt, and Danny decide to go up to the Control Room and fuck around with the microphone and the P.A. system. They walk up to the camera room and manage to get in with the help of one of the janitors. Flaco grabs his phone and hooks it up to the system with an auxiliary chord; now he can play anything throughout the whole food court.)

Flaco: (hits them with the Schwarzenegger accent) Let's give them a lil Arnold, Yah! If

     Herbie doesn't want to pay us, then I'll make some money for us. I'm going to

     "subliminal message" the fuck out of these people. Pizza, Pizza, Pizza, Pizza.

Matt: Hurry up, Danny, keep an eye on that Camera right there; once you see them running up

those steps you tells us, then we got about 30 seconds to get out of here.

Flaco: What do you think the judge would say, if we get caught and tomorrow were in front of

him again. (starts laughing)

Matt: You know exactly what he would say; he would say it with that smug, arrogant, and

slightly condescending tone. Something I really don't care to listen to again. So

please, pretty please, let's not get caught; ok.

Song: Arnolds Pizza Shop – Justine Milliam (0:00 - 1:46)

(Speakers at the food court stop playing music as you hear laughter and then….)

heLLO,

YoU've reaCHed ARnold's PIzzA sHOp, I'm NoT heRE nOw, I'm oUt kiLLin PePPorONi.

iF yOu WaNt tO rEACh ME, IF yOu WaNt A PIzzA; I dON't CArE beCAUse IM noT hErE.

COmE TO REaLIZe tHAt; IdIOt!! ☺ BuTT, iFF yOu NeeD A PIzzA sOMe TImE DUrInG tHe

neXT FEw dAyS… i CaN hAVe iT DeLIveRed tO yOu; OR mAYbE I wiLL sTAbLe IT tO

yOu. I dON't cARe WHat yOu wANt oN iT; eVeRy PIzzA cOMes wITh PePPorONi aNd

wITh 9 miLLimEtEr bULLEts oN iT. iF yOu dON't lIKe iT, I dON't cARe beCAusE yOu'LL

ReCEIvE oNe aNYhOw. tHe oNLy diFFerENce iS mAYbE tHe 9 mILLimEtEr bULLeTs wILL

Be iN tHe gUn oR mAYbE tHey'LL bE oN yOUr PIzzA. IF yOu dON't fUCk arOUnD I'LL

gIVe yOu gOOd PIzzA. IF yOu dO fUCk arOUnD I'll TAkE a PePPorONi aNd pUNch IT

tHRouGh yOUr hEAd. SO! IF yOu wANt mUSHrooMs ShUt UP!!…IF yOu wANt

BrOccOLI…wHAt tHe hEll iS BrOccOLI aNYWay?? SHUt uP wITh tHe BrOcOLI!…IF yOu

wANt soMEthInG crAZy lIKe piNeaPPle…I'LL KiLL yOu!! IF yOu LIkE PePPorONi aNd

buLLetS yOu cOMe tO tHe riGHt pLACe. IF nOt yOU'rE aN idIOt aNd yOu deSErVe tO dIE.

sO leAVe A naMe , nuMbEr, seRIaL nuMbEr, hOw tAll yOu aRe, weTHer yOu susceptible

tO aNy disEAseS; aNd iF yOu aRRe, I'LL coMe ovEr aNd mAYbe I'LL gIVe yOu A PIzzA oR

maYBe I'LL brAKe oFF yOUr aRm.

(Everyone at the food court was laughing there asses off; you could hear one man laughing hysterically as he dropped his soda. The look on this one older lady was priceless; also the look on the cleaning ladies was pretty funny too. Kids, Teenagers, grownups, the working crews, employees at other food stores; everyone was laughing.)

Damien: Oh shit, oh shit; here comes security, Run! Run! Run!

Matt: Flaco, unplug; let's go! let's go!!

Flaco: Got it; let's go..

(Leaving just in the nick of time, they avoid getting caught by the team of security guards running down the hallway. As they make it back to the food court, they see a bunch of people starting to line up at the pizza shop.)

Matt: See, I told you it would work; now let's go work hard and steal that money from Herbie.

Damien: We really doing this??

 Flaco: You bet your lily white ass we are!!

(As they make it back inside the pizza shop they see that John was back; finally. They all decide to eat some edibles whilst they smoke off some odorless THC vape cartridges, back behind the oven. As they reach a certain level of toastiness and stupification, everybody goes back to work to their respective positions. After an hour goes by, Flaco ends up double daring John into a bet; the worst kind of bet possibly imaginable. Flaco convinces John to take a shit on a pizza box and then throw it into the oven. Strangely enough, it doesn't take John but half a heart beat before he drops his pants, bends over and takes a dump on a pizza box he laid down on the floor. Danny walks back there and as soon as he turns the corner and sees what's going on, he turns right back around immediately and heads back to the bathroom. As more and more people are lining up at the pizza place ,the guys leave the front unattended for a few minutes; until Herbie shows up. He looks around and sees none of his employees present; he walks up to the register talking out loud.)

Herbie: Oh' that's ok guys, I'll take the orders; I'm only the fucking owner!! (He sees Matt
      coming back from his break) Matt!! Get your short ginger ass over here, I gotta go to
      the bathroom real quick.

(Matt who was now at the cash register starts smelling something disgusting and so does everybody else. Out from the line of people a lady screams, FiRE!!!!!! Everybody starts running around screaming like crazy, thinking the whole place was going to collapse or something. As all the chaos ensues, Herbie comes running out of the bathroom with white powder smeared all under his nose and upper lip. Finally some security guards and cops put the fire out where the oven was at. Cops along with the mall manager looking all pissed off asking to see who was in charge there; everybody that worked there immediately points at Herbie. Herbie, caught off guard and with still some coke-residue on his nose and mustache.)

Herbie: What the hell you guys looking at?? (Flaco and Matt can't contain their laughter)

Head of Security: (pointing at Herbie) Somebody put the cuffs on this, TWATT!!!

(As Herbie is getting arrested a couple of people start clapping at the situation; and as usual Herbie starts laughing at them because he's on a whole different level.)

Herbie: Don't get comfortable, I'll be out before dinner time; you'll be hearing from my lawyer,

Mr. Mall manager. (looking at the young security guard) Big day for you huh??

Young Guard: Shut the fuck up, Herbie.

(The security guards take Herbie away as they are accompanied by the State Trooper stationed there. As the smoke cleared and the oven fire now being taken care of, the mall manager starts making an announcement over the loud-speaker. He issues the customers an apology and a reminder of the centennial celebration of the mall; especially the super discounts for the weekend. He also reminds all the mall employees of the mandatory staff meeting later on in the afternoon concerning the weekend events. Needless to say that this was a pretty big event going down; seeing though as how all the big companies present at this mall were promoting hardcore. Employees didn't seem too excited in hearing this breaking news; it's they themselves that have to do all the bullshit work for little to no extra money, when it comes down to it. So buckle up and put on your fake smiles, it's time to deal with "a shit load" of customers and get yelled at. Managers just point at shit and give orders; they don't do any of the work, bunch of lazy assholes. In the midst of all this, there is a person standing there watching all the commotion happening as he sees Flaco come out, laughing his ass off and recognizes him right away.)

(In pure disbelief this person's facial expression changes immediately from the amazement; he quickly grabs his phone and calls out. He just hit the jack-pot and he knows it; the phone rings a bit and then someone answers on the other end.)

Stranger: Hannibal, you are not going to believe who I just found; you can tell the Black Frog to stop looking. What was it; $50,000 for finding them??

Hannibal: That's right, keep me posted; and whatever you do, do not engage them or you'll end up dead like the rest of our guys.

Stranger: I'm not stupid, I'm not going anywhere near those fuckers. I want a chance to spend that money, you know what I mean.

Place: Hannibal's Crib

      Trenton, New Jersey

Hannibal: I'll pass the message along, see what he says; just keep an eye on them.

Stranger: Oh don't worry, this is where they work; we got them.

Hannibal: Remember, the most important thing is finding out where they have that weed of theirs. We have to get our hands on the weed itself or on the grower responsible for it; that's priority number one. Call me back if anything changes and remember; be careful, we've already lost more than enough people to these mutha-fuckers.

(By this point in time, within the city limits of Philadelphia recreational marijuana was now in full effect. The old poor drug infested areas like Kensington, Germantown, and Fish-Town were now a thing of the past; they no longer existed. Koppel and 10 Pak bought up those areas and invested in the people; therefore creating plenty of construction jobs at first and then retail jobs with the marijuana related companies. Philadelphians were put to work on the reconstruction of the area and then received financial aid to set up businesses like; dispensaries, coffee-shops, and a plethora of other different kinds of small business. The heroine dealers and the coke dealers had been pushed out by the economic boom being offered by the weed industry; let's just say that it became more profitable to join the "marijuana fever" than to keep shooting each other to death.)

(More and more people were switching to Marijuana products as they left beer, liquor, and hard drugs behind as a thing of the past. This was a united society looking towards the future with more acceptable social behavior; as weed brought more of a free thinking hippie Beat-Writer mentality to the Philadelphia scene. All kinds of businesses started booming and everyone in the East-Coast was making their way to Philadelphia to spend their money on legalized recreational marijuana. 10 Pak's and Koppel's efforts had not been in vain because they made it possible for the city to be self sustainable due to the profits earned by the legalization act. For the first time since its inception, the city was running on a surplus; ALL schools were now funded and healthcare was available to everybody along with cheap affordable housing. More importantly, the wrong people were kicked out of city government and were replaced by honest middle-class community minded people. The city was now in the hands of "Decent People" that would see to it that no one in the city of Philadelphia would ever again go hungry or live in poverty and despair.)

Song: Lil' Ghetto Boy - Dr. Dre/Snoop Dog (0:00 – 1:30)

Place: Police Station Central Lock Up

       W 36th and Ward St.

(Over at Central Lock-Up where Herbie was being detained at, it was never a dull day; worst than the GOD-DaMN Emergency room at a hospital. Through the corridors of the jail you could hear the screams of the staff and the inmates reverberating through its walls. Not your usual type of place; people in and out all the time, needless to say this was one of the busiest Precincts in the city.)

(at a distance)

Cop: Get all those New York assholes in there; I don't give a fuck if they're uncomfortable.

      That's what you get for coming to Philadelphia to sell that shit. Take that shit back

      to New York you fucking degenerate Monkeys!!!

N.Y. Prisoners: Fuck You!! Fucking PiG!!!! Die Asshole!!

(In the cell where Herbie was presently at, he was more than fine because he was amongst some of "Budha The West's" people who knew who he was. Everything was going perfectly peachy until one poor idiot decides to fuck with Herbie; like I said, poor idiot.)

Poor Idiot: (talking to Herbie) Hey You!! Yeah I'm talking to You!!

Herbie: What the fuck do you want??

Poor Idiot: Nice shoes; how about you let me take a closer look at them?

Herbie: I rather eat a bowl of shit, then let a north jersey piece of shit like you touch my shoes.

Poor idiot: How do you know I'm from north jersey?

Herbie: Your Accent you stupid shit; now guess what's going to happen next??

Poor Idiot: What??

(As soon as he says that, three guys that were already standing behind him go ahead and grab him and pin him to the wall. Poor idiot never saw it coming; three big mutha fuckers start laying in on him medium style, leaving him stunned and disoriented on the floor. Another cop with a clipboard walks over to their cell.)

Assistant Cop: Bostwick, Herbie???

Herbie: Yo!!

Assistant Cop: You made bail; time to go.

Herbie: (addressing Budha's guys) I'll tell Budha The West to take care of you guys, plus I'll throw something extra in there for you fellas.

(As he exits the building, a nice ass S.U.V with some serious looking individuals pulls up and they get out and open the door for Herbie; Herbie scoots down a little to see who's in there. As he sees the person in there, he puts out this huge smile and starts laughing.)

Herbie: About time you came back; it's good to see you again brother, we missed you. I knew the lawyer would get a hold of you.

(Herbie enters the S.U.V and gets comfortable, he is handed a bottle of Fire-Ball. He takes a couple a big sips and starts laughing.)

Herbie: Hail to the King, baby! You know, you were right; it's not easy being in charge by

yourself. I don't have time to do any of my extracurricular activities anymore; not my

idea of fun.

(Herbie also starts mentioning to the "stranger" that they weren't completely in the clear quite yet. He starts confessing that when all the commotion started at the pizza shop with the oven fire; he noticed one of Hannibal's men, noticing them. Herbie, being the ole Wiley fox that he is; picked up on it before he was detained by mall security.)

(later on that afternoon…………)

Place: King Century Mall

Philadelphia Out-Skirts

(Back at the mall, it was now time for the staff meeting to begin; slowly but surely one by one all the mall employees entered the meeting room. The room was pretty much packed by the time everybody was all in there. It's kind of cool to see all the different employees from all the different stores all in one place; looks like those crazy funny posters with all the different characters on it. Flaco, Damien, Matt, and Danny are late as usual; they stroll in like a pack of "Jack-Asses" into a barn. Literally, everyone turned around when they came in; after a brief moment of silence the whole room starts clapping and laughing at them for the oven fire at the food court. Matt walks past the Yuppie assholes that work at the GAP and purposely bumps into one of them.)

Gap Employee: Keep walking asshole, you don't want any of this.

Matt: Awh, somebody forgot to drink his Mocha Chai Latte?? You know you're supposed to

take your "Midol" before you come to work.   (A whole bunch of girls start laughing)

Gap Employee: Whatever…(gives Matt the middle finger)

(The boys keep walking to the other side of the room and take their respective seats; the meeting begins as the Mall Manager walks to the center of the room. He starts by addressing the importance of this weekend's event and the amount of old and new sponsors, investing money into the mall. The Mall Manager starts going down the list of the "guest celebrities" that will be attending the weekend festivities.)

(There was one name on that list that caught most of everyone's attention; it was the name of the wrestler with the most "Flair", the one and only Rick Flair. WHOOOOOH!! ☺ Needless to say, this was going to be a weekend to remember. As they sit down, Flaco grabs one of the booklets and opens it up to read it; for some reason the words on the paper seemed blurry; Flaco couldn't make out what they said. Everything else around him seemed fine, except only the words on the paper; these still seemed blurry no matter how much he rubbed his eyes. Flaco, starts panicking for a second and then he stops.)

Flaco: Oh wait, I ate all those edibles; damn things got me seeing all crossed eyed and shit.

(An hour goes by when the meeting was pretty much now adjourned. A couple of girls from the Pet Store in need of some weed and a good time come over to talk to the boys. The one girl Molly and her friend Vicky approach Matt and Flaco.)

Molly: What's up Geniuses; nice going with the oven fire.

Flaco: Well you know; never a dull day with us.

Vicky: That goes without saying. Although the thing with the pizza and the accent; Classic.

Molly: That's kind of what we need to talk to you about; a couple of us at the pet store are in need of some weed and other goodies. Also, I got some girlfriends visiting from out of town; if you guys want to hang out, we can come over if you have drinks and weed.

Matt: I like how you think, stop by the house tonight; make sure you call me on your way over.

Molly: Sure thing; see you tonight then.

Matt: For sure

Flaco: Bye bye ladies..

Damien: Alright, how about that..sounds like we're partying tonight huh fellas??

Flaco: WE?? We, sounds like an army bro.

Damien: Whoah, what the fuck you mean??

Matt: It means that myself, Flaco, and Danny; Danny you want to come to a party tonight.

Danny: Sure; okay.

Flaco: See, Danny's coming; that's plenty of guys already. Damien, you got to understand that

　　　three guys at this kind of party is okay; four is just one wiener too many, way too close to

　　　a sausage party.

Matt: Sorry bro, you understand though right??　(they're all trying hard not to laugh)

Damien: You fucking kidding me right now!!!

(They all start laughing at Damien because he could be so gullible at times, that it made it way too easy to fuck with him every now and then.　The room starts clearing out and all the employees go back to their jobs.　The day comes to an end, as the sun tells us so with its departure and the sudden entrance of the high yellow moon.)

Song: Hits from the Bong – Cypress Hill (0:00 – 1:00)
Place: Matt and Flaco's House
　　Chi-Chester Suburbs

(As the different kinds of smoke collide into each other up high by the ceiling; the black-lights and the lava-lamps set the perfect tone for the occasion.　Matt, Steve, Liam, and Flaco are chilling with a couple of girls in the living room; while Danny is serving drinks to three other girls by the bar as he tells his Joke about the Mexican, a Texan, and a Donkey.　In the other room John and Damien watching TV by themselves; Flaco and Liam walk into the room just to fuck with them for a bit.　Flaco sticks his head through the door and sees Damien on a chair bored as hell and then starts making crying noises.)

Flaco: Whahhh, what's this, the fucking "SAD" room; Whahhh. LOL

Damien: Eat a dick asshole.

Liam: C'mon you dorks, time to talk to some real girls; you'll thank us later.

John: That's what I'm saying, let's meet some hoe's.

Liam: You know what, better yet; John you're going on a liquor run.

John: You gotta be kidding me; alright fuck it, but you better have a bitch for me when I get

　　　back.

Flaco: The ladies are going to love you. (sarcastically) Alright get going and don't be cheap

you hear me; get shit for everybody. Alright later, Damien lets go get you a girl.

(As John leaves for the liquor store, the guys all go to the living room to join the rest of the party. Steve starts telling the story about the time they were hanging out with some college girls and they bet her they could make her orgasm with Alka–Seltzer in less than a minute. She didn't believe it one bit; so for "posterity" sake, they put it to the test. She grabbed a piece of Alka-Seltzer and placed it on the clit of her vagina; about 15 seconds later this girl looked possessed. As Steve keeps telling the story about how the girl started buckling around on the couch like a wild bronco; all the girls attention was fixed on Steve's story and the look on their faces was priceless. The night progresses into a fine evening full of positive energy, combined with questionable women and a dash of depravity thrown into the mix. ☺ Flaco sits next to the lovely Molly and starts throwing some game at her; and starts lying his ass off.)

Molly: Wow you are smart and so brave; I can't believe you got rid of all those zombies by

yourself.

Flaco: Well you know; my friends helped a little.

Molly: But how did you know what words to read off the book??

Flaco: It happens so quick you know; it's pure instinct, my quick reflexes and a cat like

mentality. I was skimming through the pages trying to find the right spell and I saw the

words come at me in my mind. It's like when you're stoned and certain key words come

out of left field.

Molly: I know what you mean; it happens to me all the time when I'm shopping.

Flaco: See, there you go; we have so much in common.

(John finally gets back with more liquor and other beverages of the alcoholic nature and the party continues on.)

Vicky: So let me get this straight; all of you worked together at the same spot before. This is

including your friend; the one that was involved with all the crazy strange days that

we had in the city.

Matt: Yes, that is correct.

 Vicky: So why did ya'll stop working there.

(The guys start laughing because all of them had worked there at one point; including Steve and Liam. John, in an attempt to aggrandize himself, only makes it worst for himself.

John: My firing was political. (all the guys start laughing at him)

Steve: Dude, cut the shit; you got fired because you got caught doing that stupid dance in front

of every camera in every room.

(Everybody in the room including all the girls started laughing at John for being such a pretentious little asshole.)

Vicky: What dance was it??

Matt: The floss; you know the back-pack kid dance thing on TV.

Molly: You got be kidding me; you got fired for dancing around too much, that's a new one

for me. (starts laughing)

Flaco: Well, I got fired cause I lost my shit and I snapped on one of the little Vietnamese ladies

working there through a temp agency.

(Flaco has a quick Flash-Back of him screaming no pee-pee at a little Vietnamese lady who simply asked him where the bathroom was.)

Temp Lady: Excuse, where bathroom??

Flaco: (with no sleep in the last 48 hours) What? No Pee-Pee!! No Pee-Pee! AWH!!! PEE-PEE!!

(Crabs cakes are flying everywhere as he begins to kick boxes up in the air as the little old lady is trying not to laugh too hard. They all went around the room telling their fucked up versions on how and why they all got fired.)

Flaco: Yeah, sleep deprivation can be a bitch; never try this at home people because I'm a

trained professional. (starts laughing at himself)

(As far as old clichés go; there is none truer than "time flies when you're having fun". Perfect example would be our present company here at this particular point in time. Molly goes to the bathroom upstairs to try to sober up a bit as she takes a shit.   In a matter of a bout thirty seconds into taking her dump; Molly falls asleep on the toilet seat. Thirty six minutes and 49 seconds elapse when she finally comes too.)

Molly: What the fuck: I can't believe I fell asleep on the toilet again.

(After reminiscing for a few minutes on how she passed out, Molly gets up after wiping front to back; that's right ladies. ☺ She heads downstairs; for the moment the only one present in the living-room is Matt.)

Matt: Whoa, where you'd come from?? We thought you left.

Molly: Hey Matt, where did everybody go??

Matt: I'm guessing you're wondering about your sister??

Molly: Yes, as a matter of fact, where is she??

Matt: Well, your sister and your best friend left with Liam and Steve.

Molly: That bitch! Fuck, how the fuck am I going to get home now?

Matt: Well, let me finish watching this movie and this joint and I'll go drop you off.

Molly: What movie you watching? (scoots over on the couch next to Matt and grabs the joint

off his hand and kicks back and puffs away.)

Matt: BraveHeart.

Three hours later………..

(Driving down the road on Chi Chester Ave Matt swerves a little bit right after he passes an intersection. His mistake doesn't go unnoticed and a cop comes out of nowhere and turns on his lights in pursue of Matt's vehicle. As Matt pulls his car over, the officer also pulls over right behind him; he walks up to the car and shines his flashlight at Matt.)

(To the officers surprise when he shines his light on Matt; Matt was wearing face paint. Better yet, he was wearing blue and white face paint because of the movie "BraveHeart". Molly and himself had gotten so into the movie, that they actually went and found face paint and did the warrior face paint for the major battle scene at Sterling, or was it Bannockburn??)

Officer: Holy shit boy!! Why in the world is your face painted blue??

Matt: I was watching the movie "BraveHeart" with this really cute chick and we decided to

       paint our faces; I lost track of everything at that point.   (Matt starts laughing)

Officer: That's quite the story, but how do I know you're telling me the truth? You could be an

       armed robber who just did a hit wearing blue face paint. How's that sound so far??

(Molly comes out of nowhere from Matt's lap.)

Molly: I say that sounds a little bit too farfetched.

Officer: What the fuck?? (he looks at Matt and sees a stupid grin on his face) Get the fuck out

       of here; just go don't say anything just go. Just drive carefully okay and don't do

       anything stupid. I mean; stop doing dumb shit while you're driving; who am I

       kidding; this fucker isn't going to listen.

Matt: Thank you officer. (Matt throws him a military salute)

Officer: Not the Army; lucky son of a bitch.

Place: SpringField – Philadelphia Suburbs

Song: Minerva - Deftones (0:00 – 1:00)

(Matt finally arrives at Molly's house in Springfield without realizing that he had been tailed the whole time, since he left his place. The song Minerva by the band "Deftones" starts playing on the radio as Matt turns the music up; still unaware of his surroundings, Matt and Molly resume to being intimate. The people watching Matt were some of the Black Frog's men; but strangely enough, they were unaware that they, also, were being followed. They were being followed by an even deadlier bunch and they were about to find out whose bite was deadlier. Two of the black frog's men get out of the car and start walking towards Matt's car; as they get closer and closer they hear someone whistling at them.)

(They both start looking around; as they scan the landscape, the guy in the back gets dragged up to the tree by his head; something very strong and powerful just picked him up like he was picking up a towel. The other guy, unaware of what had just happened, realizes that the sound was coming from up above in the tree; as he looks up, he sees the "Grim Reaper", a hit-man out of North Philadelphia.)

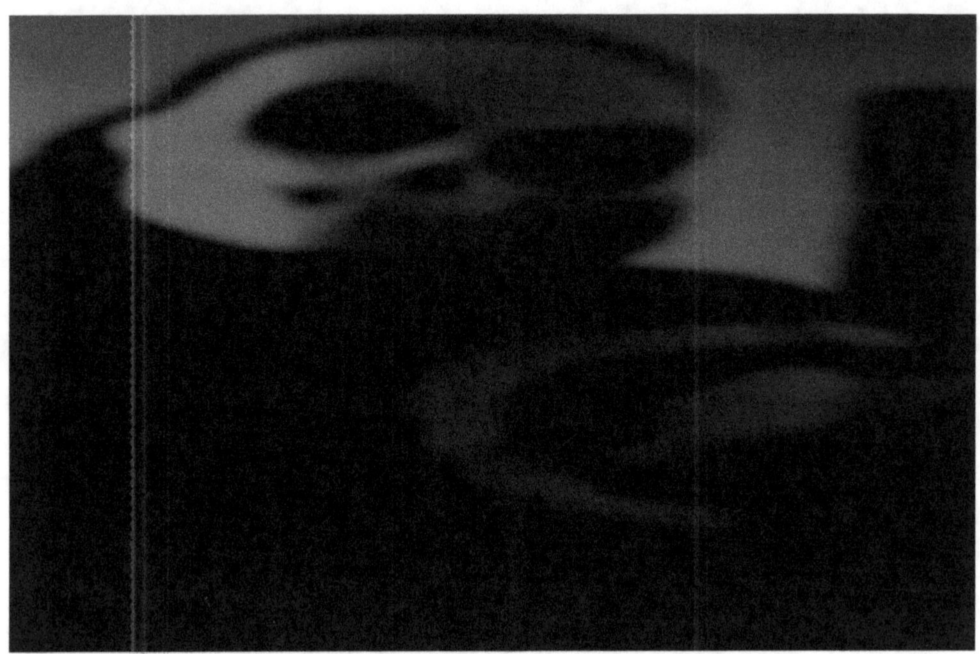

(The other two guys waiting in the car, unaware of what had just happened are surrounded by 4 men all in black carrying fully automatic weapons with silencers on them. These guys were known as the four horsemen of the apocalypse who precede "Death", in this case, our Grim Reaper. You know; the quote from the bible, Revelations: Behold the pale horse and the man who sat on him was death; and hell followed with him. Hell meaning the apocalypse that was to be set upon by the four horsemen called Conquest, War, Famine, and Pestilence. As all of this transpired, Matt being the horny little devil that he is, didn't have the slightest notion as to what had just happened; someone with great influence was looking over him. Next thing you know, these guys start emptying round after round of bullets; they light up that car and the "south jesrsey devils" inside it like a Christmas Tree.)

Next day………..

Place: Public Park Moyamensing St. and Moore St.

(It is Saturday morning and The Annual Three Corners of Philadelphia Jump Rope Competition was about to start. This was a pretty unique event set up for the students with an affinity for Jump Rope. A charity group was hosting this social event, involving young high school and middle school students; they were competing in an advanced jump rope skills competition. As part of their community service sentence, the boys were there to assist as greeters and cleanup crew. In such an uncertain world, it's good to know that some things never change; and as usual, it's never a dull day with these restless assholes. It was now 15 minutes till 9 and the competition was set to start at 10. The venue was actually nice; it was a small park and they were setting up at the Basketball court. The teams from North, West, and South Philadelphia were arriving with their respective cheering sections; this was comprised mostly by friends and families of the competitors. There were prizes and awards for everybody competing; but, the most coveted prize obviously was that of 1ˢᵗ place, obviously.☺ 1ˢᵗ place team would not only win the bragging rights, but also $500 cash for each team-member and a round trip all expenses paid to Ocean City, MD. A whole weekend of fun in the sun; this is considered to be a pretty cool place to chill at in the summer time. By the way, Myrtle Beach, South Carolina is the top spot in the East Coast in case anybody was wondering. ☺ Damien finally arrives and he sees the guys and starts walking up to them. Matt was chilling on a bench in the shade under a tree along with Flaco.)

Flaco: (on the phone) Whoa whoa whoa, hold on a second girl; I thought we were past this shit.

No, what the fuck; I didn't cheat on you twice? That's bullshit, I only cheated on you

once; there just happened to be two girls there. (phone hangs up) Hello? Hello?

God dam bitch hung up on me; how rude. What's up Damien??

Damien: Chillin, just trying to get this shit over with so we can go the fuck home. I don't work

here, remember. ☺

Matt: Don't start with that shit bro; we're here all day thanks to this little asshole .

(points at Flaco)

(More and more people start showing up to the event; it really was a beautiful day out. The street vendors, contestants, parents, and event staff started showing up as the day progressed. The street vendors started setting up their spots first for the neighborhood customers among others. As the day started getting busier, it also started getting louder with more voices in the air accompanied by the sounds of traffic. So, the day starts out without a glitch; no problems whatsoever. Until it all started coming to shit when Damien accidently bumps into Matt, Matt falls on Flaco; and Flaco ends up dropping a bottle of FireBall he was drinking on the punch over by the hot dog vending machine, next to the Cotton-Candy. At this point there were a lot of people around now; this included the fire department, the cops, the Reporters and their Camera crews from the News stations. A while later………)

Song: Rhinestones in the Sky – Gorillaz (0:50 – 3:00)

(It all started slowly, but surely it became very apparent; the crowd in the stands started getting a little bit too rowdy for a jump rope competition. Rowdy to the point where shit was being thrown from one side of the stands to the other; old ladies cussing each other out in very creative ways. In the meantime the contestants were still competing and to the amazement of the crowd the talent was pretty good. The moves and styles being put in display were no joke; they were really good. As things were getting even more heated, a couple of guys walk close by as they were sporting New York Giants Jerseys. The noise died down significantly enough for everybody to notice; everybody quickly realizes who the odd man out is. Out of nowhere you hear one old lady scream out…)

Old Lady: SHOVE A CHEESTEAK UP THEIR ASS!!!!!!!!

(And that my friends, was all it took to get that whole crowd to get up and start chasing those two guys down the street. Couple of older ladies stayed back laughing their asses off, enjoying the day more than anyone; but of course no one was laughing more about it than our anti-heroes Matt, Flaco, and Damien. As they laugh their asses off over by the watermelon fruit stand, an unexpected guest shows up right in front of them. Much to their surprise, it was Herbie; accompanied by five of his men.)

Herbie: I'm guessing that all of this is your doing; Jesus fucking Christ!! Everything you guys

touch really does turn into shit!! You little fucking pricks; hope you enjoy working at

the Pizza Shop now; I sold the place and your new boss is expecting you guys there for

the weekend festivities. Otherwise the judge is going to bend you over, grease you up,

and aim for penetration; you understand?? (Herbie starts walking away laughing) If I

were you, I'd be there on time; see you later fuckers.

(Herbie and his men start walking away)

Flaco: How the fuck did he get bailed out so quick?? I thought for sure he'd be stuck in there

till Monday.

Matt: I'm more concerned about that new owner; we got to play ball with him or her, otherwise

we are going to be stuck doing this community service shit for five more years.

Damien: No fucking way! No way dude, I can't be stuck doing this shit anymore; so whatever

we have to do to finish this, let's just fucking do it

Flaco: Oh yeah?? Well what the fuck do you think the judge is going to say about today??

As soon as he gets wind of this, he is gonna come pay us a visit at the fucking

Mall, of all places.

Damien: No no no no no no…

Matt: Now you got him going again; Damien chill out bro, it's all going to work out fine.

Damien: (stops pacing back and forth) How!! How will this be alright??

Matt: (all calm, cool, and collected) I don't know; it's a mystery. (starts laughing)

Damien: (with an even more worried look in his face now) I can't believe I'm going to be

doing this shit till I'm thirty.

Flaco: See, now you got him going; nice.

(Herbie and his men arrive at their S.U.V; he gets a phone a call.)

Herbie: Yo, talk to me. Okay will be right there.

Dizzy Rane: Who was that??

Herbie: That was the CandyMan, we gotta go meet up with him at the club.

Dizzy Rane: Did you tell the guys that he is back and that he is the one that bailed you

  out??

Herbie: No I did not.

Dizzy Rane: So you didn't mention to them that he is this new owner you told them about; you

  really want to fuck with them don't you??

Herbie: Yes I do; I got one big fat huge fucking problem with them. Paybacks are a bitch, I got

  Lady Hue working with them as their supervisor; they are going to think that Lady Hue

  is their new boss. They are going to shit their pants because they have no choice but to

  put up with it; or go to jail, not a hard choice. Besides, 10 Pak wants to surprise them

  and I have to respect that.

Dizzy Rane: Why do you have to respect that??

Herbie: Because 10 Pak is my friend; so stop with the twenty fucking questions and drive the

  fucking car, okay.

Dizzy Rane: Yes Boss, sure thing Boss; whatever you say boss!!

(Herbie and present company start heading over to the Club at the beginning of Spring Garden
Boulevard. 10 Pak has now made it known to certain associates that he is back and that there is
no reason at this point, for him to be hiding anymore. Nobody goes around looking for a dead
person; and legally he was declared dead, so he was pretty much in the clear. Having gotten rid
of the people that really were looking for him saved a lot of people some unnecessary
headaches.)

Place: Gentleman's Private Club

    Spring Garden, Old City

Song: Gravity – Perfect Circle (3:35 – 4:30)

(A beautiful dancer glides with magic across the stage, as her eyes become fixated on our very own 10 Pak. She ignores everything and everyone around her; as if 10 Pak were the one standing at the end of the tunnel, where the light shines once more. She approaches him very directly but gently, as if trying to hold a butterfly in the palm of her hands. He sings some of the lyrics of the song to her and she sings some lyrics back. She keeps whispering sweet secrets into his ear and by the look of his smile; they seem to be good ones. A few rows behind 10 Pak, a jealous customer makes a stupid comment and starts walking towards 10 Pak. In less than a second; about six guys stand up and make a wall between 10 Pak and him; these lively men were 10 Pak's security detail. Having gone with the dancer to the champagne room for a while; their conversation room comes to an end; they switch info and say their goodbyes. Herbie is on his phone calling him letting him know it's time to bounce and take care of business; the CandyMan exits the building.)

Later on that afternoon at the mall……….

Place: King Century Mall

    Philadelphia Out-Skirts

(Mrs. Hue was already present at the pizza shop by the time the boys got there. Mrs. Hue was a funny nice old lady, that didn't take shit from anyone; the type that would quickly pay money to the biggest mutha-fucka in the room to have your ass whooped. She was known around some very dangerous circles as a very shrewd business person, with a keen intellect and particular proclivity for violence.   Danny was already prepping the food when Matt, Flaco, John, and Damien walk in; Mrs. Hue walks up to them.)

Mrs Hue: You late; fuck you!!

Flaco: What the fuck!!

Matt: Fuck this shit bro.

(As soon as Matt says that, a massive, huge, big, cocked diesel mutha-fucka comes out from behind them. This guy was A.J; Mrs. Hue's personal body guard.)

A.J.: What the fuck was that Matt?? I don't think I heard you right?? (Matt turns around)

Matt: Holy shit!! A.J. When did you get out!! I mean, my brotha. I didn't mean any disrespect,

    I was talking about something else; you know me.

Hue: Yeah E.J. fuck you up! Bam! (because of her accent whenever she said A.J.

    it sounded like she was saying E.J.)

(This was something that A.J. hated, but had to put up with because Mrs. Hue had been taking care of him since he was a little boy, from back in the day. Plus, Mrs. Hue paid him a ton of money to take care of her and watch her back at all times. Flaco starts laughing quietly and then it gets louder.)

A.J.: What the fuck are you laughing at you little weasel??

Flaco: She's still calling you E.J.?? (Matt and Damien start laughing as well)

A.J.: Hey, she gets away with it; the rest of you can shut the fuck up!!

(They keep laughing at A.J. when all of a sudden Mrs. Hue throws a big ass knife and hits the wooden cutting table hanging up behind Matt's and Flaco's head. The knife makes this crisp sharp sound as it hits the wood and puts everybody in alert; they are quickly reminded that Mrs. Hue is the head of her own gang in South Philadelphia.)

Mrs Hue: Go to work; lazy, fuck you!! E.J., they make fun you; you fuck up them okay!!

A.J.: Yes Mrs. Hue, I will.

(The whole time this had transpired, 10 Pak was in the small office in the back of the pizza store. He couldn't help but laugh and reminisce about the good old days.. A couple of hours go by when the girls from the pet shop stop by to talk to the guys of bout their presentation together.)

Molly: Matt, help me look good and I swear; I'll give you the best blow job in the world.

Matt: That sounds good; sure I'll do my best,

(Flaco looks over to Vicky and winks at her)

Vicky: You're out of your fucking mind, if you think you're getting a blowjob from me over

     this dumb shit.

Flaco: Hey, I'm not a greedy person; I'll settle for a hand job. See this is the kind of

     situation that defines character; I think this just says more about you.

Vicky: Nice try asshole!! That shit doesn't work with me, so just keep your thoughts on the

     dance and nothing else.

Flaco: Fine!! Whatever!! The day we're having already, F.Y.I; I will be staring at your tits the

     whole time just to let you know.

 Vicky: What time does this thing start anyway; I can't wait to go the fuck home.

(Mrs. Hue comes up to the front and signals Matt and Flaco down; she starts pointing at her watch as if telling them to hurry the hell up. Just as they are getting ready to head back to work, Flaco and Matt both see the one and only Rick Flair walk by. The man is a legend of wrestling and I think you could even see his aura glowing as he walked by he's so cool. He was accompanied by a couple of people that seemed to be his assistants and some body-guards by the looks of it.)

Flaco: Yo!! That's Rick fucking Flair walking by over there bro; he's like a super hero or

     Something, you know.

Matt: Looks like this shindig is about to get started soon. Well ladies, will meet you over at the

     pet store in like an hour; and uh I'll be thinking about what you said.

Molly: Later guys.

Flaco: Later beautiful.

Vicky: Whatever, asshole.

(The girls make their way back to the pet store, just as the boys head back to the kitchen area for the moment. Rick Flair and his Entourage make their way to their private dressing rooms next to the food court to freshen up and start preparing for the evening. The Mall manager arrives at Rick Flairs room and welcomes the wrestling superstar to the mall and thanks him for being a part of the 100th year celebration. Unlike other celebrities that looked like they were forced to be there; Rick Flair still remained in a good positive mood and looked forward to doing his appearance. The meeting with the mall manager and his people was now over; Rick Flair closes the door to his room and was now all by himself. He goes to the bathroom and turns the light on and stands right in front of the mirror and just stays there; looking at himself. His smile, slowly but surely started turning into a frown; all of a sudden this really depressed look, took over his face. He then proceeds over to the couch and lies down without saying a single word.)

Place: Mall - North Entrance

(Out by the North entrance of the mall, about ten cars with jersey license plates park close to the entrance next to the handicapped spots. The Black Frog had sent Hannibal himself, to go take a look at the boys working at the mall, with about twenty-five of his men. So seeing though as how stubbornness can be considered to be a human fatal flaw; in this crazy case, it was the mother-ship of flaws. Not contempt with losing more than half of his men to the Philadelphia Alliance, now he was about to screw up in public, in plain sight, in broad daylight; broadcasting to the world what they were about to do.)

Place: Mall – South Entrance

(At the South Entrance, Herbie and company arrive as back-up for 10 Pak's crew who were stationed at the East entrance by the "California–Mexican-Vegan- Taco-Shop". Also set along the Eastern entrance near the Movie Theater, was "Buddha the West" and all his people. 10 Pak wanted to make sure that the Black Frog finally got the message; that he wasn't going to win this dogfight in PA.)

Dizzy Rane: Yo Herbie!! Lets order some food Yo!! I'm hungry as shit man!!

Herbie: How the fuck is it that your skinny ass can eat more than a 300lb man and remain so

fucking thin. I eat a cheesesteak; my ass jiggles for a week.

(Back inside the mall, the final preparations were being made for the main shows. The mall event is under way, Flaco and Matt have to participate in a televised dance presentation dancing duo with the girls from the pet store; along with like thirty other people. As everybody is gathering up around the middle of the dance floor with their respective partners; Flaco starts looking up to the ceiling and notices that the lights were changing shapes. It also sounded like muffled sounds were coming from the direction of the light. Flaco, was sure it was the drugs making him feel weird, but then he started remembering that he had only smoked a joint earlier and hadn't taken any pills. Something very suspicious was a foot, in his mind as he kept looking at the lights on the ceiling.)

Matt: Bro, you okay??

Flaco: Yeah I'm good bro; just a bit light headed.

(Back at the pizza shop in the office, 10 Pak takes out a pocket mirror wrapped in a piece of nice silk cloth out from his shirt pocket. He opens it up and out comes "Charlie The ghost" creator of the ghost bud.)

10 Pak: My friend, go have some fun, but while you're at it check out how far away the bad

guys are; after that, you know what to do.

Song: "Echoes" Pompeii – Pink Floyd (2:00 – 3:00)

(10 Pak takes out a vape-pen with a Sticky Icky Ghost Bud Cartridge on it; he begins to puff away in a rising motion, blowing the smoke towards the vent on the ceiling up above him. Charlie follows the Ghost bud scent into the room next door; which happened to be Rick Flares dressing room. Over head is Charlie, hanging motionless upon the air and deep beneath the rolling waves as he now descends upon the depressed and lonely Rick Flair. Now that Charlie is in Rick Flairs dressing room and starts fucking with him. Being a fan himself Charlie took upon himself to cheer our champion up. Rick Flair in his room starts hearing a weird sound coming from his bathroom; he gets up and checks it out.)

Rick: What now??

(Rick Flair turns the light on in the bathroom and sees nothing; and now hears nothing as well. He walks up to the mirror and takes a good look at himself; he lets out a deep breath and then inhales and then exhales again all depressed.)

Rick: Come on Rick!! It's a fucking mall in Pennsylvania. You got this baby!! Georgia Dome

      60,000 people, Dallas 80,000 people, Phoenix 50, 000 Come on! AWWWHHH!!!

(As he sorts things out in his head by screaming, he slams the side of his fists on the wall and the paper towel dispenser comes undone; with a little bit of help from Charlie yes, but it was mostly Ricks actions that lead to this moment. Rick notices that inside the paper-towel dispenser, a huge bag of coke was just sitting there; another one of Herbies secret stash spots. Rick Flares eyes start twitching and his lips start trembling.)

Rick: Oh no……

(Next door at the pizza place, Lady Hue unaware of the event going on in a few minutes; she is looking for Flaco and Matt so they can start prepping up the pizza sauce. She grabs A.J.)

Lady Hue: Where the two little cocksuckers??

A.J.: I don't know they just dissapoeared; like they were ghosts.

Lady Hue: Fuck you E.J!! They not ghosts, they just white!!

Back to the televised dance event……

(Right in the middle of the dance floor the music starts for about 5 seconds when suddenly out of nowhere it gets interrupted by the Black Frog's men. By this point they had already made it to the middle of the dance floor to grab and take Matt and Flaco with them. As that transpires, coming in from behind them was Herbie and crew and then next to him shows up 10 Pak and his boys. On the other end, a good amount of mall security is gathering up in order to deal with the issue at hand; they start moving in as well. As all groups are making it to the middle of the dance floor, a yell so loud and so recognizable stops everything and I mean everything in its tracks. It was the famous Rick Flare yell that had everybody frozen; he came out in his wrestling gear, hair all spiked up, and a raging look so intense it could challenge the Gods themselves. He does the yell one more time and then everybody in there starts fighting. Rick Flare starts running towards the middle of the dance floor as he just plows into people making them fly away as he hits them. As all this goes on, Flaco keeps hearing other noises and again starts seeing strange lights up above him. Vicky grabs Flaco's hand as she starts to worry a bit about that look on his face.)

Vicky: You okay??

Flaco: I'm okay

Vicky: Well, under these crazy circumstances; here goes nothing. (She grabs Flaco by the face

and kisses him.) There, you feel better??

Flaco: I actually do.

(Not paying much attention to his surroundings because of the kiss, Flaco fails to see Rick Flare coming at him from the side. Rick Flare pops one on Flaco, on the top of his head and knocks him unconscious. Flaco slowly starts seeing everything disappear right in front of him; he felt this sensation as if he were being lifted in the air as he falls to the ground. He starts hearing voices again and in a daze he looks up and the bright light above him is getting brighter and brighter till….he wakes up in the hospital; it's the mental ward on the 14th floor at the Thompson building Jefferson Hospital in Center City. Flaco finally wakes up and he starts believing that everything that happened was all a dream, the whole story, just a dream. A really hot looking nurse, way too hot to be a nurse, walks in and starts checking up on Flaco.)

Nurse: So you finally woke up; how do you feel??

Flaco: What?? God damn what did they give me??

Nurse: You bumped you're head when you fell off the table you were jumping on in the

cafeteria. You had a concussion, so that plus the medication must of made you

have an interesting dream.

Flaco: Holy Shit…it would appear so…..I thought…it felt so real.

Nurse: The mind is pretty powerful.

Flaco: You have no idea. In my dreams; I wasn't able to read anything, how come??

Nurse: That's because when you're dreaming, your using one half of the brain; the other half

that is at rest while your sleeping is the part of the brain that controls your reading

ability. The doctor will be with you soon; by the way you're getting discharged in a

couple of days so cheer up.

Flaco: That's good news; I guess.

Week later..........

Place: Chester, PA

   Crab Cake Factory

(First day back to work for Flaco after his discharge; this last relapse really did a number on his head, reality had been twisted around and then some for him. It wasn't easy for him to come to terms with the reality that was beholding him in this plane of existence. As he enters the halls of the noisy Factory, he makes his way to his locker as he says his hellos and wuzzup's to his peoples. He opens up his locker and he sees that there is a note for him. He slowly reaches for it and opens it up; it was a letter from 10 Pak letting him know that everything that happened wasn't completely all in his head.)

10 Pak s letter

"First, take a deep breath before you get all excited; everything you just went through was to throw the cops off your scent for good. You might be thinking that this was all a dream; well, it wasn't. To show you that I didn't mean you any ill will; there is a million dollars in Bearer Bonds stashed in a little duffel bag right next to you in my locker. Here's the combination to my locker 06 - 30 – 20. Flaco, take this money and go make a life somewhere else, get away from all this shit bro. Don't be more like the norm, we are not like them and be proud of that; we will do things our way. Why do we have to conform to an establishment that wants to keep our dreams away from us, just because we look and sound different?? Find your way to what makes you happy in some little corner of the world away from all the noise; that's exactly what I have done.   Flaco, by the time you get this, I'll be long gone to a place where no one can find me, somewhere where time doesn't exist, where life is simple, a place where I can find peace. There's a car for you waiting at Ramon's to take you wherever you want; be safe and live everyday without regret. Don't worry about me brother, I am finally happy in my own little corner of the world."

Your Friend Always

10 Pak

Place: Lulea -North Sweden

Song: Ancient Herding Call – Jonna Jinton (0:00 – 2:14)

(10 Pak is walking out in open field, in the middle of a farm-land facing the mountains. He's following the girl singing with a heavenly voice as they he grabs her hand and walks with her toward the lake.

The End